how I trade options

how I
trade
options

JON NAJARIAN

John Wiley & Sons, Inc.

New York • Chichester • Weinheim • Brisbane • Singapore • Toronto

I wrote this book to describe how I trade options. No statement in this book should be construed as a recommendation to purchase or sell a security, or to provide investment advice. You should understand that as a professional options market maker, I have significantly lower commissions, interest rates, and tax rates than any retail investor. You should always consider commissions and taxes prior to making any investment. Options involve risk and are not suitable for all investors. Prior to buying or selling an option, you should receive and read *Characteristics and Risks of Standardized Options,* a document written and provided by the Options Clearing Corporation (OCC). Copies of this document may also be obtained from your broker or from any exchange on which options are traded. If you choose, you can write to the Options Clearing Corporation at: 440 S. LaSalle St. Suite 2400 Chicago, IL 60605. You can also download pertinent information about options from their Web site: www.optionsclearing.com.

This book is printed on acid-free paper. ∞

Published by John Wiley & Sons, Inc.
Published simultaneously in Canada.

This publication is designed to provide accurate and authoritative information in regard to the subject matter covered. It is sold with the understanding that the publisher is not engaged in rendering professional services. If professional advice or other expert assistance is required, the services of a competent professional person should be sought.

Library of Congress Cataloging-in-Publication Data:

Najarian, Jon, 1957–
    How I trade options/ Jon Najarian.
        p. cm.—(Wiley online trading for a living)
    ISBN 0-471-31278-9 (cloth : alk. paper)
        1. Options (Finance) 2. Electronic trading of securities. I. Title. II. Series.
HG6024.A3 N34 2001
332.63′228—dc21

                                                                00-043738

Printed in the United States of America.

10 9 8 7 6 5 4 3 2 1

For my daughter Tristen, because when she smiles at me
it feels like I'm kissing God.

preface

When I set out to write a book about my career thus far on Wall Street and my experiences in the options markets, I didn't realize I would be triggering the most volatile period in history. Call it paranoia, or sheer coincidence, but as any trader will tell you, the market just seems to make extraordinary moves as soon as you begin a vacation, or when you leave for an out-of-town business trip. From the week I began writing this book, the Nasdaq exploded higher by 50 percent, lost 40 percent, and was just beginning to claw its way back as I finished the final chapter. Armed with this inside knowledge, if I ever decide to write another book, you may want to switch your money into T-bills and wait out the storm.

I didn't write this book to teach you how to make a million dollars in a week or how to day trade your way to riches. There are plenty of books about that out there already. I wrote this book to help investors like you learn how to manage your money more effectively through the use of listed options. I wrote this book with the experience that I earned through trading millions of options and billions of shares of stock over the past 20 years. I've used these strategies through the greatest bull market in history and through some of the most volatile trading periods imaginable. I've used these strategies to manage hundreds of millions of dollars worth of positions in stocks like IBM, SUNW, MU, EBAY, CMGI, and AOL and I continue to use these strategies today.

Proper use of options and the strategies I teach you in this book have helped me and my trading firms protect and profit through whatever the market has thrown at us. I know from experience that derivatives and spreading strategies can lessen your exposure to adverse market conditions, whether you're bullish or bearish. Controlling or limiting risk is a key factor to staying at the tables longer in games of chance and for my money, no casino offers better odds than you can get on Wall Street once you understand how to use options correctly. Options can also significantly increase your profit potential and, as a result, your rate of return on invested dollars. Proper use of derivatives and related strategies allows you to keep considerably more of your hard-earned dollars in safe havens such as government bonds or CDs, while you invest substantially fewer dollars in defined risk instruments. Any way you slice it, comparable upside performance with reduced risk means you've put yourself in a position to win.

Additionally, I wrote this book for investors who want to know how to protect their existing investments in stocks or mutual funds, or perhaps create some cash flow from their long-term holdings.

Finally, because investors regularly ask me what the life of a floor trader is like, I thought that this book could answer some of their oft-repeated questions: What amounts of risk do market makers take? How much can we make? How stressful is this job?

I have tried to use examples from my actual trading experiences to answer these questions and illustrate how you can expect option strategies to react. My goal was to make this book both interesting and comprehensible, so that you can begin using options to manage and build your financial future. I hope you share your knowledge and success with other investors.

JON NAJARIAN

Chicago, Illinois
October 2000

acknowledgments

I would like to acknowledge many people who have helped in my growth as a person and as a trader. For shaping me as a person, I have to thank my mother Mignette and my father Dr. John Najarian, for raising me with love for all God's creatures and respect for my fellowman. Without your support during my multiple college careers and at the launch of my trading career, I could not have made it. You are shining examples of how good we can be and I love you for teaching me so much. I hope my wife Brigid and I can give our family as much love and support as you have given me. I also want to thank my brothers David, Paul, and Peter. You guys make enjoying life a full-time job and remind me that what we do for a living is only part of what makes our existence special. I must also thank my wife Brigid for her love, for her support, and for providing time for me to write this book.

I want to thank my friend Tom Haugh for giving me my start in trading and for his friendship and stewardship of our many business ventures. I want to thank Bill Ray, Dan Haugh, Dan Sheridan, my brother Pete, and Mary Gallagher-Parks for doing such a great job trading and managing the Mercury Trading Group, so I can work on projects such as this book. I want to thank the traders at the Chicago Board Options Exchange for their entrepreneurial spirit and their willingness to push the envelope to bring more customers into our markets. Likewise, I want to thank my competitors on the AMEX, PHLX, and PCX for keeping my focus on improving customer service and making our marketplace more efficient. Thanks to the shareholders and staff of PTI Securities & Futures, including Dan Haugh, JD, Dave, Bill, Cliff, Larry, Robin, Margaret, and Matt. I want to thank Rance Masheck and his team at StockMarketWorkshop.com for bringing thousands of investors into the options markets. I want to thank the attendees of our trading seminars, individuals who use 1010WallStreet.com, and our clients at our brokerage firm for keeping me in touch with what's really important to them. Your input is a thousand times more valuable than any focus group.

I want to thank Bob Sirott and Fox television for believing in me enough to give me a weekly investment show. I want to thank CBS radio and WSCR, Sports Radio 670, for creating a daily outlet on the radio for my financial reports and for giving me a weekly investment show. I want to thank my editor Pamela van Giessen of John Wiley & Sons for keeping this project moving. I also want to thank the animated and talented Tricia Commins for her patience, skill, and hard work, without which, this book would not have been completed.

J.N.

contents

chapter 1

the making of a trader

Options trading can be a crazy business, with thousands of shares of stock traded every few seconds to hedge positions with face values in the millions of dollars. But if you like action, there is no better business. I intend to show you how options can become a part of your portfolio, whether you have $50,000 in stocks and mutual funds or whether you're a multimillion-dollar speculator. With proper training and dedication, you can use options to both increase cash flow and safeguard your investments.

Trading, like life, does not come easily, and my career in trading is no exception to this rule. My success has been the result of seizing opportunities, enduring losses, and adapting strategies to changing times. The options market is where I earned my graduate degree in making money. Now, I want to share my knowledge and experience. Why? Because a healthy options market benefits all of us—professional traders, retail investors, and speculators alike.

breaking into the markets

What made my success possible was a focus and a dream—quite simply, I wanted to distinguish myself in whatever field I played. I played on the football field for most of my life before becoming a trader. I made it to the NFL, fulfilling my dream to play professional football, an accomplishment that still makes me proud. But like many dreams in life, it was cut short. In my case, after four exciting, but all-too-brief preseason games, I was cut from the Chicago Bears. In September 1981, I went home, bruised in spirit and probably in body as well. I was down, but certainly not out.

Ironically, it was the football field that led me to trading—a classic example of one door opening when another door shuts. After I was cut from the Bears, my agent asked me if I wanted to play football in Canada. I declined, but said I thought I would like to become a stockbroker. When he asked me why, I said that I had met a number of brokers before and after our practice sessions with the Bears. Who else had time after finishing their working day to be out there watching us sweat under the summer sun? If stockbrokers earned a good living with such great hours, that's what I wanted to dedicate myself to become. Hearing my ideas, my agent told me, "You don't want to be a broker, kid. You want to become a trader on the Chicago Board Options Exchange."

He reasoned that the hours were the same as a stockbroker and that my physical attributes would serve me much better on a trading floor than sitting behind a desk. While I weighed the advantages of each situation, my agent made me the magnanimous offer of trading for him for free. When he threw in a free apartment in Chicago, my mind was made up. That's how, at the age of 22, with my ego still bruised from my failure on the football field, I found myself standing on the floor of the Chicago Board Options Exchange (CBOE). It was a hive of activity that swarmed around me. Traders in loose-fitting jackets with three-letter badges clipped to their lapels shouted at each other about bids and offers for puts and calls. Clerks screamed block stock trades. Computer screens glowed. Time clocks clicked and teletype machines rat-a-tat-tatted. It might as well have been some strange land where an incomprehensible language was spoken—I understood so little of what was going on.

Nobody had taught me the ropes. What little I learned in the first three months I picked up on my own—the jargon, the hand signals, and the pit culture where muscles and bravado were considered good traits.

Luckily, I hung in there. In many ways, I suppose I had no choice. I wanted to distinguish myself just as my father, a noted organ-transplant surgeon who made the cover of *Newsweek* and *Time,* had in his field. None of my three younger brothers or I grew up in our father's shadow, but we were certainly aware of what a famous, successful, and wonderful person he was. It would be exceedingly difficult to achieve success that would rival my father's in Minnesota, so Chicago seemed like my best bet at being someone other than Doctor Najarian's son. But in my early days in the options pit, my career didn't seem too promising.

It was 1983 and I had moved up from runner and arbitrage clerk for a New York Stock Exchange (NYSE) Specialist firm, to a floor trader at the CBOE. I was making a living on scalping and small spreads on the Midwest Options division of the CBOE. The CBOE had purchased the competing Midwest Options Exchange and absorbed its 350 members into the CBOE in the late 1970s. Those of us who traded on the brown badges (versus the blue badges of full CBOE members) could only make markets on 16 option classes. The remainder of the CBOE was off limits to us. Fortunately, I could afford the $19,000 for a brown badge with the remainder of the money paid to me by the Bears. A full CBOE seat was eight times more than that—$155,000—and since neither could be used as capital in your trading account, the full seat was out of the question. But I knew if I was going to make it to the big time, I had to find a way to get the full seat. Luckily for me, the man for whom I was working wanted to take the summer off and offered me the chance to trade on his full CBOE seat. I seized the opportunity to be part of the big show. Nearly 19 years and billions of dollars of stock options later, I still remember the day my opportunity came and I stepped up to the challenge.

It was as if I, as the linebacker I once was, had intercepted the ball and now had a chance to run for a touchdown. But the trading pit, like the football field, tends to have many people standing between you and the goal.

One of your obligations as a market maker on the floor is making a two-sided market. So if a broker has a customer order to execute—whether it's buying or selling puts or calls—the traders on the floor have to make a market for both the price at which they will buy and the price at which they will sell. Because of this obligation, the Securities and Exchange Commission (SEC) allows market makers to be exempt from Reg-T, a part of the 1934 Securities Act that mandates customers have a minimum of 50 percent of the value of the stock that they are buying in their trading accounts. Without customer margin requirements, we option market makers can trade hundreds of thousands or even millions of dollars of stock per day, so long as we meet minimum hedging requirements and provide that two-sided market.

The options pit, like other traditional exchanges, still operates as an open outcry auction where bids and offers are called out by buyers and sellers. In the pit, the brokers congregate in the center, like the target of the bull's eye. Traders stand in concentric rings, with the veterans and those who have earned their place standing nearest that center where the brokers hold court. The brokers yell out their customers' orders to the traders who surround them in the pit. When the pit is crowded, chock full with hundreds of traders, the brokers' voices don't project more than five or ten feet. And when a broker yells out an order, the traders chime in at once, with varying bids and offers. A millisecond after the bids and offers are shouted aloud, the broker determines which trader made the highest bid for the broker's customer who is selling or the lowest offer when the customer is buying. That's why a trader's proximity to the brokers is very important.

Brokers have two primary concerns when they are trading for their customers. First, they want a trader who won't stiff them. Trading floors don't have cameras trained on every trader, recording every shouted word. It's just not feasible. So the broker and traders depend on each other's word that when they agree on a trade, it's done. No backing out when the market is 200 points lower. In our business, if the other traders and brokers don't trust you, you might as well be invisible. Second, they need a trader who will bid and offer large quantities, so they don't have to break down an order into many small pieces. The more names a broker has to write on a given ticket, the greater the chance for a mistake, either in quantity or price. The broker's job is a lot easier when he or she can depend on your ability to take on reasonable and sometimes even unreasonable size to fill their order. Keep in mind that brokers don't get paid for bidding or offering. They get paid for filling orders. An honest trader who will do size is every broker's favorite trader.

Up to this time, I had been virtually invisible to the brokers in the IBM pit because I had just moved up from the brown badge—the minor leagues. I hadn't had an opportunity to establish my reputation yet, and I hadn't broken into the inner circle.

To break into that inner circle, you have to know what you are doing. After a year of fighting for two and three lots on the Midwest seat, I was ready to trade some size (twenty and thirty lots) and rock-and-roll. Being six-foot-two and, in those days, 230 pounds, I did have a physical edge when it came to making my way through the ranks. But bulk alone would not earn me a place in the inner circle. It would take intellect and ability to do that.

At nine o'clock that morning, I started on the edge of the IBM options pit, where I had been trading for nearly a month. It was the biggest and busiest pit on the floor. As traders ebbed and flowed into and out of the pit over the next hour and a half, I made my way closer to the inner circle. By late morning, with the ranks thinned by traders who were having a late breakfast or an early lunch, I made it to the center. There I was, on the trading floor's equivalent of the one-yard line. I was eye-to-eye with brokers from the biggest houses—Salomon, Merrill Lynch, Goldman Sachs, Morgan Stanley— and I was the newcomer. It was as if I had intercepted the ball and now had a chance to run for a touchdown.

Then, as luck would have it, the IBM pit started rocking and rolling.

"Jan '95 calls!" a broker yelled out.

That was verbal shorthand for January call options with a strike price of $95 a share. That meant, if you bought that call you'd have the right to be long IBM shares at $95. In those days, IBM was trading around $88 a share, and put and call options with strike prices from $80 to $100 were actively traded.

Since the big traders the brokers usually relied on had left for lunch, the broker who wanted January 95 calls had to rely on me. I had both the best bid and the best proximity to that broker. Here was the opportunity I was working for; now I had to prove I was prepared to handle the action.

"Even to a quarter!" I yelled back.

I quoted both the bid price—buying at $4.00-even—and the ask price—selling at $4.25. But at that point I did not know if the broker was looking to buy or sell, or how many options were involved in the transaction. Brokers, working on behalf of their customers, never disclose more information than is absolutely necessary.

"Buy 'em at four-and-a quarter!" the broker responded.

"Sell you 20!" I yelled out. I threw out an amount that I felt comfortable selling. I wasn't going to look like a lightweight by offering five options, but I wasn't going to sell 100 either.

"I'm looking for 10," the broker replied.

"Sold!" I yelled triumphantly.

At the end of this seemingly complicated ritual, which took about 10 seconds, I had sold 10 January IBM call options with a strike price of $95 a share for a premium of $4.25. Since each options contract is worth 100 shares, I was short 1,000 IBM shares at $95 ($4.25 × 100 shares × 10 contracts). Those options were worthless until IBM shares rose close to $95 a share, but I still had an open position to cover to hedge my risk.

The more sophisticated you are, the more choices you have to hedge your position risk. In a perfect world, you'd sell 10 calls at $4.25 and buy 10 from someone else at $4.00, and make $25 per contract. If I could fully capture the spread between the bid and the offer on that 10-contract trade, I would have made $250. Since I was a rookie, I took the safe way out and decided to hedge my position with stock. I signaled for a "crowd clerk," whose job was to facilitate stock trades for the options traders on the floor. Getting his attention, I pulled my index finger toward my forehead and then held up my clenched fist. This told the clerk that I wanted to buy 1,000 shares. (A single finger pulled toward my forehead told him I wanted to buy. Having my palms out and facing away from me would have told him I was a seller. A clenched fist indicated that I wanted to buy at the whole number, in this case $88 a share). Moments later the clerk flashed back his confirmation that I had bought 1,000 shares of IBM for $88 a share.

Trade 1:   Sold 10 Jan '95 IBM Calls
            Strike Price $95/share
            Premium Collected $4.25/share
            Hedge: Bought 1,000 IBM shares at $88 a share

Trade 2:   Bought 10 Jan '95 IBM Calls
            Strike Price $95/share
            Premium Paid $4.00/share
            Hedge: Sold 1,000 IBM shares at 87⅞ a share.
            Net result: Made $0.25 a share, or $25 per contract, for profit of $250 on 10 options contracts. Lost $0.125 a share on 1,000 IBM shares for loss of $125. Net profit on trades before commissions, $125.

From that trade on, I was not invisible to the brokers. I'd be short the stock one minute and long the next. Sometimes I had a profit on the put and call spread, and on the stock I bought and sold to hedge my position. Most often, I scratched—or made no profit—on the stock, or lost an eighth on the stock, while making most of my profits scalping in and out of the options (for example, buy at an eighth and sell at a quarter). When the traders came back from their lunch, they expected to be able to move me out of the way, but that didn't happen. Then they hoped I'd be forced to step behind them and get shoved to the back because I failed to respond with markets and size for the brokers, but that didn't happen either. I stayed on the front lines the rest of the day, buying and selling puts and calls all day and making bigger and bigger markets. The more I traded, the more confident I became. I knew the other big traders didn't appreciate the fact that I'd moved into the neighborhood, but that was their problem. Like thousands of traders before me, I saw my opening and went for it. Once I had my feet under me, nobody was going to stop me. This was pure unadulterated excitement and I knew at that moment that I could make my place in this business.

the front lines of capitalism

My "marketplace" for options, for most of my 20 years of trading, has been the trading floor of the CBOE, which I consider to be the front lines of capitalism. This business is fast and a trader needs to be hedged at all times. We half-jokingly compare this business to dashing in front of moving bulldozers to pick up dimes off the ground. Fumble for the dime, and you could be flattened.

Since I trade, increasingly, off-the-floor myself these days, I know the "upstairs" traders at the desk of any brokerage firm or trading house have the same ego and attitude as the floor traders. Those off-the-floor traders may be trading huge sizes—500 or 1,000 option contracts at a time, and each contract is worth 100 shares of stock. Many of those upstairs traders long to be on the floor where the action is. There is an immediacy we experience on the floor that does not translate to a screen upstairs. You may be a Nasdaq dealer, wheeling and dealing large lots of shares, but when you have an options trade to execute, you still have to call the floor to trade.

Today, much of my time is spent managing trading firms that operate as separate entities under the "Mercury Trading" umbrella. Our firms, located in San Francisco, New York, and my hometown of Chicago, are designated primary market makers—or specialists— in 95 different stocks, such as Micron Technology, Sun Microsystems, and Biogen. Each day we trade nearly 35,000 option contracts and nearly $100 million worth of stock.

Options trading has changed since I started out in 1981 when there were 70 stocks with options on them and no index products. Today, we have options on 1,600 stocks trading on the floor of the CBOE alone. Seats at the Exchange were worth $155,000 in 1981; today, they're worth about $600,000. Volume on the New York Stock Exchange can easily top 1 billion shares on an active day, a dramatic rise from the 48 million shares per day when I began trading.

The floor has also changed. We trade much more now, given a strong influx of both institutional and retail paper. But more and more, the ranks on the floor are young traders with handheld computers the size of a Palm Pilot that record their trades automatically. Many of those computers automatically analyze the market, letting a trader know if an option is "expensive" or "cheap" by color-coding— red for overvalued and green for undervalued. Some of these novices can't even buy or sell unless the computer tells them.

It rankles veterans like me to see a floor dominated by traders holding their miniature computers. But I know why they're there. Trades have become yet another commodity. Why pay veterans like me to trade when you can get computer-savvy youngsters who are more than willing to stand on the floor and trade for $40,000 to $70,000 a year, following the instructions of a handheld computer. It's not so amusing when the computers go down and the trading pits become silent, either because the traders don't know how to trade unassisted or their firms have instructed them not to trade without electronic guidance.

Granted, it's not as "pure" as some of us old-timers (at age 42) would like. But there's no denying that this new breed of trader has accompanied a large influx of capital to the floor. Even trading firms with millions of dollars in backing can't just hire 100 experienced traders to go down to the floor. There are 70 different pits or "posts" on the floor where we trade options on 1,600 stocks. That means you need a minimum of 70 traders on the floor. That means 70 salaries plus 70 seat leases at about $10,000 a month. That puts the overhead of a trading operation at more than $1 million a month. With seat leases being a fixed cost, the only variable is salary. And that means hiring younger traders who are willing to work at a lower salary. Frequently, I refer to this style of management as "Fat Brain," as the young guns are directed by a group of traders, or in some cases even computers (the Fat Brains), that generate buy-and-sell levels and do most of the hedging, as well.

At my firm, we make sure all our traders know how to trade. Although we use computer assistance, the electronics do not tell us when to buy or sell.

For retail investors, this change in the dynamics of the market has been part of an overall change for the better. With more big money coming to the floor and a proliferation of stocks with options on them, there is a greater depth and liquidity in the market than there has ever been. The four U.S. options exchanges list about 20 to 30 new issues every month, some of them initial public offerings (IPOs) that are only six months old.

It's a different landscape now than when I first came to the trading floor as a 22-year-old, left largely on my own to cull insights into the market where I could. But some of the changes have been for the better. Traders download their "sheets"—lists of put and call option prices and values—at night from the Internet. In many ways, this embracing of technology will help the options pit to survive in the electronic era.

Unlike many of the traditional futures-trading exchanges, which have fought the encroachment of technology, in options we have embraced technology and brought it into the pit. Ours is a hybrid of open outcry and electronic trading, which many of us believe will extend the life of the trading floor, so that when we become fully electronic we won't have an exchange that looks like a ghost town. We will be ready, because we have been at least partially electronic for a decade or more.

The electronic revolution on the floor will continue to bring dramatic change in the experience of the retail customer. Response times—from the placement of an order by a customer to execution on the floor—is being narrowed to just seconds. That means virtual instant gratification for the public. We'll be seeing this, increasingly, with electronic communication networks (ECNs) in stocks, which bring the market to the retail customer. We've also seen the explosion of volume that this direct access to equities has produced. In options, technology will mean virtual interaction between the public and market makers, and that leveling of the playing field should likewise result in massive increases in the volume of options traded.

When I began trading nearly two decades ago, the average response time was two minutes. First, a customer's order would leave a desk at a brokerage-house office upstairs and be sent to the pit. There, a teletype machine would print the order out at a desk on the floor, where a clerk would separate carbon copies of the order and hand one to a runner (who may or may not be waiting there) who would bring it to a broker in the pit.

In those two minutes, the market could very well have moved, meaning the customer might not get anywhere near the price anticipated. Or, if the customer placed a limit order—with a specified price—it may never be executed if the market moved substantially higher or lower.

Today, 90 percent of the orders come to the floor fully electronic. Orders go from a brokerage office upstairs to the trading floor at electronic speed. By the time the order is offered in the pit, the response time is something like seven seconds. This means slippage—the difference between the price a customer sees on the screen when an order is placed and the price at which the order is executed—is greatly reduced. The result is a more efficient market and a better experience for the customer.

When I began trading, virtually all the trading capital was held in the accounts of individual traders on the floor. Each trader was capitalized to the tune of tens of thousands—and in a few cases, hundreds of thousands—of dollars. Since late 1998, the average firm on the options floor has multimillion-dollar backing and a cadre of young traders. Some of the firms that are offshoots of the major brokerages may have $200 million to $300 million in backing. From a customer perspective, this amount of capitalization means there will be ample liquidity in the market to handle large trades when a Fidelity, a Dreyfuss, Goldman Sachs, or a large hedge fund—which we almost never saw in the market in my early days—comes into the market.

The marketplace may change, but the attributes of a good trader have not. The most important commonality among traders is discipline. If you're an independent trader, discipline is your single most important quality; without it, you have a slim chance of succeeding on your own. If you work for a firm, discipline will help others have confidence in your ability to trade and carry out a plan. At my own firm, I can only put my trust in traders who I know are disciplined, abide by the rules, and carry out our strategies. I need to know, for example, that when one of my traders is long more than 5,000 shares, he (or she) will cut his losses or start to take profits. If they can't carry out those directives, they won't be with our firm very long.

To trade in the pit, you must have stamina, as well. To earn a place in the front ranks nearest the brokers, you must stand your ground—literally. Among the brokers in that inner circle, the most sought after are those who handle orders from the public. These brokers, working for firms such as Charles Schwab or Fidelity, often have 10- and 20-contract orders to execute on behalf of a retail customer. For independent traders, these are prime orders that offer us a chance to sell 10 call options on Dell, for example, and then buy 10 a minute later in another transaction and make the quarter-point spread between the bid and the ask. That's why the crowd is usually the thickest around these "public" or retail brokers.

The orders these brokers execute are generated when a retail customer reads an article about a company or gets a tip from a friend and decides to invest in the stock via options. As I'll explain a little later, options are a relatively low cost way to speculate in stocks and take advantage of leverage. These retail orders are not based usually on sophisticated technical analysis that shows an option is under- or overvalued. Nor do they reflect a careful study of a company based on concerns over upcoming earnings or product development.

The crowd of traders is a lot thinner around the institutional brokers for major houses such as Goldman Sachs, Morgan Stanley, or Lehman Brothers. These brokers are executing large orders on behalf of institutional clients. The size, alone, precludes many traders from trading, since these brokers are dealing with a "lot of paper"— often in the hundreds of contracts. Since each options contract represents 100 shares of stock, the exposure is considerable on each trade. Additionally, these orders do tend to be based on sophisticated analysis of either the price of an option or the fundamentals of a company. For example, if an institutional investor expects an earnings surprise—either positive or negative—from a company, they may become big buyers of either puts or calls. The market maker who takes the trade must be disciplined and always hedge those large positions because these institutional customers are usually acting on time-sensitive information. Thus, the market makers must be fast and accurate on their hedging against these trades.

To be a floor trader, in particular, you must be a competitor who will go the distance. For example, when the CBOE prepared to list Dell options in 1999, traders were vying for a place even before trading began. Traders were staying overnight in the pit to mark their spots so no one else could muscle in on their floor territory. At first they were coming in at 2 A.M. to secure a spot on the floor, but quickly learned that they needed to arrive by 10 P.M. to get the best location. One of our traders brought an inflatable mattress to work and slept on the floor of the exchange so he wouldn't lose his spot. There were 20 or 30 traders sprawled out on the floor, using telephone books for pillows. Finally, the Exchange drew the line and no one was allowed to spend the night on the floor. Spending the night to protect your position on the floor may seem a little extreme, but in a business where your position on the floor could mean the difference between getting the other side of a broker order or not, you'll do whatever it takes.

Moreover, trading on the floor is a "people business." The observer sees only the screaming and yelling of prices and the bantering among the traders. But when you're quoting a market to a broker who may be buying 10 options or 500, there is a good deal of negotiating going on. You have to have some kind of personality that makes you stand out, even if it's a friendly combative one. You have to get along with people in the pit; it can't always be war. There are literally hundreds of traders in the stock index options pits. There might be 70 or so in the popular stock options pit, like the AOL. With this kind of population, you must be able to hold your own as a trader and as a human being. If there aren't at least some people with whom you get along, it will be you against the whole pit. That, obviously, doesn't work very well.

Beyond these qualities, you must also have a quick mind and an ability to focus on several things at once, such as the premiums quoted on puts and calls on several options and the price fluctuations of the underlying stocks. That's why some trading firms like to recruit bridge players and chess players, who can think multidimensionally, strategically planning several moves ahead. Others like card-counters, who can keep track of numbers and combinations quickly, as well as the odds of certain events occurring. Many former athletes go to the trading floor. At my firm, I have seven former football players, including my brother, Pete, and myself.

my path to the options floor

I came to the options pit directly from the football field. It was not a career path I had planned, but it all worked out better than I might have ever hoped.

By nature, I am an optimistic person. But I also know my limitations, even though I might extend myself to the end of those limitations. Part of what makes up my trading and business acumen is that I can get out there and dance on the edge. I respect what could happen, but I don't live in fear of it. If fear dominates your thoughts, you're not going to see the opportunities that are available to you.

When I am focused on a goal, I give it all I have. But when I know, realistically, that I have no chance of succeeding, I switch to an alternate plan. That is a personality trait that has served me well in trading, in life, and in football. A critical assessment of where I am and where I want to be is the reason why I, in time, became an options trader. And it's also the reason why my college football career spanned five schools. Unless I was going to be among the starters, I simply wasn't going to play. I'd go somewhere else.

I always wanted to play football, a dream that really took shape for me when I was a 12-year-old "ball boy" for the Vikings, after my family moved from the West Coast to Minneapolis, where my father became the Chief of Surgery at the University of Minnesota. My football dream began to take shape when I played at Central High School in Minneapolis, a school that was racially and ethnically mixed. Among my classmates and friends were "The Artist Formerly Known as Prince" (a slightly built musician who did not play football) and his brother (who did), and two other famous musicians and producers (Janet Jackson's Control), Terry Lewis, and Jimmy Jam.

A torn-up ankle, repaired with two surgical screws and synthetic ligaments, killed my football-scholarship offers from Ohio State and Notre Dame. Instead, I went to the fall football camp at the University of Minnesota, but my ankle wasn't good enough for me to play on the team. So I sat out that season and enrolled in Normandale Junior College in the spring of 1976. There, I met football players who were good enough, in my estimation, to play at

Division I schools, from which most of the pro-ball players are drafted. Because most of us at Normandale were overlooked by those Division I schools, either because of physical or academic reasons, most of us played with a chip on our shoulders. This was great for our team, but bad for our opponents, as we led the nation in several categories and our defense, which I co-captained, was one of the tops in all levels of college football, allowing just over five points per game. We went on to win a bowl game and sent several of my teammates to Division I teams, and four of us to professional ball teams.

After graduating from Normandale, I went to the University of California at Berkeley for the spring quarter. But I didn't stay because the team initiated a switch from a four-linebacker defense to three, and I was concerned that I would become the odd man out among the four linebackers. So rather than stick around and be the backup, I transferred to Cornell University in Ithaca, New York. Although Cornell had a good team, it wasn't Division I. Besides, my brother David was playing football at a small Minnesota college called Gustavus Adolphus College and he and I had always talked about playing together. Figuring this was my last chance to play football with my brother and in front of my parents and friends, I transferred there and became captain of the college football team.

Our team won its share of championships, and my brother David and I were scouted by most professional teams. After practices, the scouts would ask you to run a 40-yard dash, do vertical or horizontal jumps, or press 225-pounds for maximum repetitions. And, if they represented a team like the Dallas Cowboys, they'd run an IQ test on you. With a degree in art history and design, my "Plan B" was to go to graduate school and become an architect. My "Plan A" was to play professional football.

I was contacted by a number of professional teams, but I did my homework and decided to play for the *worst* team, which in 1981 was the Bears. I figured that on a comparatively bad team I had the best chance to stand out as a rookie and would have a better chance of making the cut.

I headed for Chicago where the starting middle-linebacker, Tom Hicks, had suddenly quit in a salary dispute. Tom was making more money in the off-season as a trader at the Chicago Mercantile Exchange without getting beaten up to do it. So the Bears (whom, famed ex-coach Mike Ditka once said, "throw nickels around like they were manhole covers") lost their starting middle linebacker and any leverage they had over their second round draft choice, Mike Singletary. I guess Mike and his agent understood leverage as well as any options trader on the floor of the CBOE, because he held out, forcing the Bears to sign me as a free-agent. That opened the door, at least for a short while, to play linebacker for the Chicago Bears.

The practices were tough, but the camaraderie was excellent. Walter Payton, the Bears' best-known running back, was on the team. (Walter used to call me "Elvis," because I had hair in those days—a lot of hair—which has since been replaced by a bit more forehead and a short ponytail in back.) Mike Singletary had signed with the Bears by the time the preseason began. It was obvious to me that Mike was a real talent, but I wasn't about to quit . . . I was ever the optimist. I was going to give it my all, but I knew that Singletary was the star of the future.

If events had played out differently, I could have held on and been a back-up. Or, perhaps I would have gone to another team and had a satisfactory career for five or seven years. But my career in football was not to be. My last preseason game was against Kansas City. To this day, I remember how big that stadium was and how large the crowd. It seemed surreal, because when you're on that field, all you can focus on is the play you're executing. It was as if the crowd was silent. My last play for the Bears was on the suicide squad covering a kickoff. I made the tackle and broke my helmet in the process. It was a pretty good collision, and my tackle had knocked the back down inside the 20-yard line. Unfortunately, there was an offside penalty against us, so we had to back up five yards and re-do the kickoff. On the next play, the running back downed the ball in the end zone and, thus, ended my brief professional career.

After that fourth preseason game, I was told at breakfast on Sunday to "bring your play book. The coach wants to see you." Those are never the words you want to hear as a pro ball player. I handed in my play book and was given a return ticket to Minneapolis. I went home a 22-year-old ex-NFL player with a few choices, but no real plan. I decided against playing football in Canada because, true to my nature, if it wasn't the big league, I didn't want to be part of it. One of my driving motivations has always been to distinguish myself in whatever field I choose.

That's when I decided to become a trader. You see, when I was practicing with the Bears during the long hot Chicago summer, the fans who came out to watch us at three o'clock in the afternoon were stockbrokers and traders. Why? Because as soon as the market closed around 3 P.M. Central time, they were free. I was fascinated by the markets and by the fact that it would be wonderful to finish your day at 3 P.M.! Minus another plan, a career as a stockbroker seemed to be the best choice for me.

So I told my plan to my football agent, Dick Lurie, who also happened to be an options trader. "If you want to get into the market," he told me, "you ought to trade options."

The notion of options trading was completely foreign to me, but I agreed to give it a go. A few days later, I was a clerk at the Exchange, completely in another world.

Dick was a good guy, but he didn't have the time or the temperament to show me the ropes. I was left to absorb what I could about options on my own. That was probably the most difficult thing for me. I was used to being in a world—most recently football—where I knew exactly what was going on. Things were pretty regimented for football players: Break down tendencies on film. Put in new defensive sets. Practice against the other team's offensive formations. But in the options pit, nobody hands you a play book and puts you through the paces. Everyone is expected to learn to "read the tape" on his or her own. Options trading was so new that those who really understood calls and puts were desperately trying to keep the knowledge for their own benefit. It would be like giving a prospector a map to your gold mine. Why would you do it?

The main reason I was unhappy was that I thought I would never be good enough at options trading to distinguish myself in that field. I was lost half the time with no one to teach me while the market swirled around me. (As a teacher and a lecturer now, I remember how that felt. I believe this experience as a rookie helped me to become not only a better options trader, but a better trainer, as well.) But I was as tenacious about this career as I had been about my football career—I wasn't about to quit. I had been raised to believe that if I was going to be successful, I would have to give it my all.

Being the son of Dr. John (with an "h") Najarian is a wonderful, but difficult, role. My father was famous for his skill as a surgeon who performed some of the earliest organ transplants in the country.

His picture on the cover of *Newsweek,* in surgical gown and mask and performing a transplant, is framed on my office wall. I am immensely proud of him and the rest of my family, which also includes my brother, Pete, a former linebacker with the Seattle Seahawks, Minnesota Vikings, Sacramento Surge, and Tampa Bay Buccaneers and now an options trader; my brothers, David and Paul, who live in Minneapolis and operate several fast-food franchises in the Twin Cities, and my mother, Mignette, who raised us to try to be our best. But as my father's son, I knew what it was like to grow up in the shadow of a famous and accomplished man. He was both my role model and my challenge.

my education on the floor

Through hard work and innovation, I managed to learn about options trading during my time as Dick's clerk. He hooked up with a New York stock specialist firm, a partnership that enabled us under "Reg T" to trade stocks without putting up any margin. When I started, options traders had to put up a margin on the stocks they used to hedge their positions. Later, that rule was changed and options traders, like stock specialists, could trade without margin as long as they had sufficient hedges in options against the stock they were trading.

Through our partnership with the specialist's firm, we had an opportunity to make good money in stocks, especially shorting them in a hedged transaction known as a *reversal.* Interest rates topped 16 percent in those days. Imagine selling 100 shares of IBM at $100 a share, or $10,000. With interest rates at 16 percent, you could earn a lot of interest on that money, and the margins were huge since the other option market makers didn't have access to our Reg-T exemption.

I would arrange the stock loans (because the person shorting the stock must borrow from someone who has access to lendable securities) with Merrill Lynch or Drexall Burham for hundreds of shares at a time. There were months when our rebate checks (interest paid on the stock we sold short) would exceed several hundred thousand dollars. As lucrative as that was, those proceeds never seemed to trickle down to me, the clerk. So when another trader named Thomas Haugh, whom I had met playing softball in my off hours, asked me to come to work for him, I jumped at the chance. Tom paid me $100 a week and taught me all that I needed to know about options. He was—and still is—a brilliant trader. In fact, we still work together in PTI Capital Management LLC, a Chicago-based proprietary trading firm and iTradem.com, our all-electronic brokerage for securities, options, and futures.

Tom's strength was as a market technician, particular in spreading techniques (which I'll explain a little later in this book). Working with him, I began to understand the possibilities in this market that, for six months, had eluded me. I saw that if I bought "this" and sold "that," I had the potential of making more money than just trading one position with a hedge.

Unfortunately for Tom and me, we were trading in the "dark ages" of 1981 and 1982 when computers were extremely slow. Printing our "sheets"—endless lists of options prices—took hours. We came in at six in the morning to get ready to trade at nine. Often, after the close, we'd go to the gym to work out and then come back to the office and work until 10 P.M.

We'd scan the sheets for options that, based on our analysis, were under- or overvalued, which we would then want to buy or sell. Perhaps there was an option trading at $3.50 that we thought should be valued at $4.00; we'd want to buy those. Or, perhaps an option was trading at $5 that we thought was more fairly valued at $4; we'd sell that one. Even though options were trading on only about 80 stocks in those days, we'd find enough opportunities to have spreads all over the floor.

By comparison, with faster and more powerful computers, the analysis that used to take Tom and me hours to do can be accomplished in six to eight minutes—and for 1,500 stocks instead of just 80.

Tom began to let me put on the spreads that I would find, which introduced me to trading on the floor with the money he was managing. Then I wanted to trade for myself. Tom knew I didn't have enough money to back myself, so he set me up with a friend of his who put up my trading capital and let me keep 50 percent of my profits. For the first time, I not only knew the game, but I had a plan to succeed.

Then I made it to the front of the IBM options pit one day and traded in the big league. The rest, as they say, is history.

In football, some people can't get past the big bodies slamming into each other to truly understand the intricacies of the game. For a long time, I was like that in the market. I saw the action, but I did not fully comprehend what was really going on. I couldn't see the strategies that the players were using or understand how the market was reacting and why.

In 1981, the money supply was everything. It was the one economic factor that everybody waited for and reacted to. Then, by 1987, it was the trade deficit. There were even some who believed the trade deficit had become so large it actually caused the stock market crash of 1987.

Through early 1999, it was inflation. All eyes were on the unemployment figures for signs that the economy was growing too quickly and the Fed would have to raise rates. In late 1999, the dollar had our attention. In early 2000, we're mesmerized by the gyrations of Nasdaq and the Internet.

As I have seen countless times in the past 20 years, just when you think something is the answer to all of the market's questions it turns out that something else is wielding more influence. In the investment world today, anything "dot-com" is the rage. But while the Internet is useful technology, it's really a twist on an old theme. Once it was railroads that connected towns and markets. And then radio was the hot new medium. Who knows what will follow the Internet.

One thing is certain: Whatever appears on the horizon will somehow become a traded security, and securities will always need market makers like me. But that doesn't mean the opportunities will be limited to only a small inner circle. On the contrary! What the e-trading explosion has showed us is there are the vast legions of retail investors willing to trade and invest in stocks on their own—and online. Once the options market becomes demystified for them and electronic access is improved, the options market will become as fertile a field for these retail investors as the stock market has been.

how investors can use options to their advantage

While my arena has been the trading floor and my off-the-floor trading operation, Mercury Trading, there is increasing interest in the options market among retail investors and speculators. The retail audience that has poured billions into the stock market, speculating in stocks from Blue Chips to dot-coms, is learning more and more about options. At the same time, the options industry is eagerly educating the retail market about trading options, including how to use these derivative securities to participate in the market with limited risk.

Options carry no guarantee of return, just as with any investment. There are strategies that can help you to maximize your return while keeping your risk within defined parameters. Trading options successfully will require you to do your homework and to plan out your strategy. But it's not impossible, and as you'll read in later chapters, there are many strategies to profit in bull markets, bear markets, and when the market (or a particular stock) is in a range. This is a message that I bring home at the myriad of options seminars that I speak at around the country every year. I teach investors that, with the proper training and dedication, you *can* use options to increase profits and protect your investments. Investing in options is not a "get rich quick" scheme, but with a long-enough time horizon and a little homework, it's possible that options will become the most important part of your investment strategy.

The options market—where I had my baptism by fire—is the place in which I "grew up" professionally. As I stated at the beginning of this chapter, a healthy options market benefits all of us, professional and retail speculator alike. As you'll read in Chapter 2, retail investors don't compete with professionals. Our games are entirely different. But the liquidity that each group brings to the marketplace can only make it a healthier and more profitable place to be.

chapter 2

the marketplace

The floor of the Chicago Board Options Exchange (CBOE) is a hybrid environment. Like its parent exchange, the Chicago Board of Trade, the options-trading floor has pits where traders in colored loose-fitting jackets call out their bids and offers. But electronic technology has made strong in-roads onto the floor. Large, electronic screens flash above the pits—or posts, as they're also called—where stock options are traded. These big screens bear a close resemblance to the departure and arrival monitors at airports. But the technology doesn't end there.

In the pit, the market maker, whose job is to make a two-sided market for put and call options, is more than likely holding court around a cluster of computer screens that display the orders to be executed. Traders with handheld computers scan their screens for the latest analysis of bids and offers. Headsets and computers abound. Traders have every gadget from Palm VII's, cell phones and beepers, to strings of batteries to run everything.

One trader passed me on the floor the other day wearing a headset (a kind of limited-range cell phone that only works on the trading floor) and a computer in a ballistic nylon case slung over his shoulder. In his hand, he clutched a Palm VII and a calculator. All he was missing was a satellite dish on his head.

Technology will extend the life of our trading floor and our pit, as other exchanges debate the futures of open-outcry. Even though purists like me have been irked at times by "Gameboy traders"—so named for the handheld computers they use that resemble the popular video game hardware—technology is our future. As I stated in the opening chapter, technology will speed the flow of customer orders to the floor and technology will allow firms to hire legions of young, inexperienced traders who are willing to take direction from a computer screen.

To be honest, the hybrid trading floor, where traders and computer screens commingle, is fitting for a derivative marketplace such as options. Think about it. Our stock and trade is the next generation of financial instruments. We trade speculative instruments that, in virtually all cases, no one wants to buy and hold (unlike those shares in the electric company your grandfather bought and put in the desk drawer for 30 years).

But when I buy an option, I do not own a piece of a company or a bond that will pay me interest. I own the right to own or sell something. In form, options are a speculative opportunity in case a stock price does, indeed, move your way. And in function, options (at least when they're bought and not sold) act as a kind of insurance policy potentially to limit risk.

Within this marketplace, there are key players, each of whom plays a vital role in making an efficient and liquid market. There is the market maker, who provides a constant, continuous market with a bid and ask spread. There is the broker who executes customer orders on the floor, and the local traders who speculate on market movements. Behind the scenes, in trading offices around the country, are professional traders who sit at computers off the floor, as I do the majority of my days. As an owner of four trading firms and a partner in a Chicago-based brokerage operation, I am trading on the floor less and less. But I trade on a regular basis in either our 15th-floor proprietary trading office adjacent to the Options Exchange or help manage our option fund, across the street in a room filled with computer screens.

To understand options, I believe you must understand the role of each of those players, and where you—as a professional trader or a retail speculator—fit into the game.

market makers

First there is the market maker who is obliged to make a two-sided market—meaning he or she may have to sell an option that, as speculators, they'd rather buy. In return for the obligation quoting both bids and offers on options, the market maker is exempt from Reg T, meaning we can buy or sell stock without margin requirements. (If an investor or speculator wants to buy a stock, they must buy the shares outright or put up a margin equivalent to 50 percent of the value of the transaction.) All we have to have is enough capital in our accounts to cover the risk, which is called—inexplicably—a "haircut."

For each stock, there is a designated primary market maker (DPM), a kind of overseer market maker whose job it is to make sure there is a liquid and orderly market for individual options. The DPMs are analogous to the specialists who oversee trading of a stock on the New York Stock Exchange. The American Stock Exchange (AMEX) and Philadelphia Stock Exchange (PHLX) call those people responsible for smooth and orderly trading of their option classes "specialists," and the Pacific Stock Exchange (PCX) calls them Lead Market Makers (LMMs).

There are a few other advantages that come with the responsibility of being a market maker, namely leverage and the absence of Reg T, which allows us to buy and sell stock and options for a relatively small, up-front investment. For example, if a retail customer wants to buy 10 options that have a $6 premium, he or she must have $6,000 in their account. (Each option represents 100 shares; thus 10 options are equivalent to 1,000 shares. With a $6 premium for 1,000 shares, the total value of the transaction is $6,000.) A market maker, on the other hand, could purchase the same 10 options for as little as $150, thanks to leverage we receive for the obligations we take on.

Leverage and the opportunities that come from being a market maker (and, at the risk of sounding boastful, being experienced in options trading) can bring some very big rewards. Neither the Exchanges I trade on nor my fellow market makers, specialists, DPMs, and LMMs would appreciate it if I touted my performance, but I can suggest a range of returns that is representative of the sort of numbers we are capable of achieving. First, let me say there is no average. Average doesn't cut it on the trading floor. Boarding houses are full of average traders. The reason for that is simple: Overhead will take all the profits of a so-called average trader.

Consider that the seat you need to trade on the Exchanges costs from $5,000 to $16,000 per month, depending on which exchange you intend to trade on. The seats are in demand because people are making money down on the trading floors. Most Exchanges have a fixed number of seats. But the CBOE, which was started by the Chicago Board of Trade (CBOT) in 1973, has an elastic membership since every full member of the CBOT can trade on the CBOE. Even so, the demand for seats on the CBOE is intense. Each month, anywhere from 30 to 60 new members plunk down about $2,500 to take the test for membership. Even with the elasticity created by the unique CBOE/CBOT structure, those new members mean that about the same number of CBOE members had to leave the business. When you do the math, you see that nearly one-third of our floor, which averages about 1,400 members, turns over every year!

I think there are two primary catalysts for the surge in demand for seats on our exchanges: (1) the rapid growth of retail option business and (2) the groups that have proliferated as computerization enabled them to link multiple floor traders with upstairs risk managers. When I started in 1981, there was really just one such group on the CBOE—O'Connor, which was purchased by SBC Warburg Dillon Read in the late 1980s. Today, there are 15 such groups, each employing as many as 100 traders and, thus, pressuring as many Exchange memberships (seats).

Given the cut-throat competition for seats and position in the trading pits, you can understand why average doesn't cut it. A reasonable amount that a good options trader takes home after expenses is $150,000 per year. With some seasoning, proper discipline, and sufficient capital, the numbers probably average between $200,000 and $800,000 per year. Exceptional traders, maybe the top 5 percent, push into the strong seven figures.

Other than the lack of proper discipline, the greatest obstacle facing the trader is access to satisfactory capital. For that reason, the majority of traders do as I did and find a financial backer to help insure their success. Profit splits range from straight salaries to sliding scales of profit-sharing. Some traders must sign noncompete agreements that obligate them to a certain number of years of service for the backing, while others gets 50 percent, 60 percent, or even 75 percent of the profits they generate from their trading activities.

When you look at these kind of returns, you might say to yourself, gee, if I had two or three winning trades and the kind of leverage that a professional has, I'd really make a killing in this market.

But you have to remember that the same kind of leverage that can compound a reward will also compound the risk. Leverage puts risk on steroids. As a professional trader, when a trade goes against me I'm losing from 20 to 100 times as much as a retail investor would lose on the same dollar-amount of investment.

Another consideration is my cost, starting with a seat at the CBOE. The Chicago Board of Trade, where commodities such as corn, soybeans, and wheat and financial instruments such as futures on 30-Year U.S. Bonds are traded, founded the CBOE in 1973. At that time, every full member of the Board of Trade—about 931 members—had a right to a seat at the options exchange. The seats were originally priced at $10,000. The all-time high was about $750,000. Today, the seats are valued at about $600,000. To lease a seat, the cost is about 1.75 percent per month, roughly $10,000 per month. To be a trader on the floor, that $10,000 per month lease is quite an up-front cost.

Once you have a seat and pass the membership test, you need a clearing firm, such as the one I use—First Options of Chicago, a Division of Speer Leads & Kellogg—to clear your trades. As a trader or broker on the floor, who buys or sells puts and calls on nothing more than a verbal agreement, there must be a firm that stands behind your trades. You can usually tell by the color of the jacket that a trader wears—black is Bear Stearns; red is Schwab; steel blue is Merrill Lynch; and black jackets with planets on them are for Mercury Trading, my firm.

Traders' connections with a clearing firm and trading firm provide the assurance that any trade they make is good. Another trader doesn't need to know your financial situation. All they need to know is that your clearing firm backs any trade you make, and along with that there is the Options Clearing Corporation (OCC), which is the only AAA-rated clearing facility in the world. All listed

---

Here's an aside on the naming of my firm: One day I was sitting in my office, which overlooks the CBOT, and found myself staring at the statue of Ceres, the goddess of the harvest, that stands atop the CBOT. That gave me a little inspiration for the naming of my own firm, in this case for Mercury, the god of markets and commerce and the protector of traders.

options in the United States clear through the OCC, which stands behind every trade with the full faith and credit of all its members, which include the likes of Goldman Sachs, Merrill Lynch, and Morgan Stanley Dean Witter. When you're trading on the floor, you're identified by your trading badge. On the CBOE and CBOT, we have from one to three letters that create our acronyms. Mine is "DRJ." I first sought out "JON," but that was taken. So I opted for DRJ to honor my Dad, because he, too, is known as "Doctor J." Traders on the Chicago Mercantile Exchange can choose up to four letters for their badges, while traders at the AMEX, PHLX, and PCX get numbers on their badges.

As a professional trader, I pay miniscule commissions—10 cents or less to trade an option and only a fraction of a penny a share to trade a stock. That's one reason why I'm not in competition with the general public. As a professional trader on the floor, I have a time and place advantage that no retail investor can replicate. If you try to compete against someone who has one-tenth or one-hundredth of your costs in any business, you are going to lose no matter what and no matter how good you are. Additionally, floor traders, with our time and place advantage, can buy and sell in fractions of a second, while the fastest cyber-trader still has to point and click his or her trade into a brokerage, which then routes the order to the trading floor.

No, my competition is not the public, but rather the other 1,399 traders on the floor of the CBOE. With the time and place advantage of being on the floor, and trading within shouting distance of the institutional and retail brokers, I can trade repeatedly. That sheer volume of trades means that even if I make a profit on only 50 percent of my trades (keep in mind that a market maker is obliged to quote bids and asks that may result in losing trades as obligations are fulfilled) I can make money overall. How? Because I hedge myself against risk, cut my losses short, and let my profits run.

Within this realm of professional traders, there are the market makers who are drawn by opportunity. Where there is the greatest perceived opportunity—whether it's Dell, IBM, or the latest dot-com stock—there will be the greatest number of market makers, all vying with each other for the brokers' bids and offers.

When a new stock options out such as eBay or Broadcast.com (which premiered briefly on the CBOE before the company was taken over by Yahoo) players compete to be the DPM. It's not a bidding war with money involved. Rather, it comes down to who will make the best market. First, you need to show you are an experienced market maker. In the case of Mercury Trading's Chicago office, we handle 30,000 options and several million shares of stock each day. Then you propose your specifications to create a deep, liquid, and tight market that will encourage people to trade. Based on the various proposals, the Exchange's committee chooses who will be the DPM for the new issue.

The first time Mercury Trading was given DPM status was for Capital Cities Broadcasting. That was a great one. At that time, the management of Capital Cities went to Warren Buffett with what turned out to be a valuable discovery about New York properties that ABC's owned: They thought ABC's New York City properties were not properly accounted for on the balance sheet. These hidden assets meant, in effect, that ABC's stock was grossly undervalued. So when Capital Cities' made its bid to buy ABC back in the early 1980s, both stocks went up. (Normally, the buyer's stock goes down because of added debt to pay for the transaction or dilution due to additional shares being issued to finance the deal. Shares of the firm to be acquired usually rise to near the buyer's bid price, with a slight gap in case the transaction should fall apart.) As you may recall, takeovers like this and others engineered by people such as Carl Icahn and T. Boone Pickens were the rage as so-called vulture capitalists sought value from the stocks that management was unable or unwilling to emancipate. (It's strange to imagine that now in early 2000, the government may unintentionally take on the same roll in the Microsoft case, as they negotiate whether to split the software giant into two or more companies.)

The CBOE didn't always have DPMs. In the beginning, Chicago, being fiercely entrepreneurial and very competitive, wanted to draw a distinction between itself and the New York Stock Exchange, which has the specialist system for trading stocks. Instead, the CBOE set up its marketplace as a very egalitarian arena where anyone who was fast and aggressive could get the trade. Remember, anyone on the floor of the Exchange has to perform one of two functions: they're either a *broker* executing customer trades or they're market makers who make a two-sided market. That made for a very independent environment.

Then in 1987, the CBOE created DPMs. We needed a specialist-like entity to compete in the newly competitive battle for multiple-listed stocks. Until 1987 there was a lottery for stock options. Each time a new stock was eligible for an option, it was offered to Philadelphia, Chicago, the Pacific Exchange, American Stock Exchange, or the New York Stock Exchange. (In 1997, the CBOE bought the New York Stock Exchange business.) Under a Securities and Exchange Commission mandate, options could only be listed on one Exchange.

What ensued prior to 1987 was a little like an NFL-draft. The Exchanges acted like the team management, accepting the stock options they wanted when it was their turn to pick or passing it on to the next Exchange. With options, it's completely up to the Exchange to choose which options it will list. The company doesn't receive any compensation for its options to be listed, nor do they have to pay the Exchange to list its options.

But that practice changed in 1987. Now, when a new option is available, it is more than likely to be listed by all four Exchanges. When this happened, the CBOE found its lack of a "specialist," one individual who centralized all trading and brokerage, was a detriment. Large institutions such as Salomon or Merrill Lynch wanted to deal with one person in the options market who was in charge of that stock. Thus, to compete and survive, the CBOE gave birth to the DPM.

The DPM must always have a presence in the pit to ensure an efficient and orderly market. In return for that responsibility, the DPM gets a minimum of 30 percent of the trades. That means if 100 lots are traded, at least 30 of them go to the DPM. If there are 1,000 options, at least 300 go to the DPM—regardless of price. But that doesn't mean a DPM can set any price. Options are usually multiple listed so even if you tried to quote a price that was too high or too low, the other Exchanges wouldn't move. When the market returned to equilibrium, you'd be eating the price difference all the way up or all the way down.

Now, with 20 new stocks eligible for options every month (and bearing in mind that these options are likely to be multiple-listed), firms must bid to become the DPM. Their proposals must show that they will not only create the best possible market to attract volume to this option, but also win a majority of the business away from other Exchanges that may list the same security.

My firm, Mercury Trading, specialized in biotechnology firms in the 1980s (a reflection, perhaps, of my own interest in the biotechnology field, given my father's specialty as an organ-transplant surgeon) and in high-technology stocks in the 1990s. Whatever the stock, it's important to remember that customers want volatility. If the underlying stock price doesn't rock and roll, there will be fewer opportunities to buy or sell the option.

At the same time, the DPM must be aware of the dynamics of the options marketplace. For example, when a big order comes in, the effect will extend beyond the option to the underlying stock as well. So if there is a big seller of Micron options, say 5,000 options or so, that's equivalent to 500,000 shares of stock. If someone sells that much stock to hedge an options position, you know the stock price is going down. Although options are a derivative of the underlying, there are times when the catalyst for the market movement begins with the options, sort of a tail-wagging-the-dog scenario.

In most situations in options, the only player bigger than the DPM is going to be a large mutual fund or, in the case of an NYSE listing, the stock specialist. For example, on the occasions when Fidelity is getting into the options market, they're going to dwarf everyone else. It's like in the movie, *Jurassic Park,* when the T-Rex is approaching. You can hear and feel the ground shaking as big funds trade 200,000 shares the way customers trade odd lots. But as the DPM, entitled to 30 percent of the volume of a big stock such as Sun Microsystems (SUNW), I'm going to make some noise, too.

At the same time, it's the responsibility of the DPM to create an orderly marketplace to facilitate both large orders and small. For example, say a broker has 5,000 options to sell, although he won't tip his hand in the beginning regarding the size of the transaction or whether he's buying or selling. He has to begin this ritual with a shout to the pit, for anyone within earshot to hear. Even with all our electronics, we're still an open-outcry auction marketplace. And so it begins like this:

"What's the market on Jan double [meaning, in this instance, 55—get it? Double 5s] calls?" the broker yells out.

"Four to a quarter, a thousand up," the DPM replies. [This response lets the broker know the bid is 4 and the offer is 4¼, both for 1,000 contracts.]

"I've got 5,000 to go," the broker adds.

Now, the DPM, specialist or LMM has to estimate how much impact that half-million shares is going to have on the price of the underlying security. To buy or sell a large order, a market maker is going to want to build in a little price protection for himself.

"For 5,000 my best bid is 3¾," the DPM shouts, estimating he needs another ¼ point to get the majority of his hedge in the underlying stock. If you do the math, a quarter-point price adjustment on a 1,000 lot is worth $25,000, or $125,000 for a 5,000-lot. But before you begin to think trades like this are free money, consider the fact that if the DPM misjudges the impact of his hedging, the stock could fall by ½, ¾, or more, thus locking in a loss of $125,000, $250,000, or more! That's why I spend so little time at the tables in Las Vegas. I get plenty of action every day, and I think my odds are better on Wall Street.

Or perhaps the deal is best done in increments. That scenario goes like this:

"What's the market for Jan double calls?" the broker begins.

"Four to a quarter," the market maker replies.

"I'm a seller," the broker tells him. "How many are you buying?"

"Five hundred on that bid," the market maker says.

"Sold!" Thus the first 500 options are purchased by the market maker for a $4 premium.

"Where can I move some size," the broker continues.

"3¾ bid for 2,000," the market maker responds.

If the broker is still selling, then it could be a large order. That means the options and the underlying stock price are likely to go down.

"Sold you two thousand," the broker adds.

"Done," the market maker agrees.

Perhaps the next 1,000 lot is down at 3½, and then at 3¼ and then at 3 and so on. The market maker is protected from what is expected to be a drop in the stock price, and the broker has staggered the selling price on the way down. For the market maker, this risk protection is crucial, because when he or she must hedge their risk by selling 500,000 shares of stock to offset those 5,000 options that were purchased, the specialist at the New York Stock Exchange is going to go through a similar price discovery ritual. And, there's no guarantee that the market maker will be able to purchase all the stock that is needed to offset the options position—particularly if it's late in the day. It's not that there is a right or wrong way for the broker to execute the order, but as the scaled price example above illustrates, a single price execution is often the better route for such large-block option trades.

The conundrum the broker faces is just how much information can be disclosed to get the trade done at the best price for the customer. The broker-customer understands that a 5,000 lot in-the-money (ITM) option trade will necessitate a hedge of up to 500,000 shares of the underlying security. But if after opening up to the specialist, DPM, or LMM, the broker sees blocks of stock hit the market, or option prices dropping like crazy, that would be the last time that broker would open up to that crowd. These are the times when the market maker must forget about trading the market, and concentrate only on making one.

There are times when trading a customer's order goes against your own best interest, including if you get stuck in a position that goes against you. I remember vividly the biggest loss my firm ever had in one day. We lost $1 million on my birthday, September 29, 1991. Here's what happened:

> One of our traders was trading options for SciMed LifeSystems, a medical device company that has since been acquired, and we were the DPM for this stock. SciMed (SMLS) was very active in those days, and the stock was up sharply that year based on a strong performance to date. On September 29, late in the session, the stock was around $94 a share.
>
> It was two minutes to the close. Goldman Sachs came into the market to buy 2,000 put options with a strike price of $70 a share. In other words, that customer was either betting that the stock was going to go down sharply, or looking to hedge some downside exposure after the big run up. We knew that earnings would be announced after the market closed, and thus, volatility was trading near its zenith.
>
> So the trader made a bet against Goldman Sachs, which is never a wise gamble, as they clear a number of very well-informed, fast-money hedge funds. Our trader figured those puts were only disaster insurance. The chance of the stock actually going down $23 a share, in his mind, was very slim. So he sold those puts, which meant he was obligated to be long the stock at $70 a share, and did not hedge the exposure by selling the physical stock. For one thing, it was two minutes to the close, and it would have been difficult to hedge 2,000 options—the

equivalent of 200,000 shares of stock—in two minutes. Besides, the trader was convinced that we'd make a small fortune selling those puts, anticipating the volatility would zoom out of the options after the earnings, and he'd be able to buy them back and make a big profit.

Keep in mind that our policy has always been to be flat overnight. We massage all our long and short positions until everything is hedged, even if that means carrying millions in stocks to offset our long and short options positions. The goal is always to be hedged, so that we are less than one percent long or short.

The SciMed Life options scenario was a deviation from that policy. And it turned out to be the worse-case scenario. SciMed Life came out with earnings that were, on the surface, quite good. Then one of the executives dropped what turned out to be a bombshell. The company was involved in patent litigation that potentially affected a large part of its product line. This was widely known by the Street, but that executive for SciMed then did the Wall Street equivalent of screaming, "Fire!" in a crowded theater. He said the litigation may force the company to drop its most-profitable product.

During the course of a conference call with analysts, the stock in third-market trading fell from $93 a share to $68! By that time, those puts we sold were $2 in the money instead of $18 out of the money. In plain words, a stock price target of $70 a share was already a done deal instead of a long shot. The next day, the stock traded down to $50 a share, and keep in mind those puts we were short obligated us to buy the stock $20 higher at $70.

I'd say we lost about $1 million on our stock exposure in about two minutes. The pain was horrendous, but at least it was administered all at once. Ultimately, there was a good conclusion to this financial bloodletting. We made back all the money we lost over the next month, in part because we got back to our knitting and didn't let the order flow make us come in long or short. In other words, we can't end up with a net long or net short position simply because a customer wants to do a trade that, because of circumstances, we can't cover. If you can't sell 2,000 options and cover with stock with only two minutes to go, then you'd better build some massive edge into the trade, because with no minutes to trade, my money is on the customer who wants to buy 2,000! You do the trade and get it hedged, or you don't do the trade. Simple as that. And while exercising your duty to create a fair and orderly market, you also protect yourself on a large order by seeing how much the customer is willing to pay for those last-minute, large-volume options trades.

Luckily about a third of the volume that we handle on the floor involves 200 contracts or more. That level is generally assumed to be the minimum size an institution will play. The vast majority is comprised of smaller-volume transactions. Most of our day is spent trading 10, 20, or 30 contracts.

But that may be changing. For years there was an "anti-churning" rule imposed on mutual funds that prohibited them from making too many short-term trades, which although they could be profitable, would absolutely generate significant fees which would impact the return to investors. If the fund made too large a percentage of its profits from short-term trades, the penalty would be tax imposed on the fund before the distribution to investors. That put the brakes on churning, but it also hurt options trading by the funds, since most options plays are short-term (90 days or less) transactions.

A change in the tax law some two years ago has resulted in an increase in short-term trading by mutual funds, which has been part of an overall rise in options trading volume. According to the Options Clearing Corp. Web site (www.optionsclearing.com), since the start of the bull market in 1990, cleared contract value increased 142 percent, yielding an average daily volume of 2,015,442 contracts. The options industry also achieved a milestone when cleared contract volume surpassed 5 billion in mid-October 1999, underscoring the momentum of the market. Total options volume across OCC's participant Exchanges amounted to 507,891,483 contracts cleared, marking the first year options trading at over a half-billion:

OCC Annual Statistics
Year Ended December 31, 1999

AMEX Total Contracts	129,662,442
Equity	126,821,529
Index	2,840,913
CBOE Total Contracts	254,331,851
Equity	198,086,825
Index	56,202,720
Interest rate	42,556
PCX Total Contracts	75,801,209
Equity	75,770,940
Index	30,269
PHL Total Contracts	48,095,981
Equity	44,085,930
Index	3,189,587

I expect that increase will become more dramatic, in the options traded to help hedge and manage the trillions of dollars worth of stock positions that they manage. I addressed a buy-side conference in Washington in November 1999, with an audience that included many mutual funds and hedge funds. I was not surprised to hear how they plan to expand their trading of listed options—such as the stock and index options listed by the CBOE.

Many of these funds have been trading over-the-counter (OTC) derivatives, which are subject to pending legislation that would limit their use. Many funds have opted to buy OTC derivatives because they've been told there is not the necessary liquidity to buy and sell options on a listed Exchange. Think about it. If you're trading a $1 billion stock fund, you need to make some very large trades to make a difference to your bottom line.

Instead, a growing number of investment banks and large brokerage firms—who shall remain nameless—do OTC transactions for mutual funds and large institutional and private clients. There are no commissions. Just the net transaction. The brokerage firm will devise an option product with the size that the fund needs for speculation or to hedge existing positions. The only time we traders on the floor get a glimpse of the deal is when the brokerage houses then come to the floor to buy or sell listed options to lock in a profit or lessen their risk on a big OTC trade.

As a market maker and professional options trader, I'd like to see more funds using listed options. Without a doubt, the floor could handle the size trades that these funds are seeking. Granted, a few years ago there was not the liquidity. But there is much more liquidity now, some of it due to multiple listing of options on major stocks such as Dell, Microsoft, and IBM. Those multiple listings have created opportunities for new specialists, which have received funding from banks, insurance companies, brokerages, and so forth. The upshot is, there is considerably more capital on the floor than there has been in the past.

There is another advantage for the funds to trade listed options: open competition. Rather than just receiving one bid or offer from a given firm for an OTC option, wouldn't it be better to have quotes on 5,000 listed options from 20 to 50 market makers, many of whom are backed by the big banks and brokerage firms? Chances are, the funds would find an efficient market with a narrower spread between the bid and the offer than in the OTC products.

Here's an analogy that might illustrate the point. Say the Rolling Stones are in town, and you call a ticket broker to buy a ticket. That's the equivalent of calling a Wall Street broker and asking for an OTC option. What the ticket broker is likely to tell you is it will cost you $500 per ticket for the Stones concert. But if you go over to the United Center, Chicago's arena where the Chicago Bulls play and a variety of events are hosted, chances are you could get far more offers to sell you a good ticket for the concert. And guess what as you get closer and closer to the United Center? The price of those tickets will probably drop. Why? Competition. One guy is offering to sell you a ticket for $250. Another guy overhears his offer and counters with two tickets for $250. And to carry the analogy a little further, being a trader I understand the concept of "time decay." If I'm holding an option that expires in three days, I know I have to do something with it TODAY. Because on the fourth day, it will be as worthless as a ticket you're trying to sell today to last night's Billy Joel concert.

Get the point? When there is a centralized marketplace where buyers and sellers meet, the competition makes for a more efficient marketplace with a narrow spread between bids and asks. Anyone who has used the Internet understands how competition creates better opportunities for buyers and sellers when you gather a crowd in a centralized marketplace. The dilemma facing those of us who would like to see a hybrid that merges open outcry and electronics is how to keep the costs of the open outcry (with market makers in trading pits shouting bids and offers) in line with the completely electronic competition.

I believe the efficiencies and the depth of capital in our marketplace will draw more participants, including the funds. Market makers like me will be ready for the challenge, with greater capital behind them. As a routine, we see 2,000—and 5,000—option trades, which are the equivalent to 200,000 and 500,000 shares of stock, respectively. That kind of size and volume, I would project, will only increase.

The good part of those trades for the market maker is you normally get a reasonable edge. The broker handling those large-volume trades normally wants a single price, moving all 2,000 or 5,000 options at once. The negative part is, now you've got 20 people all buying the stock and you're trying to hedge the position. It comes down to whoever has the fastest connection to the stock

Exchange or ECN that will be able to put on the best hedge at the best price.

But as I've said before, stock is not the only way to hedge an options trade, and that's why the centralized marketplace is so important. When you're on the floor, you may remember, for example, that a broker on the other side of the pit wants to buy 1,000 options that may now be a perfect hedge against my purchase of 1,500 contracts moments ago. The best pit traders remember where the resting orders are and use those to establish better hedges and, thus, make more trades with less risk. The more often I can hedge option-to-option, the better the use of my risk capital and, equally important, I get an immediate hedge rather than waiting to see if I missed the stock and have to chase it up or down. And, if I'm really creative, maybe I can wait to buy or sell my stock after the buying or selling frenzy subsides.

The challenge for the market maker is always making a two-sided market. Even when I'm a raging bull on the floor, I must have an offer to sell. A broker could take me up on that and I'll end up with a short position, even though I think we're going higher. That is the trade-off for being the risk taker for the customers who come to the floor, via their brokers, to trade. Market makers act as a kind of insurance company. We assume risk on their behalf by buying and selling what they need. Our challenge is then to transfer that risk with another position, be it in stock or an opposite position in options as fast and efficiently as possible.

Assuming risk in a volatile business environment is not for everyone—particularly if you have to think out every move you make. You might do okay in an off-the-floor trading room where you can take more time to research and plot out your trades. On the floor, you must think and act simultaneously. When a broker yells out an order, you just have to react.

Luckily, some personalities can adapt to that intense and unpredictable world known as the trading floor. In everyday life, my brother, Peter, thinks everything to death. He's the kind of guy who will spend six months shopping for a new couch. In the pit, however, he's a different man. He can make rapid-fire trades as well as anyone. He's a prime example of someone who slips into a different personality on the trading floor. Perhaps it's the competitiveness of that arena or the adrenaline rush of trading. Whatever the cause, I've seen little, mousy guys turn into Rambo traders. You'd think your eyes were deceiving you when a five-foot-five, 140-pound guy takes on a bulldog mentality.

But that is the pit. It's an arena where physical presence does matter, but it's not the determining criteria for success. However, you need to be seen and heard to get your share of the trades. That's why it helps to be like Mike Suarez, one of our traders, who stands six-foot-five and 275 pounds. A former professional and college football player, Mike knows how to take his space in the pit and occupy it. Then there are guys who stand five-foot-nothing, but are all mouth. What they lack in stature, they make up for in decibel-level. The brokers have no troubling hearing them, but they have to work harder than Mike or my brother, Pete.

The pit, however, is not the only arena for the professional trader. Increasingly, veterans like me are moving upstairs to trade from the screen. It's not that it's easier (except, perhaps, on the knees since you don't have to stand for six hours a day). But it is different.

At the screen, you don't have the machine-gun pace of buying and selling virtually everything the brokers have to offer. There is a natural progression among experienced traders from the floor to the trading room. Market veterans like myself get tired of standing for hours on end and our vocal chords get strained from yelling. But that's not the only entrée into the profession of off-the-floor trading. Many people come to options trading from other businesses that have left them well-capitalized and versed in risk management. If you're trading off the floor, you're probably like me, surrounded by computer terminals with 20 flashing phone lines at your side. When the market makes the move you've been waiting for, you either call your broker on the floor and put in your order to trade, or point and click to trade. Maybe it's not the same adrenaline rush as being on the floor, but it definitely has its own appeal. For one thing, trading off the floor is a strategist's game. Virtually everything that you see in the outside world can be applied to the market.

One of my favorite scenes in the movie, *The Player,* is when the producer/director played by Tim Robbins opens a newspaper and starts scanning the headlines. Mergers. Murders. Mayhem. It's all fodder for a script, Robbins believes.

The same could be said for trading. When you read about the latest gadget or a new twist on Internet technology or the fact that baby boomers are likely to buy more X-Y-Z, you can find some way to apply it. What company or industry would benefit from that, you ask yourself? Who's likely to win as a result, and who is going to lose out.

This strategy is what differentiates trading from gambling, an analogy that many people like to draw because of the speculative, risk-taking nature of both. When you trade without the market maker's obligations, you have a very good chance of moving the odds in your favor. Just like a card-counter in Vegas, you wait until the deck is stacked in your favor, then increase the size of your wager. The biggest differences are that Wall Street doesn't buy you drinks, but it doesn't shuffle the deck or switch "dealers" either! But you have to have a bit of the gambler's nature in trading or in any entrepreneurial, risk-taking venture.

You "gamble" when you give up your job and start day trading. Bill Gates "gambled" when he dropped out of Harvard. People take risks every day, especially in trading. The key is to take risks because the reward is much bigger.

This is much easier to practice off the trading floor, I believe, than on. When you're in the pit, it's easy to be swept up in the emotion. You're so busy trading that you may not have time to stop to think about your position. You could be extremely bullish based on the fundamentals, the technicals, or even biased due to the time of year. (October is notoriously volatile in odd-numbered years ever since the Crash of 1987 and the Correction of 1989.) You can go to the floor, convinced that you're going to be a buyer and then let the emotion of the floor take your bias away. You'll find yourself leaning toward the bears, just because the floor has that tone.

The tone of the trading pit is communicated in many verbal and nonverbal ways. First, there is the market talk. If you want to know what a trader is thinking, just ask. People on the floor who shout for a living aren't shy about expressing their opinions. Then there is the floor activity itself. When a broker's first five orders are all sells, the mood is decidedly bearish.

From upstairs, I can trade more easily without regard for the emotion. At the screen, I am governed by my own opinions and my own emotions. It's similar to a card-counter at the poker or black-jack table who can move the odds in his or her favor by what they've seen and what they know. For instance, I know there is an earnings announcement due the next day, or a new product is being announced, a litigation settlement, a major trade show—whatever the event, there may be an opportunity to position myself in a stock in front of an expected announcement. If I expect the announcement to be positive, I'll be a buyer. If I'm expecting negative news, I can be a seller.

I can use this and other means to push the odds into my favor. Here's an example of what we do all the time when a company is about to announce earnings: Hewlett Packard is notorious for being extremely volatile around its earnings. The more Wall Street can predict a company's earnings, the less volatile the stock is likely to be since volatility is a measure of market uncertainty. In Hewlett Packard's case, its earnings tend to be volatile because it is really a combination of companies involved in printers, computers, and Internet routers.

Hewlett Packard's earnings may miss earnings expectations by 20 percent on any given earnings cycle. Because of that, the stock is very volatile ahead of those earnings. Typically, I'm the seller of that volatility. In other words, I'm taking on the risk that Hewlett Packard will not move as much as expectations in the market. This is best illustrated with a bell curve as shown in Figure 2.1.

Let's say Hewlett Packard is trading at $100 a share. Under normal circumstances, the weekly range is between $92 and $108⅝. That's normal volatility of around 60 percent. But around earnings, that volatility may increase to around 85 percent or 90 percent with a price range extending between $88⅛ and $112½ (Figure 2.1).

(As a reference point, utilities tend to have very stable stock prices and a low volatility value, some as low as 20 percent. Internet stocks that are very volatile, perhaps reaching 120 percent, indicate we could see wide swings in share prices. On the food chain of volatility, the lowest are the utilities, then the multinational companies, then the computer companies, and then higher risk issues such as Internet companies, and genetic engineering and biotechnology stocks. The higher volatility reflects the greater number of unknowns regarding this company.)

Back to our Hewlett Packard example, during normal "nonearnings" times when the stock is trading between $94 and $106 on a weekly basis, a $100 call might be priced at $3.25. But just before earnings are announced, that same call might have a premium of

Figure 2.1   Hewlett Packard—$100 share, volatility 85 percent, weekly standard deviation

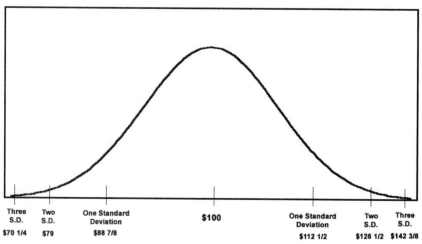

Three S.D.	Two S.D.	One Standard Deviation	$100	One Standard Deviation	Two S.D.	Three S.D.
$70 1/4	$79	$88 7/8		$112 1/2	$126 1/2	$142 3/8

Source: Chicago Board Option Exchange.

$5.50. (The higher the volatility, the higher the value—or pre-mium—on an option. Why? Because the more a stock price bounces around, the greater the chance a particular strike price will be hit.)

In these instances, you're looking for an event outside the norm. In plain words, you want a stock to rise above your strike if you buy a call option or fall below your strike price if you buy a put. With this in mind, you set your parameters for a trade. In this case, I'd sell puts with a $90 strike price and sell calls at $110. The pre-mium on the $90 put might be only $1 a share and $1.50 for the $110 call. But if the stock doesn't open higher than $110 or lower than $90, I can keep that premium as my profit, because the buyer of those calls won't exercise the option.

In this instance, I act like an insurance company that will in-sure your seaside house during hurricane season with a big enough premium and an understanding of the calculated risks.

Conversely, perhaps the range for Hewlett Packard is $94 to $106 (or 60 percent volatility), and I don't expect volatility to in-crease to more than 70 percent. So I'm going to sell the $100 calls and the $100 puts, because I think it's likely that the stock will trade within the projected range. The option prices reflect what Wall Street thinks the range for the stock will be. So if you buy options—particularly ahead of earnings—you're buying much higher volatility because the earnings are unknown, and the stock must move outside of that wider range for you to make money. In other words, you must have an extraordinary move to profit from buying that pumped up call or put.

Here's another analogy we use a lot. Say you're in Florida and you're watching the Weather Channel, when suddenly you hear that a hurricane is fast approaching. If you called the insurance company right then to try to increase your coverage, you'd pay a very high premium (if they'd give you a quote at all) because conditions at that moment indicate there is a high probability that the storm will hit and cause a lot of damage. Of course, there is a chance that the hurricane may miss the area completely or do only minimal damage.

But from the insurance company's point of view, the premium they collect for that insurance policy has to be high enough because there is a good probability that they will have to pay for damages. And, if the hurricane is downgraded to a storm or goes out to sea, the insurance company can keep the premium and make few or no payments. Likewise, a market-maker who sells an option ahead of an earnings event when volatility is increasing will want a higher premium. Why? Because the likelihood of that strike price for the option being hit increases with volatility. So if the put or call is exercised, the market maker has to buy stock at a higher price or sell at a lower price than the current market. For that possibility, the market maker will have collected a good enough premium to make it worth his or her while—and hedged the position with physical stock. And in the event the earnings announcement from the company isn't outrageously good or horribly bad, then the market maker gets to keep the premium because the options weren't exercised.

Whatever the scenario, as I set the parameters on my trade based on historic stock-price patterns and an analysis of the value of the put and call options, I can move the odds in my favor. I can look at the trading volume for both the stock and the option and the price pattern two or three days ahead of earnings. That will indicate to me how other people are positioning themselves for that event. These are some of the ways that I can be like the card-counter at the table who waits until there are a lot of face cards in the deck before making a big bet.

If you're playing Black Jack, the card counter wants to know when there are a lot of face cards with a value of 10 in the deck. As the game continues, the card-counter knows what's left in the deck and will increase or decrease the wager accordingly. On Wall Street, if you've got a "hot hand" because your analysis is right on, you have been doing your homework, managing your capital, and making disciplined trades, there is nothing to stop you.

But one word of caution: Strategies that involve selling options and collecting premium should only be used by professional traders and very sophisticated investors. I would strongly caution against any retail investor speculating in options by selling premium—meaning selling puts and/or calls. As we'll discuss in the next chapter, when you are a buyer of a put or a call, you automatically limit your exposure to the amount of money you paid for the premium. But when you sell puts or calls and collect the premium, you could end up with an unhedged stock position as the market moves sharply against you.

Let's go back to the bell curve to illustrate the risk when the "unlikely" does happen. In our previous illustration, we saw that the first portion of the bell curve is what is likely to happen 68 percent of the time, namely the stock ought to trade between $94 and $106 (assuming a current price of $100 a share). Moving farther out on the curve, we see that 98 percent of the time—taking in more of the variables from aberrant conditions, events, and so on—the stock should trade between $85 and $115 a share. But that wider range of possibilities encompasses many "once-in-a-lifetime" probabilities. In fact, it's so far down on the bell curve that you'd expect to see Hewlett Packard trade below $85 or above $115 once in your lifetime.

But that's where the models break down because these once-in-a-lifetime events happen much more frequently than the models predict. Stocks (at least at this writing when 24-hour-a-day trading is still only conjecture) aren't continuously priced, but rather trade actively for six and a half or seven and a half hours a day. That means that price moves are often exaggerated when an event occurs or an announcement is made after the stock market closes.

Take an example of what happened to Xerox on October 8, 1999, when the company predicted a 10 to 12 percent drop in earnings per share for the third quarter ("USA: FOCUS—Xerox Sees Results Shortfall, Stock Falls," by Matthew Lewis, Reuters English News Service, October 8, 1999). The stock had closed the night before at $42 a share. That gives it a range of $39 to $45 for 68 percent of the time, a range of $37 to $49 98 percent of the time, and, in the outermost reaches of the bell curve, a range of $33 to $51 99.5 percent of the time.

But after the news came out, Xerox's stock price fell 25 percent to close at $32 a share on the New York Stock Exchange. The day after, Xerox opened at $30. That move was significantly below the once-in-a-lifetime range for XRX, but it happened and similar events will happen again.

The mathematical formulas say this should only happen once in your life. So either XRX has used up its once-in-a-lifetime move (for the second or third time) or (1) the math is wrong or (2) the formula doesn't take into account the fact that stocks are not continuously priced because we don't have 24-hour trading. The bell curve formula is still helpful, but it doesn't give you an absolute guarantee of what can or will happen.

In fact, the occurrences of these once-in-a-lifetime moves show why an average investor ought to be a buyer of puts and calls rather than a seller. Remember, if you've made the decision to sell premium—meaning you're selling puts and calls and collecting the premium—you're acting like the insurance company who will guard against catastrophe. Sure, it's great to collect the premium when it's all blue skies and fair weather. But hurricanes do hit the coastline occasionally. When that happens, do you want to be an insurance company? Do you have deep enough pockets to withstand that kind of risk?

There are three basic rules for any trader: (1) Make money. (2) Do not lose money. (3) Come back tomorrow to trade again. As we'll discuss later, there are ways to limit risk and enhance potential profits by trading options.

Options are gaining in popularity among retail investors, both as part of the day-trading craze that has turned attention to the market and as speculative instruments. Some investors may have started out as employees who received stock options from the company. Perhaps an executive was given stock options with a $20 strike price when the stock was trading at $17 a share, and now the stock is at $22. Those options are suddenly worth a lot more than the executive may have realized.

From this exposure, many retail investors become intrigued with options as an investment and speculative vehicle. As I'll explain in a later chapter, it's possible to trade options with less risk than buying stock outright. Here's a preview of a strategy that might be used.

Say I'm interested in buying IBM, which is a $105-a-share stock. If I wanted to buy 1,000 shares, I'd have to come up with the $105,000 or have $52,500 in margin to buy the stock. My premise (just for the sake of illustrating a point) may be that the stock is likely to rise from $105 a share to $150 in three months or so.

An alternative to buying the stock is to buy 10 three-month-out call options for a premium of $5 a share, or a total investment of $5,000. If the stock, as you expect, rises from $105 to $150 a share, you're going to make $20,000 or $30,000. If the stock doesn't, the maximum you could lose is your $5,000 investment. There isn't a perpetual downside in case a stock makes a big move against you. You've defined exactly what your risk is going into the trade and you've only tied up one-tenth of the money you would have needed to buy 1,000 shares on margin, which has additional risks.

And if you give yourself enough time to be "right"—in this case three months—you may see an appreciation in the value of the calls that you bought.

When it comes to trading options, the two keys are timing and volatility. With enough time and enough market movement (volatility) there is a greater chance than an option will be "in the money."

But that opportunity doesn't mean trading options is a "slam dunk." So often at the investment seminars I speak at, people ask a logical question: Can I make a living doing this? The short answer is you can if you have enough money. Remember the higher the return you *must* make to live, the greater the risk you will have to shoulder. So if you have $250,000 to trade and you are looking to make 20 percent return, or $50,000, you'd have a shot at this. But if you only have $100,000 to trade and you're looking to make a 50 percent return, it may be far too risky a proposition. Don't get me wrong. It is possible to make six-figure money investing and trading a $100,000 account, but rather than playing the odds, you're betting you are one of the 0.1 percent of the population who can accomplish that feat. Setting realistic goals for your investing is one of the most important facets of managing your money. Options can definitely help you define risk and take less of it when you invest, but to make 100 percent returns requires some luck as well.

That doesn't mean there are no opportunities for the retail investor. But you have to do the proverbial crawl before you walk, and walk before you run. So begin with learning the trading methodologies, which you can practice with simulated trading. Then once you build a confidence level, you can put some money on the line. But as in most new ventures, you must begin small as you learn—because the name of the game is risk management.

chapter 3

a case for options

If you're interested in equities, you might ask for one good reason why you should use options to invest and speculate instead of purchasing the stock outright. To answer that, I will give you several good reasons.

stretching your capital

As a leveraged instrument, options allow you to participate in the upside potential of a stock with far less capital than by buying the stock outright. For example, if you're bullish on IBM when it's trading at $100 a share, you could buy 100 shares for $10,000, or get super-aggressive and buy that same 100 shares with $5,000 of your own money and $5,000 on margin (which would require you to pay interest to the brokerage firm).

Alternatively, you could buy one options contract for a premium of $5 a share, or a total cost of $500. (Remember one options contract equals 100 shares of stock.) Let's say your option has a two-month timeframe and a strike price of $105. That means if the stock were to rise above $110 a share—the $105 strike price plus the $5 a share premium you paid—you can exercise your option and own the stock at $110 a share. In fact, the buyer can, at his or her discretion, call those 100 shares of stock any time from the moment they buy the call option, until expiration. Compare that to the capital requirement of $5,000 on margin or $10,000 for an outright purchase of the stock. I'd say the option investor got both a better deal and tied up a lot fewer greenbacks to accomplish the same thing.

managing your risk

There's no such thing as a risk-free trade, unless maybe you're buying short-term Treasuries backed by the U.S. government. By using options, however, you are able to define the exact amount of risk that you're willing to take when you enter the trade. The stock buyer or seller has virtually unlimited risk that can escalate in the event of a margin call, or a short squeeze. If you buy 10 call options with a premium of $5, your total risk—if that option expires worthless—is $5,000. If the underlying stock drops from $100 to $5 a share, you still can't lose any more on those call options than the premium that you paid—in this case, $5 times 1,000 shares (10 options contracts, each representing 100 shares).

With the outright purchase of a stock, however, you could, conceivably lose all of your investment. If you bought 1,000 shares of a $100 stock, that, theoretically, means you've got $100,000 at risk. If the shares decline sharply in value or (as happens only rarely) lose all of their value because of some underlying problem, a stock could potentially go to zero. Those problems might be alleged corporate fraud, such as in the case of Centennial Technologies Inc., which has faced lawsuits rising from allegations of inflated sales and net income (Dow Jones, April 30, 1998, "Centennial Tech/Final Court"), or legal exposure, such as in the case of Dow Corning and the breast implant litigation (Dow Jones Business News, April 13, 2000, "Appeal Hearing Over Dow Corning Breast-Implant Settlement Plan Ends").

The trade-off, however, is time. If you buy a stock, you own it; you can hold it for a day or the rest of your life. An option only has value for a defined period of time. If you buy March calls in January, those options will have value for two months. After the third Friday of the expiration month (March in this example), the option is no longer exerciseable or assignable.

sophisticated trades

When you buy a stock, you're long that security. To make money, the share price has to increase. Or, you could sell a stock to take a profit or—as we'll discuss in a moment—short a stock because you think it's going down. Basically, there are two ways to play stocks—you buy 'em or your sell 'em.

But there are myriad of ways to play options. Even retail investors can undertake at least a half-dozen options strategies, combining buying and selling put and call options. (We'll discuss these strategies in later chapters.)

taking advantage of a trading range

If you buy a stock and it stays in a trading range, your investment is on hold. You don't make money unless the stock price moves in your direction. But options, as we'll discuss in Chapter 5, also allow you to make money if you believe a stock or an index will stay in a trading range.

There are many reasons stocks stagnate in a trading range, such as a recent acquisition, the cyclicality of its business, or a recent earnings announcement that leads Wall Street to believe there are no surprises ahead in the short term. Not surprisingly, playing a trading range for an index is even more popular than playing the range for an individual equity. This is because the very nature of an index is that its diversification of stocks smoothes the performance and volatility of its individual components.

playing the downside

One of the clearest examples of why it's better to use options instead of dealing with shares directly, is playing the "short side." Admittedly, there are many professional traders and "vulture funds" that make money by shorting stocks that they believe are going to decline in value. When you short a stock, in effect, you're agreeing to sell shares at a certain price—say $10 a share—even though you don't already own the stock, because you believe the price is going to decline and you'll be able to deliver those shares later at a lower cost—say, $8 a share.

Many retail customers think it's "un-American" to short a stock. They want share prices to go up; that's why they buy a stock. They don't want to think about stocks that might decline in value. But day-traders—particularly professional ones—know differently. They play the stock market from the short- and long-side. But to do that, you have to literally borrow the shares of the stock that you want to short until the time that you can deliver the securities for which you're obligated.

Problems may arise, however, if you need to "borrow" a stock that has a very thin float, meaning there are only a few shares outstanding. In such a situation, a majority of the shares are in the hands of company "insiders" and institutions. Perhaps only 15 or 20 percent of total shares are in the hands of the public, whereas 80 to 85 percent of the float is held by company insiders and institutions.

With only a few shares around to "borrow," it may be difficult—and potentially very costly—to short the stock, adding to your overall risk. As you'll see, an easier way to play the short side would be to invest in put options. But first, let's discuss how the stock-shorting scenario would play out.

You believe that Company XYZ shares are overvalued. If you actually owned the stock, it might be a good time to sell. But what if you didn't own the stock? One possibility would be to short the stock. When you short a stock, your brokerage firm has to go out and borrow stock certificates electronically. Remember, every time shares are bought and sold, these certificates have to be sent to the buyer. Instead of Brinks trucks full of stock certificates going to and fro, today it's all done electronically. But these stock certificates still have to change hands, they just do so with the click of a mouse.

If you're shorting the stock, certificates also have to change hands. But the process is far more complicated than a simple sale. When you short the stock, you're promising to sell something you don't already own.

Here's how it works: First the short-seller commits to sell 100 shares of XYZ at a certain price, say $100 a share. In this scenario, the short-seller believes the shares are currently over-valued and will be available for purchase in a few days or a few months at a lower price. Once the commitment is made, the seller then has three days to settle the transaction. That means that the seller needs to fulfill the obligation to deliver to the buyer stock certificates in three days. The seller's clearing firm normally goes out and borrows the stock certificates from someone who owns the stock—often a larger brokerage or financial institution. But those lenders don't loan out their stock certificates as a "favor." It's often a very lucrative transaction.

The brokerage or institution that agrees to lend the stock is already charging some customer margin on the shares. For example, if 100 shares of XYZ are priced at $100 a share, you'd need to come up with $10,000 or $5,000 on margin. In return for putting up that $5,000 on margin, the brokerage firm will charge an interest rate anywhere from 6 percent for a major trader to 12 percent for a small investor.

But that margin interest is just part of the money the brokerage stands to make if they can lend the shares to a short-seller. The brokerage firm also earns interest on the proceeds of the short sale. A large trader who makes a short sale collects the bulk of the interest on the sale proceeds, often 90 percent of the interest, while the brokerage firm that loaned the stock certificates collects the other 10 percent. A smaller professional trader may keep 70 percent of the interest, while the brokerage gets the other 30 percent. And a retail investor who chooses to play this risky game may get zero interest, while the brokerage keeps it all. (That interest on the proceeds of the short sale is in addition to whatever margin the brokerage house may also charge. Margin and interest are some of the most lucrative businesses for brokerage firms.)

The most dangerous thing that can happen when you sell a stock short is what's known as a "short squeeze." That usually occurs when the lender demands the stock back. The short-seller then has no choice but to go to the market and buy shares at the prevailing market price. And if the short-seller doesn't do it, the lender will do it—perhaps at not the most competitive of prices. Take it from me, every time a firm has bought me in on borrowed shares, they paid the high of the day.

In options, we can usually tell when there's a short squeeze on a stock because the puts become very inflated. The pricing model may show that a put should be trading at $6 a share; instead, it's at $10. The reason is either a short squeeze in the stock or a back-end on a takeover deal, and in either case, protection seekers or arbitrageurs, they'll pay anything for puts.

When there's a short squeeze on a stock, you face considerable risk of the share price rising sharply—the exact opposite of what you'd hoped would happen when you shorted the stock. (Remember, in this scenario the short-seller committed to sell 100 shares at $100, hoping that the share price would decline, enabling shares to be purchased at a lower price—say, $90 or $80 a share—to replace the borrowed certificates.)

You might even be right about the stock; it is overvalued and shares will eventually drop. But in the meantime, you can get caught in a short squeeze.

A far better way to play a price decline in a stock is to buy put options. If you think a $100 stock is overvalued, you can buy puts with a strike price of $100, $95, $90, or lower. (Remember, the farther an option is "out of the money," the less premium you'll have to pay.) If the stock doesn't go down as you expect, all you'll lose is the premium. But if you short the stock and the market goes against you, your potential loss is almost unlimited. Put another way, if you short sell 10,000 shares and the price goes up by $3, you're facing a $30,000 loss.

avoiding margin calls on stock

An adverse move in the market may result in another problem for stock investors—margin calls. For example, if you buy 100 shares of a $100 stock on margin, you agree to put up $5,000 while your brokerage puts up the other $5,000 (and charges you interest on that loan). Now, say the stock declines sharply in value and the $5,000 you put up is virtually exhausted. The brokerage firm is going to demand more money to cover the difference, which is known as a *margin call*. If the money isn't immediately forthcoming, the brokerage will liquidate your position to cover that debit. Keep in mind that, with volatile shares such as Internet stocks, brokerage firms may demand the investor put up a higher percentage—75 percent or 80 percent—instead of the usual 50 percent on margin.

In the worst-case scenario, a stock is bought on 50 percent margin. Then, the share price declines dramatically, resulting in a margin call to cover the shortfall—plus the brokerage firm raises the percentage that an investor must put up to 75 percent or 80 percent. You'd then be in the unenviable position of putting up more money to hold onto a losing position.

That, in and of itself, is a good reason to own options instead of stocks. Granted, options may be brand new territory for many investors. But people "invest" in options all the time. Consider taking an "option to buy" in real estate, a common practice among many developers to secure the rights to several parcels of property before buying. Or, consider insurance which, in its simplest form, is nothing more than a "put" option to protect you from downside risk—in this case decline in your property value because of damage or destruction.

In fact, the easiest way to understand how options work is to look at puts. If you buy a put, you're acquiring the right to sell a stock at a given price within a certain timeframe. Let's say a stock that you hold in your portfolio is trading at $50 a share and you're concerned it may decline in value. To protect yourself, you can buy a put to sell the stock at, say, $45 a share. So if it declines to below your target, you can exercise your right to sell at $45. (Remember, the theory behind all trading is to sell at the highest possible price and to buy at the lowest.) If the price doesn't go down, your stock portfolio will register the gain. And all you'd lose on the options trade is the premium that you paid for the put.

For that reason, options trading is analogous to purchasing insurance. Think about it. Would you drive out of a dealership with a $12,000 Hyundai or a $130,000 Mercedes without insurance? Of course not. But not every insurance policy is the same. The larger the deductible, the smaller the premium that must be paid. And, it costs more to insure the Mercedes than the Hyundai. But let's assume that you have a $500 deductible on your $12,000 Hyundai, and the car is totaled in an accident. You only have to pay the first $500 in the loss. The other $11,500 is paid for by the insurance company. In options terminology, you paid $500 (the deductible) to guard against a $12,000 loss. When catastrophe strikes, the party that sold the put—in this case the insurance company—pays the difference.

If you drive for the life of your car without an accident, you've "lost" the premium you paid for the insurance policy. But you had the protection of that insurance policy just in case.

Legal requirements aside, no one would buy a car or a house without insurance. But people buy stock all the time without downside protection. To most of us in the industry, this is as unfathomable as owning a $400,000 home without an insurance policy.

Say you hold Microsoft, a blue-chip stock if ever there was one. This champion only goes up, so why waste money on buying protection that will doubtless go unneeded. On the other hand, let's say you started to feel a little nervous about whether or not the government's antitrust division could get the software giant declared a monopoly. I know that's just silly supposition, but let's say you were feeling it was time to protect some of the thousands of shares you own that cost $5 a share but that are now trading at $90 a share. You're willing to pay a $5 "deductible" in case of a loss, so you buy the $85 put. That put may be exercised any time during the life of that option. But obviously, you would only want to exercise the right to sell Microsoft at $85 a share when it's trading below that price. And even if Microsoft should trade to as low as $50 or $60 a share, by exercising that put, you may sell at the $85 strike price—and the party that sold you the $85 put must buy from you at that price.

What happens if Microsoft goes from $90 to $110 a share? Obviously, you're not going to exercise that option to sell at $85. All you've lost is the premium you paid for that put option, which expires worthless. But that option gave you the peace of mind to hold Microsoft through $100 a share, knowing that you were covered if the market suddenly made an adverse move. There is no way you can say that you "wasted" your money buying that put, any more than you could say you "wasted" money on your homeowner's policy because your house didn't burn down!

Options are more than just an insurance policy, though. They are also effective means to trade the market, regardless of whether you have a small or large stock portfolio. Options can bring balance into your holdings, helping you to guard against risk and minimize exposure—and also to reap returns based on how you think a particular stock will perform. Stated simply, you can use options to capitalize on certain market moves—buying calls when you're bullish and puts when you're bearish. Options also provide leverage, increasing the buying power of your investment capital. And they offer greater diversity in your holdings.

For example, say you want to buy 1,000 shares of IBM, which is trading at $95 a share. To make the purchase outright, you'd need $95,000. Fully margined, you would need to put up $47,500. (Investors can buy stock on 50 percent margin, but you still must pay interest to the brokerage on the amount of money loaned to make the purchase, as well as commissions. These fees are paid regardless of whether your investment appreciates or declines in value.)

Or, you could participate in the upside potential of IBM by buying the $95 call. This gives you the right to buy IBM for $95 a share until that option expires. You could hold an option for as little as a day—if you buy one close to expiration—or as long as two years. And in general, you want to hold an option long enough to increase the chance of the market move that you're anticipating really happening. (There is a greater chance of a stock going from $95 a share to, say, $110, over several months than in just a few days.)

Getting back to our example, let's say you decided to buy $95 IBM calls for a $6 a share premium. With each options contract representing 100 shares of stock, they would cost $600 each—or $6,000 for 10 contracts, which is equivalent to 1,000 shares. Compare that with the cost of buying 1,000 shares outright for $95,000 or $47,500 fully margined.

But there are some limitations. Your break-even price on the IBM stock is $101 a share (the $95 strike price plus $6 for the premium). And you only participate in the upside potential of IBM for the life of that option, or in this example one month. But with the leverage inherent in options, you can make greater use of your money by diversifying your holdings among options on several different stocks instead of committing large portions of capital to the outright purchase of shares in only one or two companies.

But remember when you buy an option, time is your enemy. You only have the right to control that stock for the term of that contract—the *expiration cycle.* If you don't give yourself enough time for your outlook on the stock to prove correct, you're going to lose. Most of the time people lose money in options because they don't give themselves enough time to be right. As a stock moves in your favor—either down if you hold a put or up if you bought a call—your option becomes "in the money." For example, a $90 call option when a stock is trading at $95 a share is "in the money." An $85 call would be "deep in the money." However, a $110 call option when the stock is trading at $95 a share would be "out of the money." And the further "out of the money," the option is, the cheaper the premium.

But buying an out-of-the-money option that looks cheap on a relative basis—costing only $1 a share instead of $6 or $8 for an in-the-money option—is not a sure bet. The reason is that the further out of the money an option is, the more extraordinary a market move would have to be.

Thus, time is a tricky component when you're trading options. With the exception of the professional trader, investors should not hold an option until the very end of the expiration cycle because of time decay, which accelerates as expiration nears. Time decay is so great when options are near expiration that you hear the traders "hissing" on the floor as they imitate the sound of air escaping a balloon. When an option is only a day or two away from expiration, there usually isn't enough time for a significant market move that would bring an out-of-the-money option into the money.

It's a far cry from the days when pricing models for options were very expensive and difficult to come by. In those early days, options were frequently mispriced, which led to an opportunity for investors and professional traders to pick up a valuable option at a bargain price, or sell an overvalued option at an inflated price. As pricing models have become more sophisticated and more available—thanks, largely, to improvements in computing power—options are much less frequently mispriced and the mispricings only last for seconds, not days. As a result, both public investors and professional players have a greater sense of each option's value.

As I wrote in Chapter 1, when I began trading options in 1981, I used to take hours to run the analysis on options prices—even though we only had 99 listed options in those days. I used to start printing my option runs at 6:00 A.M. to be ready for the 9:00 A.M. opening. And when we went to the floor, we took reams of computer printouts with us. Some traders carried saddle bags slung over their shoulders to carry several hundred pages of printouts of theoretical values. The rest of us stuffed our pockets with the theoretical values of options at varying price levels of the underlying securities. All day, we flipped through those pages, comparing the current quote with the optimum valuation, hoping to capitalize on a disparity in pricing. In 1981 and for the next several years, computers for option analysis were not allowed in the pits, as they would give an unfair advantage to the most highly capitalized trading firms.

Today, it's a different story: Sophisticated handheld computers operate on wireless local area networks (LAN) or wireless infrared communicators connect the floor traders with the risk manager upstairs and the outside world. Virtually every trader has onboard analytics and access to the NYSE and Nasdaq markets, as

well as the burgeoning number of electronic communications networks (ECNs). Thanks to such technology, the hedging, communication, and trade analysis is virtually instantaneous.

Another obvious beneficiary of the tumbling cost of computing power is the individual investor. For retail customers, the Internet makes a number of options pricing models available, often
through discount, or full-service brokerage firms' or other trading sites.

The most basic way to price an option is to start with the
strike price. If IBM is trading, for example, at $90 a share, and you
decide to buy a call—or in Wall Street parlance, to go long a call—
at the $95 strike price, you are buying the right, but not the obliga-
tion to own IBM for $95 a share until that option's expiration. Now,
take that $95 and multiply it times the interest rate that you would
have to pay if you borrowed money from the bank, say 8 percent. If
you're not borrowing the money, multiply the strike price times the
interest rate you would get paid if you put your capital in a certifi-
cate of deposit (CD) today, say 5.5 percent.

For the sake of illustration, let's pick an interest rate of 8 percent to borrow money to buy the $95 call:

$$\$95 \times 0.08 = \$7.60$$

Now, multiply that by the number of days for the life of the option, such as 30 days for a one-month option:

$$\$7.60 \times 30 = \$228.00$$

Now, divide that by 360, for the approximate number of days
in the year (you could use the exact 365, but nobody on Wall Street
does):

$$\$228.00 \div 360 = \$0.63$$

This would give you the value for that $95 call, assuming there
were no *volatility considerations*.

But that's like computing the value of a piece of property
based on square footage alone—and not taking location into account, like 500 square feet of land in a remote part of Utah versus
500 square feet in Central Park.

As market makers, professional traders, and sophisticated retail investors know, the biggest component in the price of an option is *volatility.*

In the simplest of terms, volatility is a measure of risk. The more volatile something is, the greater the risk. Put another way, if the price of something is bouncing around like crazy—up one day and down the next—there is greater risk that you could be caught short or long with the price moving against you. That volatility increases your risk.

At the same time, volatility is an estimate of what the expected range is for whatever stock or commodity you're trading. Again, if a stock has some pretty wild gyrations in price, such as eBay or AOL, it has a relatively high volatility and its projected trading range will likely be wide. By the same token, a stable stock with little change in price, such as a utility stock, would have low volatility and a comparatively narrower expected price range.

Here's another analogy to illustrate the concept of volatility. Everybody (particularly any parent) knows it costs more to insure a 16-year-old boy who is driving the family car than for the 30-year-old man who is married and is the father of two children. Why? Volatility!

The 30-year-old man with a wife and two kids is less likely to engage in "volatile" behavior such as drag-racing his friends down the neighborhood streets or drinking and driving to impress his girlfriend. Thus, the range of expected events—in this case the chance of an auto accident—is far greater with the 16-year-old boy than with the 30-year-old. So what does the auto insurance company do? It charges more to insure the 16-year-old driver than the 30-year-old driver because the likelihood of an accident (which would result in the insurance company having to pay for damages and/or injuries) is greater with the young boy than the presumably more mature and stable married father.

To bring our analogy back to the market, the 16-year-old driver might be the equivalent of an Internet stock, the price of which is bouncing around in a volatile fashion. The 30-year-old station wagon driving Dad might be IBM. IBM, with its far lower volatility, usually will trade in a narrower range than the high-flying Internet stock.

Based on the volatility, we can project how a stock is likely to trade in a day—say, with a price range of $3 a share. That volatility won't tell you the price at which the stock is likely to close. But it will tell you where it's likely to trade based on past price patterns and current volatility.

Using a bell curve model, you could predict that about 66 percent of the time, the stock would trade in a $3 range, 95 percent of the time in a $5 range, and 98.6 percent of the time in a $10 range.

Now, take the example of IBM. With the stock trading at $114, normal weekly volatility is around 40 percent. Its bell curve points are likely to show, for example, a $13 range 66 percent of the time, a $25 range 95 percent of the time, and a $39 range 98.6 percent of the time (Figure 3.1).

But before earnings, IBM could reflect a weekly volatility of around 70 percent. At that time, its bell curve points are likely to show, for example, a $22 range 66 percent of the time, a $45 range 95 percent of the time, and a $67 range 98.6 percent of the time (Figure 3.2).

With higher *volatility* there is a greater *probability* that a particular price point will be hit. (Think of the 16-year-old driver. What is the chance that the volatility of youth will result in a fender-bender?)

Figure 3.1   IBM—$114 share, normal volatility 40 percent, weekly standard deviation

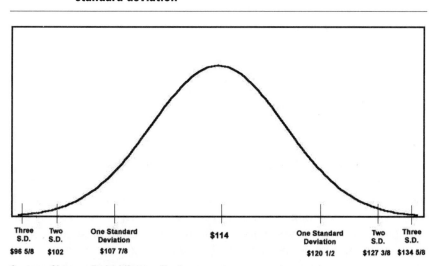

Three S.D.	Two S.D.	One Standard Deviation	$114	One Standard Deviation	Two S.D.	Three S.D.
$96 5/8	$102	$107 7/8		$120 1/2	$127 3/8	$134 5/8

Source: Chicago Board Option Exchange.

Figure 3.2   IBM—$114 share, unusual volatility 70 percent, weekly standard deviation

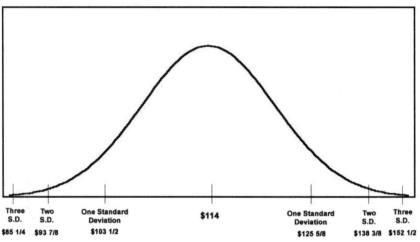

Three S.D.	Two S.D.	One Standard Deviation	$114	One Standard Deviation	Two S.D.	Three S.D.
$85 1/4	$93 7/8	$103 1/2		$125 5/8	$138 3/8	$152 1/2

Source: Chicago Board Option Exchange.

To buy an option on a volatile stock, you would have to pay a higher premium than for a less volatile issue. Why? Because the seller—like the insurance company offering coverage on a teenage driver—wants protection from the risk of an event. In the case of an option, the seller wants to ensure that the premium paid will balance the risk involved in hedging the exposure the seller takes on should that option be exercised.

If the option is exercised, the seller may be obligated to sell the stock at a considerably lower price than the prevailing market (in the case of the seller shorting a call option) or buy the stock at a considerably higher price (as could be the situation faced by a put seller) than the prevailing market.

As we'll discuss later, there are many different strategies to employ when trading options. But with some 1,200 different issues on the CBOE alone, there is the inevitable question of which options to trade. I don't recommend particular stocks to people. Rather, my advice is to trade what you know—whether it's retailing, manufacturing, the Internet, or, in my case, medical technology. Peter Lynch once recommended investing in companies you know, whose products you use. If you love your HP printer or think Ford is really making a terrific truck, you may want to consider buying their stock.

Because of my father's background as a transplant surgeon, I was active in biotechnology and medical device stocks. Why? I had a natural inclination toward medicine and medical technology. Plus, when I read that a company was developing a particular drug or device, for example, I could ask my father for his input. This, I believed, gave me a bit of an edge over the average investor.

Similarly, when I do a seminar in the San Francisco Bay area, many of those who attend work for technology companies or are interested in technology. For them, the stocks they're likely to track are Sun Microsystems, Cisco, eBay, and other similar stocks. Why? Because they know stocks in that industry.

Trade what you know. If you're involved in a particular industry, you'll know the important events. If you follow technology, you'll know that the Comdex computer trade show is the venue at which many of the new technologies and products are unveiled. If you follow Apple Computer, you know about MacWorld in January. And if you don't know about it, don't trade Apple! You'd be better off throwing darts to pick your stocks.

Follow the stocks for which you have a natural affinity. Trading involves in-depth research into an industry, specific companies, and the trends that affect them. You need to know all you can about a company, including the kind of news events that will affect a particular stock. If Company A announces a new product, it will likely have an impact on the value of its stock. But what about its competitors? Will that new product put Company B at a competitive disadvantage? Or is Company B working on a new version of its products that will put it light years ahead of Company A?

For part of the late 1990s and in early 2000, momentum investing was the rage. What does advanced DotGizmo do? Who cares! People weren't investing, they were trading. If you feel compelled to join their ranks, it's okay, just don't kid yourself into believing you're investing. You're not. There is no shortcut to investing, but there are better, safer ways to do it. You can't trade without doing your homework. The easiest and most enjoyable way to trade is to follow those companies and industries that interest you.

When you're trading options as a retail investor, you can't rely on pricing models alone. If you believe, for example, that the March 2000 call is undervalued and therefore a good buy, it's not enough.

As a retail investor, you're looking at more than just the relative value of an option, hoping to turn a quick profit on a put or a call, buying an option at, say, $3 and selling it at $3.75. Retail investors must have a longer time horizon than floor traders. As I jokingly tell investors at my seminars, floor traders like me have about a 15-second attention span. It doesn't matter what I'm doing, I can only focus for 15 seconds.

That usually gets a laugh out of people, but a floor trader (remember the emphasis is on TRADER, not INVESTOR) is competing against dozens of other traders to hedge each purchase or sale as quickly as possible. Why? Because the quickest traders will remember the resting orders in the brokers deck from 10 minutes or two hours ago and hit those orders as the market rallies or dives. Once the resting orders are gone, the last resort is to hedge with the underlying security and when the stock specialist or Nasdaq market maker see hundreds or thousands of shares of buyers or sellers hitting the market they run. Being 15 seconds late in my world is an eternity. The complete picture of the stock can change in half that time, so speed is of the essence.

Additionally, floor traders usually have a very rapid turnover. When a floor trader buys an option, we are not buying for investing purposes, we are taking on inventory and hopefully, capturing some of the bid-ask spread. That is the spread between my posted bid of say 4¼ and my posted offer of 4½. Due to the competition between upstairs traders and the other market makers in my pit, I can rarely capture that full ¼ point. Rather, traders seek to lock in ⅟₃₂ ($.03), or ⅟₁₆ ($.06) by hitting a resting option, or selling the underlying stock. Active market makers will make hundreds of trades per day, running in front of bulldozers to scoop up pennies. That's why floor traders can "day trade," entering and exiting positions— ideally, hundreds of positions—within the same day. Paying retail commissions, retail investors are better off taking a longer time-frame—anywhere from several days to a few months—for trading.

Conversely, floor traders could never use such a long-term timeframe, largely because they are continually obligated to make a two-sided market, which means selling even when they're bullish and buying even when they're bearish.

Because of our rapid turnover of positions, options are not a zero sum game. You don't have to lose for the market maker to win. You may buy a call option from me, and I may buy stock to hedge that sale. Let's say that Micron goes up $5. You make money on your call and if I hedged properly, I made money on my stock purchase. As long as we continually hedge and monitor our risk, the market maker can provide a liquid market for the customer and a potentially lucrative market for himself.

A floor trader also has much tighter parameters on trades that turn out to be a little "early." For example, you may believe an option priced at $3\frac{1}{2}$ is undervalued and is worth closer to 4 or 5. But a floor trader, trading with a very short time horizon, will sell out and cut his loss the minute that option drops to $3\frac{3}{8}$—even if it rises to 4 or 5 within a few days. A retail investor, on the other hand, will probably ride through the drop from $3\frac{1}{2}$ to $3\frac{3}{8}$ or even 3, if that's part of the strategy, on the belief that the option will appreciate in value before expiration.

Because of the short timeframe for floor traders and for professional off-the-floor traders, fundamental analysis into a company's operation is not as much a concern as theoretical analysis on the relative pricing of options. If someone on the floor is day trading, they could care less about what the company does. They're not trading the fundamentals of a company's bottom line or the strength of its industry. Instead, they're trading volatility, taking advantage of price swings and trading momentum. Or they're trading psychology when the market is panicked and oversold, in which case they're looking for an opportunity to buy, or when it's over-extended, and they're looking to sell.

So if you're set on day-trading as a retail investor, remember I am your competition. In this case, your decision to day-trade options is like playing a game of chance in Las Vegas; the odds are inevitably stacked against you. Let's put it this way, I pay pennies per trade, have instantaneous access to the market (I just have to yell!), and don't have to finance the same margins that a customer does. No matter how big a player you are, you're still paying dollars, have to wait several seconds to several minutes to access the market, and have considerably higher cash demands. How can you possibly beat me on a per trade basis? Investing for a day, a week, or a month, sure, you can make money. If you use various spread strategies you can drastically reduce time-decay and volatility risk. But day-trading options against the floor is a loser's bet.

Having said that market makers don't have the same margin requirements that customers do, I must remind you that the leverage I use means I can make 100 times as much money on a trade than the average investor—and I can lose 100 times as much money.

Here's an example: Let's say the $95 IBM calls are trading at $6, and I—as the professional market maker—sell you 20 of those calls. I'm now obligated to deliver 2,000 shares of IBM at $95 if the option is exercised. Let's say I bought 1,500 share of IBM at $95 against this option sale as a hedge.

If the stock pops in one day up to $97 a share, the option my customer bought is worth $7. The customer may opt to sell that option and make a tidy, one-day profit of $1 per contract. On the other hand, I bought 1,500 shares because I'm just as bullish as the customer and I wanted to hedge my upside exposure to that call sale. When the stock goes up to $97, I lose $1 on every option that I sold (assuming no leverage), for a $2,000 loss on 20 contracts. But I made $3,000 on that stock investment, for a net profit of $1,000. My customer, on the other hand, made $2,000 on those 20 contracts. Please keep in mind that most market makers will have turned over such a trade multiple times during that one-day period, but I am simplifying the relationship to show that both sides could have similar outlooks, and both profit despite being on opposite sides of the same trade.

As a market maker, I'm obliged to make a two-sided market, even though the customer and I were both bullish on the stock. The advantage for me, however, is that with my margin and such insignificant commissions, I can trade multiple times a day like this—hopefully netting a few dollars each time! But more importantly, because of our different roles, fee structure, margin requirements, and so forth, the customer and I are not competitors.

The only way I can effectively gain an edge as a professional is to equip myself with professional tools. For example, I have access to *all* the news feeds and brokerage upgrades and downgrades, not just a few tidbits offered from online services. In fact, my firm pays some $30,000 a month for all the news feeds, computers, and other services that we use. The wonders of the amazing Internet have helped level the field for the retail investor in terms of quick access to information, but if a retail investor has an inch of information, a prudent professional has a yard.

If you're an investor, you need to take a longer term time horizon of at least a week and preferably a minimum of one month. And, to move the odds in your favor, you need to rely somewhat on fundamental analysis. Again, I'll use the blackjack analogy. If you were a card counter, would you be satisfied with an ability to count only one deck to determine how many "face cards" (with a value of 10) are left in the deck? Or would you train yourself to count three, four, or five decks, which simulates the way most blackjack tables at large casinos play. Obviously, you'd need to count multiple decks to move the odds into your favor. Otherwise, you are really just gambling.

When you're investing, either with stocks or options, you should become a student of the game and strive to know all you can about a particular company. This knowledge will act as an edge to help you take a more controlled amount of risk. Why? Because fundamental analysis, when used in concert with technical analysis, will help you determine whether or not a stock is likely to make a particular price move within a particular timeframe.

The question then becomes how many stocks you can possibly track with research and price models? If you're not doing this full time, you could still have anywhere from 10 to several dozen positions in options. With stock you have a potential undefined amount of price risk for each company in which you invest. But in options, your risk can be defined exactly when you enter the trade. If you are an option buyer, your loss is confined by the amount of premium that you paid. This assumes that you are either buying options or doing spread trades that put limits on your exposure, instead of selling "naked" or unhedged puts and calls. For example, if you buy 10 calls (each representing 100 shares of stock) for a $2 premium, you know that the most you could lose is $2,000 if the option expires worthless. And you would still have a chance to cut that loss, even if the stock made an adverse move, by selling those calls before expiration, say for $1 or $0.75.

In fact, I do not recommend that retail investors hold an option until expiration. Even if a stock is moving strongly in your favor, you probably want to get out of that position—either by taking your profit and initiating a new position, or by rolling the option into another expiration—before the option expires.

But at what point do you get out of a winning trade? Or in other words, how much is enough? Remember, when it comes to options, the variable is not just price—it's also time. You may hold a six-month out-of-the-money (meaning the stock is trading below in the case of a call or above the current price in the case of an out-of-the-money put) option that becomes in-the-money far more quickly than you anticipated. Perhaps the $2 call you bought is now worth $4 or even $6 in just a few weeks or even days. What do you do now?

It all goes back to your original plan. Your decision to buy that call was based on your analysis that either the option was under-valued or the stock was poised for a move—or both. As part of that plan, you had a price target for the stock. When that target is reached, it's time to re-evaluate and decide what the next step will be. Most likely, if you've doubled, tripled, or quadrupled your money, you'll want to take a profit. You pull that money off the table and establish a new position based on where you think that stock will go from this point. If you're still bullish, you'll buy another call with a higher strike price. But you don't just let it ride in hopes of turning $2 into $10. You take a profit once your target is reached and re-evaluate your plan. Remember, it's not the house's money if it's in your account; it's your money!

For example, say IBM is trading at $100 a share and I'm bullish on the stock. An at-the-money 100 call would have a premium of about $5. (That means the stock would have to rise above $105 a share—the strike price plus the premium—for this trade to be prof-itable at expiration.) The $110 out-of-the-money call would have about a $2 premium (and profitable above $112 a share at expira-tion). And, let's say the $120 calls have a premium of $0.75. Now, as-sume my research indicates to me that IBM is likely to run from $100 to $130 a share in two months, based in part on the company's fundamentals and the strength of technology stocks in general. If I'm right, the $120 call could go from $0.75 to $10 a share, the $110 call could go from $2 to $20, and the $100 call could go from $5 to $25. Let's take a closer look at the scenario: The $2 and $0.75 calls rise roughly 10-fold, while the $5 call has a five-fold increase. So the biggest gains are in the $110 call (with a $2 premium) and the $120 call (with a $0.75 premium).

How do you choose your strategy? With the current price of $100 a share, if I bought the $0.75 call—which is the cheapest—I would miss out on part of that run. Specifically, my out-of-the-money $120 call would not see a significant gain on the run from $100 until $110 or so. Therefore, the best value would be to buy the $110 call for $2. If, one month from now, the stock has moved from $100 a share to $115, that premium has increased from $2 to $6 or even $8. That gives me the opportunity to sell that option out, taking a profit, and initiating another position. As I stated before, if you're still bullish based on your plan, you may decide to buy the $115 or the $120 calls, paying the premium with the portion of the profits made on the previous trade. In that way, you're preserving your capital and playing with the house's money, just make sure you pull some off the table for yourself.

Also, keep in mind what your initial investment was. If you bought 10 of the 110 calls for $2, you invested $2,000. The run to $115 brought in a profit of $4,000 ($2 paid for the 110 calls minus the sale price of $6 one month later). If you still are bullish on IBM, you may want to still limit your next investment to $2,000.

Take a look at another IBM scenario. Let's say you bought the $95 IBM calls for $6 and thus, your breakeven at expiration is $101. Then in three days, the stock moves from $95 to $112 a share—a $17 move. We "own" from $101 (our break-even price) all the way to $112. Our option has increased in value sharply—especially as an option moves deeper into the money.

The premium on an at-the-money option generally moves $0.50 for every dollar that the stock moves in favor of the option (rising in the case of calls and declining in the case of puts). When it's deep in the money, the premium option begins to move $0.75 to the dollar and keeps on tracking closer and closer to 100 percent (a dollar increase in option value per each dollar increase in the underlying security). That everchanging differential between the change in value of the option and the movement of the stock is known as the *delta*. Because of deltas, you must evaluate your option trades differently. You may see a $2.50 gain in premium on a $97 call as the stock rises from, say, $95 to $100. But from $100 to $110, that premium increases $9. So at that level a $6 call is worth $17.50.

Under our "take the money off the table" scenario, you could sell the $95 calls and, if you're still bullish, buy the $115 call options that have a $3 premium. Or, if you think it's going down because the stock is overbought, you could buy puts with a strike price below the current market. Again, it all goes back to your constantly updated plan.

Whatever the scenario, it's important to have a game plan and to follow it. If you think IBM will go up 10 percent or 20 percent, you must know where you would exit the trade. And, you're constantly reassessing that game plan based on the market movements and the relative value of the premiums. That's why the *homework* phase of trading is so important. You must know not only what looks like an undervalued or overvalued option, but also the salient fundamentals impacting the price of the underlying stock. As simple as it may sound, you must know when earnings are coming out. Four times a year, a company announces earnings and it's always a major occurrence. Plus there are major industry conferences and brokerage-sponsored events at which time the stock is likely to be upgraded or downgraded. Based on that constantly updated plan, you make your decisions in regards to the options in your portfolio.

Trade what you know. Trade what interests you. That's why investment clubs work well in options strategies. Each member of the club brings his or her expertise and interests. Maybe one guy is a doctor who knows medical devices. Someone else works for an Internet company and is familiar with breakthroughs in that technology. Investment clubs give you leverage of time and expertise. And, in the future, I believe investment clubs—and their use of options—are a partnered explosion waiting to happen.

chapter 4

beyond the basics

You've got the basics down. You know how options work and you understand the marketplace. You're ready to trade. There is far more to options trading than just buying a put or a call and waiting for the market to move. In fact, once retail investors learn the ropes, they can quickly become adept at using basic strategies to control risk and enhance potential profits.

The options plays you execute will depend largely upon two things: your risk tolerance and your portfolio goals. Risk and reward are directly proportional—the higher one is, the higher the other is as well. If you have a high risk-tolerance and your aim is to make 200 percent on your money, then you're probably going to follow an aggressive option strategy. If your risk tolerance and your investment goals are more middle-of-the-road—meaning, you'll be satisfied with, say, a 30 percent return and don't want to risk more capital than is absolutely necessary—then you're likely to adhere to a more conservative *spreading* technique.

Spreading, which involves selling one type of option and buying another, is one of the most common ways to create positions that match your outlook for a given stock or index and limit your risk. Depending on the type of strategy you choose, these spreads can limit your upside potential as well. But the trade-off of capping your risk, in return for a limit on the upside, usually is one that many investors are willing to make. Consider, for example, buying an out-of-the-money (OTM) call at the 55 strike with a $5 premium that's two months out and selling a nearby OTM call at the 65 strike for $2. The worst thing that can happen, no matter how much the market moves, is you might lose $3, the difference between the $5 you paid and the $2 you received. And the most you can make, no matter if the stock doubles in price, is $7, the difference in price between the strike you purchased and the strike you sold.

The strategies discussed in this chapter involve stock options that, by definition, are American-style options, meaning they may be exercised at the buyer's discretion at any time, from the moment of purchase until expiration. Again, the buyer of the option, not the seller, may elect to take these actions. Usually, the only time an American-style option—such as a stock option—is exercised at expiration is when the strike price is in-the-money (ITM).

The other type of option contracts are known as European-style options, which are "frozen" and can only be exercised on the day of expiration. These options involve mostly stock indexes in the United States, such as options on the Standard & Poor's 500 Stock Index, which are traded at the Chicago Board Options Exchange. This type of option is popular with institutions that normally want to stay in their short positions until expiration.

Because American-style stock options can be exercised at any time, it's imperative that you are hedged, particularly if you are selling an option. Again, the only time we advocate retail investors selling options is as part of a spread. If you are not adequately hedged, there is a risk that, if you're a seller of an option, the buyer may "call" the stock from you or "put" the stock to you when that option is in the money. And even if you are unhedged or "naked" on even one options contract, you could have a very bad day if the stock moves against you.

For that reason, spreading is a very appealing way of controlling risks, hedging positions, and ultimately, preserving capital. I believe it is a less risky way to speculate in a stock, rather than just buying the shares outright. For example, say IBM is trading at $100 a share. Do you want to hold the stock and commit that much of your capital? Or do you want to buy a call to be long IBM for a $5 premium (each option is 100 shares, so such a position would cost 100×5 or $500 per contract), which you hope will increase in value as the stock price rises and the option moves further into the money. Or, do you want to take the next step, and not only buy the $100 call for a $5 premium, but sell a $110 call and collect a $2 premium (Figure 4.1).

Figure 4.1   long 1 July 100 call, short 1 July 110 call

Source: Created by StockmarketWorkshop.com.

I do not advocate retail investors selling options naked, but using conservative strategies, such as this bull-call spread, the investor owns one option for each he or she has sold, so they are not naked any contracts. Collecting the premium when you sell an option may look as easy as picking up dimes on the pavement. But if you're not careful, a bulldozer rumbling down the street could knock you down. The only time a retail investor should sell options is when it's part of a carefully constructed spreading strategy.

Another popular hedged strategy is known as the *covered call spread*, in which the investor sells an option against stock that they own. As we stated before, the value of an option erodes very quickly in its last weeks and days. This time decay, as we call it, not only eats away at the premium, it also helps move the odds in your favor, as the option has fewer days to move against the seller.

As *the seller of an option,* you are granting the right for someone else to be long (if you sell a call) or short (if you sell a put). For example, let's say you sell a call with a $100 strike price and collect a $4 premium. That means when the stock rises above $104 and the holder of that option exercises it, you are obliged to deliver shares at $100. Unless you purchased the stock previously, you are obligated to deliver shares that you must now purchase in the open market for $104. If the stock is trading higher than $104, you are still obligated to deliver 100 shares per short option, but any price higher than $104 means you're losing money, as you only took in $4 for the 100 call. Now remember that every option is worth 100 shares. If you sell four calls, you may have to buy 400 shares, and if that stock is trading over $104, then the loss compounds four times as fast. That's how risk compounds quickly with uncovered options.

But when you sell a call as part of a spread trade, that potential loss can be defined when you enter the trade and offset by the calls in your own portfolio. And, in a covered call strategy, most of us prefer to sell calls that are ready to expire. Remember, time is the enemy for the *options buyer.* As time runs out, there is less and less opportunity for an option to be in the money for the buyer. (If a stock is at $50 a share and you have bought a call with a $60 strike price and it's a week to expiration, what are the chances you'll be able to exercise that option?) But time is the *options seller's* friend! (If a stock is at $50 a share and you've sold the call with a $60 strike price and it's a week to expiration, what are the chances that option will be exercised, obligating you to deliver stock?)

Thus, with a covered call, your strategy is to buy an option with a longer time horizon of at least several months—and perhaps one to two years, known as a long-term equity anticipation security (LEAP)—and sell one with only a few weeks left to expiration.

Here's an example: IBM is trading at $111 a share. A two-year call option to buy IBM for $120 a share is selling for $23, and a one-year $120 call is selling for $17. Let's take a look at this. The price differential for two years versus one year is $6. So for $6 more ($23 vs. $17) you can control the stock for an extra year. As a buyer of a call, you must determine which is the better buy—the one-year or the two-year, depending on your outlook for the stock and your expectation for how much the call option could appreciate in value.

Now let's take a look at the short-term options. A $120 call option that has 45 days left to expiration has a premium of $3.75. (When you consider that eight purchases of such a 45-day option—which would represent one year of purchases of a 45-day option—would cost $27.60, you can see why the LEAP is such an attractive alternative.) The same call option that expires in two weeks is priced at ⅞. The shortest-term option is the cheapest because you only have two weeks for a $9-a-share move to occur (from $111 to $120). So as the *seller* of the option, that limited amount of time and time erosion are your friends.

Among these various options, you must then find the best value. In general, your strategy will be to buy the long-term call option and sell a short-term one against it. So you buy 10 of the $120 calls for a premium of $17 a share. That's equivalent to getting 7-to-1 leverage (120/17) for the equivalent of 1,000 shares of IBM. You then turn around and quickly sell the $120 call that expires in 45 days and collect the $3¾ premium (Figure 4.2).

Now, let's say in the next 45 days IBM shares rise from $111 to $117. The 45-day call you sold for 3¾ expires worthless, and you get to keep all the premium. Meanwhile, the one-year $120 call you bought for $17 may have lost a little value to, say, $15. But the $2 lost on that LEAP is more than offset by the $3.75 in premium that you kept from the short-term call that you sold:

BOUGHT: $120 one-year LEAPS for $17 premium

SOLD: $120 45-day calls and collected $3.75 premium

Figure 4.2 long 10 Jan (02) calls, short 10 Aug 120 calls

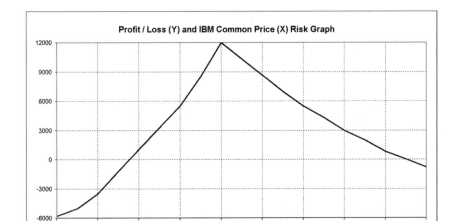

Source: Created by StockmarketWorkshop.com.

With this strategy, known as a *time-spread,* the calls that you buy and sell always have the same strike price:

Stock rose from $111 to $117

45-day calls expire, allowing you (the seller) to keep the $3.75 premium.

Premium on one-year LEAP declines from $17 to $15.

Total net profit on this trade $1.75 per share.

Remember: The key to the time-spread strategy is to buy a long-term option or LEAP that has slow time decay, and sell a short-term option that has fast time decay.

Here's another scenario: Let's suppose the stock rallies and closes at $120 a share by the time the short-term call expires. Since it didn't rise to $123.75 (the break-even point for a $120 call with a $3.75 premium), we still get to keep all the premium. Plus, the LEAP may have appreciated in value from, say, a premium of $17 to $20, since the stock rose by $10 a share. The entire profit on the trade reflects the $3 gain on the LEAP and the $3.75 pocketed from the short-term option that was sold.

SOLD: $120 45-day calls and collected $3.75 premium

BOUGHT: One-year LEAP with strike price of $120 for $17 premium

Stock rose from $111 to $120.

Since stock is not trading above strike price (for option to be exercised, shares would have to trade at the equivalent of the strike price plus the premium) you keep the $3.75 premium:

Premium on one-year LEAP increases from $17 to $20.

Total net profit on trade $6.75 per share.

Total investment was $17 minus $3.75, or $13.25 less commissions.

Return on that $13.25 investment is 50 percent.

Let's assume the stock rises to $125, and the 45-day option you sold is exercised. Now, you're obliged to deliver stock at $120, for a $5 loss per share. However, you collected a $3.75 per share premium on that option, which helps offsets that loss, reducing it to $1.25 a share. Meanwhile, the LEAP you hold has seen an appreciation in value from a $17 premium to $22 a share. The total net profit on the trade is $3.75 a share:

> BOUGHT: One-year LEAP with strike price of $120 for $17 premium
>
> Stock rose from $110 to $125 a share.

Your 45-day option is exercised, obligating delivery of stock for $120 a share, $5 less than current price. That loss is partially offset by $3.75 premium, for net loss on short-term option of $1.25.

> Premium on one-year LEAP increases from $17 to $22, a gain of $5.
>
> There is a loss of $1.25 on the 45-day call written.
>
> Total net profit on trade is $3.75.

Another variation on this theme is the *Covered Write,* meaning you sell a short-term call and either already own the stock or you go and buy the stock outright. Personally, I prefer that investors use the LEAP-Covered Write, which allows them to participate in the upside potential of a stock through a long-term call or LEAP, while taking advantage of the leverage inherent in options and the time decay of short-term options selling.

The Covered LEAP and the Covered Write are best used if you are bullish on a stock. By bullish I mean that you think the stock will outperform the market. If not, then why not just buy a Spider (S&P Depository Receipts), Nasdaq QQQ, or DJIA Diamond, since they will give you absolute performance of each of those recognizable indices.

And, as an investor, you can use the Covered Call Strategy as part of your portfolio management. Let's say you have $100,000 to invest and you're interested in technology stocks. Instead of buying shares outright, you can use the LEAP-Covered Calls to invest a portion—say 10 or 15 percent—of the money to participate in the upside potential of a stock. The remaining 85 to 90 percent of your principle can then be put into a Treasury bill making a modest

6 percent. That locks in a minimum profit for the bulk of the money, while your upside is the potential for that LEAP. Using LEAPS, you can then participate in several stocks at once, giving you, in effect, "several fishing lines in the water at once." This is especially effective within a sector. In technology, this might include LEAPS for IBM, Hewlett-Packard, Texas Instruments, Sun Microsystems, and so forth. With the leverage inherent in options, you can participate in a broader number of stocks—albeit for the time period defined by the duration of the options—than your capital would otherwise allow.

Working several stocks together you can, in the vernacular of the trading floor, avoid the "sin" commonly known as "right church, wrong pew." At times, stock investors can pick the right industry, but they buy the wrong stock within that sector. For example, you might want to participate in the Internet, but you pick Excite instead of Yahoo. (I have nothing against Excite, but remember on December 7, 1999, Yahoo rose an unbelievable 67$\frac{3}{16}$ a share after it was included in the S&P 500.)

Using this LEAP strategy, you can participate in the upside potential of several different stocks with the same investment that you'd need to buy only a few hundred shares of just one company. Then, for up to two years, you can participate in the upside potential of several companies—and not just Internet stocks. Maybe you're interested in telecommunications, but which stock to buy? AT&T? Quest? Global Crossing? WorldCom? You can leverage your money across a sector with LEAPS and, in effect, sit in many different pews in the same church. And with exposure across several different stocks, you can potentially improve your returns—especially if you happen to catch a fast-rising issue, such as Yahoo or Quest.

Similarly, you can use the LEAP strategy to participate across several sectors. Maybe you've enjoyed a good run in telecommunications stocks, but you don't want to sell, for example, WorldCom because it's done so well. And if you do sell it out, you would have tax exposure due to capital gains. (Your tax exposure and best tax strategy are something that's best left to you and your tax professional. My comments here are by way of illustration.)

So, you can leave your WorldCom stock and borrow against it on margin from your brokerage firm, and put that margined money into other LEAPS on stocks in other sectors. This is a very effective strategy for getting additional capital and freeing up capital for diversifications in other investments. That includes investments within a sector and across sectors.

There are variations on this theme. You could buy an in-the-money LEAP call, which would work much more like a Covered Write (in a Covered Write, you buy the stock and sell a short-term call), because an in-the-money option tends to move like the stock. Or you could buy an out-of-the-money option that track somewhere between 50 percent to 30 percent of movement of that particular stock. With out-of-the-money options, you don't get the full appreciation of the stock movement, but you pay less money.

The pricing of these options reflects both the intrinsic and extrinsic value. Here's an illustration: If a stock is trading at $110 a share and you buy a call with a strike price of $105, it's $5 in-the-money. That $5 is also reflective of the *intrinsic value* or the difference between the strike price of an in-the-money option and the price at which the stock is trading.

The extrinsic value is the amount of the premium in excess of the intrinsic value. For example, if you bought this option for $15, then the *extrinsic value* would be equal to $10. (The stock was trading at $110 and the strike price was $105, so that $5 is intrinsic value and the additional $10 was time premium or extrinsic value.)

But if you bought an out-of-the-money $120 LEAP call, it would have no intrinsic value, because the call is above the current market price of the stock. Therefore, the premium you pay is all extrinsic value. In other words, the price you're paying is all hope, and time for that hope to pan out. The longer that time horizon, of course, the more premium an option will normally hold.

Your strategy to use in-the-money options or the out-of-the-money variety depends largely upon your own plan and risk parameters. If you tell me that you want to own IBM, the best bet is not an out-of-the-money call, as the stock would have to make a dramatic move to reward you for your investment. Rather, if you want to own the stock, you'd be better off buying a LEAP call that will move most like the stock . If the stock is trading at $110, then a $110 call will move more in step with the underlying shares than an option with a strike price at $115 or $120.

With LEAPS, an investor can take advantage of a long-term time horizon, which, at least in theory, increases the chances of a stock move occurring. But one thing to remember, these LEAPS are not designed to take advantage of short-term moves in the market. Consider Yahoo's one-day rocket rise, up nearly 24 percent to $348 a share on December 7, 1999, the final session before the stock was added to the Standard & Poor's 500 Stock Index—and S&P Index fund managers would be obliged to own Yahoo as of that date.

As a long-term instrument, a LEAP would not be the best place to take advantage of that kind of price movement. Rather, you'd be more interested in the movement of the stock over a longer time horizon of, say, two to three months to two or three years. (Profit-taking on December 8, 1999, took $28.38 out of the stock, closing that day at $319.63.)

The LEAP-Covered Call strategy is used, when an investor is bullish on a stock over a time horizon of at least a few months. In theory, the same sort of strategy could be used with puts—buying the long-term and selling the short-term—if you had long-term bearish prospects for a company. But generally speaking, investors rarely employ such a put strategy. Puts are bought primarily for downside protection. Although vulture investors do actively speculate in put options, very rarely do most investors buy puts to bet on the downside of a company the way they buy calls to speculate on the upside.

Another options investment strategy is the *Bull Spread*, which, as the name implies, may be used if you have a bullish bias for a stock. Let's say you're interested in the Internet auction company eBay, which is trading at $150 a share. Buying 1,000 shares would require a staggering investment of $150,000. Instead, an investor might *buy $150 at-the-money calls* that expire in two months, and *sell the $160 calls* against them. You paid a premium of $11 a share for the $150 calls and collected $8.25 for the $160 calls, for a net cost of $2.75 a share. On a 10 lot (1,000 shares), that's a net price of $2,750 (Figure 4.3).

Now, instead of investing $150,000 outright to buy 1,000 shares of eBay, you have a $2,750 net investment. Here's what happens under two possible scenarios:

BOUGHT: $150 calls for $11 premium
SOLD: $160 calls for $8.25 premium

Within two months, eBay falls to $125 a share. The $150 call that was purchased is worthless. You keep the $8.25 premium

Figure 4.3   long 10 Aug 150 calls, short 10 Aug 160 calls

Profit / Loss (Y) and EBAY Common Price (X) Risk Graph

Source: Created by StockmarketWorkshop.com.

collected on the $160 calls. The net loss is $2.75 a share, or $2,750—the maximum that can be lost regardless of how far the stock drops. However, if you had purchased the 1,000 shares outright, you would have lost $25 a share or $25,000 under this scenario.

> BOUGHT: $150 calls for $11 premium
> SOLD: $160 calls for $8.25

Within two months, the stock trades up to $175 a share. The $150 calls that you purchased are worth $25, reflecting their intrinsic value (the stock is $25 over the strike price). Similarly, the $160 calls that you sold are worth $15. Thus, the spread between those two options has gone to $10 a share or $10,000. Your net cost, however, was $2.75 a share or $2,750 (which is the maximum you can lose on the trade). Thus, you're looking at a net profit of $7,250—nearly tripling your initial investment amount. The stock investor, however, made $25,000, which based on a $150,000 outright purchase of shares, is a return of about 17 percent. So based on the rates of return and the ability to sleep at night because of a limit on risk, it's easy to see why options spreads like this one are so popular with knowledgeable investors.

The advent of high-flying Internet stocks has encouraged the use of options as a speculative vehicle, particularly in recent years. Unlike some of the better-known Blue Chips, it's not uncommon for Internet stocks to trade at $300 or $400 a share or more. With this kind of price volatility, it's no wonder that investors are migrating to options for risk control and capital preservation. And, as we've discussed previously, as leveraged instruments, options allow you to participate in the upside of a stock (albeit for a defined period of time) for less capital than if you bought the shares outright.

But there is a mitigating factor (I don't want to call it a downside) when you use a strategy such as the Bull Spread, and that is the upside is limited by the strike price for the option that you sold. Using this example of buying $150 calls and selling $160 calls, even if the stock trades $25 a share higher, your upside is capped by the differential between the strikes of the two options. Yet, this seems to be a reasonable trade-off for taking on far less risk than purchasing the stock outright.

The examples we've discussed thus far for the Bull Spread have involved fairly static scenarios, meaning you bought a call at one price and sold a call at another and the stock moved in one direction or the other. But since the market is constantly moving, you should re-evaluate your position based on your view of the stock. Using our eBay example, say, as we discussed earlier, you buy $150 calls and sell $160 calls about two months out. Then 10 days later, the stock is at $165. You've made a profit on the $150 calls, but you still have the $160 calls that you sold to consider. At $165, the $160 calls with a premium of $8.25 won't be exercised as yet. But the more the stock moves, the greater the chance you'll have to deliver shares at $160 if the option is exercised. What should you do?

It depends on what your outlook for eBay is with the stock now trading at $165. You may decide that eBay still has considerably more upside and you don't want your profit limited by this $160 call that you sold. In this instance, you could buy back the $160 call, and sell a call at a higher strike such as the $170 or $175, or whatever you believe to be a price at or above the upside potential of the stock.

Whatever your decision, make sure you have a plan that includes a price goal for the stock. If the stock hits or comes close to that goal faster than you anticipated, you have to reassess that plan. You may say to yourself that, based on what you're reading and hearing about the company's sales targets and so forth, you're very bullish. Then you re-evaluate your strategy and move your price target. If there's nothing compelling to cause you to re-evaluate your previous goal for the stock, then it's time to exit.

Wall Street's stars do it all the time. A stock moves higher to their price targets and they either suggest investors take profits and leave, or they move the target higher. And it's okay for you, a retail investor, to do the same thing. You can always re-assess your plan, as long as you're doing your homework on the stock. Maybe your option has doubled in value; now you think it might triple as the stock moves higher.

With options, there is always a way to lock in your potential profit as part of your strategy. But rarely, after a substantial move, would you simply keep a winning position on and let it ride.

Let's say you re-evaluate your goal for eBay, and come up with a target of $175. You've bought a $150 call. To raise your upside profit potential, you buy back the $160 calls and sell the $165 calls. But eBay runs up to $170 a share in 10 days—not the two-month time horizon that you used to evaluate your options. So, you re-assess your position.

If you believe that $170 a share is the top for the short-term, you can "close the spread" and take your profit. To do that, you sell the $150 call and buy back the $165 call. Then you look for an opportunity in another stock to play the Bull Spread.

Or, you may decide eBay is going higher and the new target is now $200 a share. So, you may sell the spread—pulling the money that you've already made off the table—and put on a completely new trade. For example, you might decide to buy the in-the-money $195 call for $12 a share and sell the $210 call, collecting a $5 a share premium, two months out. The total risk for that spread is $7 a share, the difference between the premium you paid and the premium you collected.

The mirror-opposite of the Bull Call Spread is another popular strategy called the *Bear Call Spread*. These spreads are popular because they allow a retail investor to collect a premium, or credit, for doing the spread. The downside, in my opinion, is that the risk/reward ratio for the Bear Call Spread is not favorable. The amount that you can lose in most Bear Call Spreads is far greater than the amount you can win.

Let's take a look at an example. In the case of a Bull Call Spread, if you buy the $65 call and sell the $75 call, that's a 10-point spread. If the stock goes up to $80 a share, the $65 call will be worth $15, and the $75 call will be worth $5. Since I sold the $75 call, that $5 goes against me for a net profit of $15. It's called a Bull Call Spread because you make this trade when you're bullish on a stock.

Now let's turn it around and say that you're bearish on a stock. So you sell the call spread. You sell the $65 call and buy the $75 call. If the stock declines, as you anticipate, you'll keep the premium on the $65 call. The problem is, as the seller of that call spread, you'll lose money if the stock goes up, although the $75 call that you bought will put a cap on that loss.

Let's go through another example. As in the example of the Bull Call Spread, say eBay is trading for $150 a share. You think that the stock is overvalued, so you establish a Bear Call Spread by selling the $150 call and collecting the $11 a share premium. Next, you buy the $160 call for $8.25, for a net credit of $2.75. Since each option contract represents 100 shares, you collect $275 for each time you do this Bear Call Spread (Figure 4.4).

You're betting that eBay will trade at $152.75 a share (your breakeven) or lower. As long as eBay finishes at expiration at a price no higher than $150 a share, you get to keep the premium you collected. The problem is the maximum you can make on this Bear Call Spread is $275, or $2,750 if you did this trade 10 times.

The maximum you could lose on this spread is $10 (the difference between the two calls) less the $2.75 you collected, or $7.25 a share. That means a loss on a one contract spread of $725, or $7,525 on a 10-contract spread.

Personally, I don't like this spread from a purely risk/reward standpoint. I don't like the fact that my maximum profit is $2.75 a share, while I could lose $7.25 a share if I'm wrong. For me, as a trader, I try to find strategies that are just the opposite—with a reward that is at least twice the risk.

The appeal of the Bear Call Spread, though, is that it is a limited-risk trade. Instead of selling calls outright, which exposes

Figure 4.4 long 10 Aug 160 calls, short 10 Aug 150 calls

Profit / Loss (Y) and EBAY Common Price (X) Risk Graph

Source: Created by StockmarketWorkshop.com.

you to virtually unlimited risk, you can lose only $7.25 a share—even if eBay goes from $150 to $200 a share. By comparison, the person who has sold the stock at $150 a shares loses $50 a share in that same move.

A better risk/reward strategy to play the downside of a stock you consider to be overvalued, is to buy put spreads, which we'll discuss in Chapter 5.

As you evaluate your option strategies—including Bull and Bear Call Spreads—the question becomes how you assess and reassess your stock outlook. The answer will depend on what resources you have. Professional traders and firms pay a lot of money for information, particularly if we're trying to gain a short-term edge. For example, my firm subscribes to services such as First Call, which lists brokerage upgrades and downgrades virtually as soon as they're issued. That may gain us a 20-minute to two-hour edge versus when you hear about a change in a stock recommendation by a brokerage firm on a free service such as CNBC.

Interestingly, the Internet and the media in general—with the advent of the all-day financial news shows such as CNN and CNBC—have really leveled the playing field for available knowledge, information, and intelligence gathering. So for instance, as a stock is running out of steam, you'll probably hear about it on CNBC—if you don't see it before then through a casual perusal of an information site such as Reuters, Bloomberg, CNN-FN, or our own site at 1010WallStreet.com.

In addition to the stocks that are in the news that day, you must do your own technical and fundamental analysis of the company. Plus, you must learn to use what I call the "gut meter." What do you sense about this company? Is it out there in the news still or has it faded from the spotlight? If it has faded from attention, has it topped out in price or is it within the top of its range?

Another thing to watch for are the tails of the bell-shaped curve, those "99.5 percent moves," the once-in-a-lifetime kind of rises or falls in the price of a stock. If you're a trader on the floor or full-time at the screen, you'll be able to watch those gyrations— but most retail investors haven't given up their day jobs. So, they might be limited to watching the stock only occasionally during the day, usually via the Internet. Or, you might be willing to give up some control to your stockbroker, if he or she is knowledgeable about options. You could instruct your broker with specific directions or guidelines for where you would like to take a profit on a particular stock.

Say you were playing December calls in Yahoo on December 7, when the stock gained some 24 percent and options rose 39⅜ to 49⅜ on Chicago Board Options Exchange volume of 10,726 contracts. ("Options Report: Traders Take Profits in Yahoo! as Stock Soars and Then Bid Up Ciena Calls in Heavy Trading," by Steven M. Sears, *Wall Street Journal,* December, 8, 1999). If you didn't notice what was happening during the day, your short-term profit potential on those December calls would have evaporated as traders took profits after Yahoo's big run.

Now, lest you think that professional traders always have the edge over retail investors, here's what we did in Yahoo on the day of its now-legendary run up in price. We bought at $290 a share and sold at $293. We bought again at $310 and sold at $312 . . . That's what we do, in and out of a stock for a quick profit. But this time, instead of scalping (or making a short-term trade for a quick profit) for an ⅛ or a ¼, we were scalping for dollars. The stock was moving so fast that day, we bought at $290 and sold at $293 some 35 seconds later. Our longest trade that day latest about two minutes. We did okay, in fact, better than "okay." But as short-term scalpers in stocks, our profit was far from the full 24 percent buy-and-hold-all-day potential that the shares experienced.

We also traded Yahoo options, which were moving as fast as the stock, but much of our activity took place later in the day. Quite honestly, we didn't expect a 70-point run in options; they had already run 25 points the day before and 17 points the day before that . . . We did our analysis but, alas, in hindsight we were short of the mark. Even with the best analysis, sometimes a stock does not move according to your plan. When that happens, you either take your profits and say thanks or cut your losses quickly, reassess your strategy, and move ahead with the next trade.

So at the end of the day, we bought puts in the last half hour, expecting a sell-off in the stock. We started buying puts when Yahoo was at $340 a share (it traded as high as $351 earlier) and held them overnight. But volatility was lower the next day and, as a result, the premium was coming down. We sold out of those puts quickly for a profit, but not as large as it could have been.

We're not the designated primary market maker for Yahoo. Instead, we were speculating as professionals—and taking profits quickly as a professional normally would. But in hindsight, we kick ourselves for being too disciplined. The profits could have been far larger, but nobody ever went broke taking profits.

But when you buy an option, you have to have a short memory. Here's what I mean. You have to forget what you paid for that put or call when you re-evaluate you strategy. You can't say, "Oh, I bought this call for only $2 and now it's trading at $17. I only have $2 into it so why don't I hang on?" Rather, you have to ask yourself whether or not you would buy that option at $17. If the answer is "yes," then hold it for a while. But if the answer is "no," then get out. Take your money off the table and, from your profits, establish a new position if you're still bullish, or take your money to the sidelines and wait for another opportunity. If you won't buy an option for $17, then why hold it when it's at $17? The risk/reward ratio simply isn't there.

Sometimes this is easier said than done, particularly when you look at a five-, six-, seven-, eight-fold profit. It's so tempting to hold out and squeeze every last dime out of the profit. But you can't let greed motivate you. Instead, you have to use discipline to devise a strategy and then follow your plan.

I believe *discipline* is the number one factor any trader—be it a professional or a retail investor—must have. It may be fairly easy to get into a trade, particularly if you're a buyer and the market moves in your direction. But getting out with a profit once your target is hit can require a lot of discipline. And if it turns out that you left some money on the table, you can't fault yourself. Constantly ask yourself those crucial questions that all disciplined traders must pose: "Would I buy this option here? If not, then why would I hold it at this price?"

Admittedly, there are times when it's boring to be disciplined. But even if you're the luckiest person alive, you're not going to keep your profits if you're not disciplined. It also helps to have a disciplined mind that can do research on a company or industry and then apply what you're learned. This kind of research is even more critical for investors who have a longer term timeframe than a trader who might be scalping during the day. In fact, the closer you move to a floor trader-style of trading, the less you have to care about what a company does or any other fundamental factors. All you're looking for is price opportunity and opportunities to exploit volatility swings.

As a professional off-the-floor trader, I take a hybrid view. I do make scalp trades when opportunities arise. But at the same time, I do plenty of research—something which I enjoy—to find trading opportunities. For example, if I see oil prices rallying, I like to short the airline stocks either by buying puts or by selling calls. (Remember fuel is second only to labor as the biggest direct costs for airlines.) Or if bonds are up or down 12 or 14 ticks, then I have to evaluate the financial stocks. Or you watch the market sectors and look for stock opportunities among stocks that are not moving in step with the others. Here's a recent example. I noticed that while drug stocks, in general, were lower, Johnson & Johnson had not declined as much. When I determined that it was not event-related (none of the drug companies had just reported earnings or finished a new product introduction, for example) I decided that it was only a matter of time before Johnson & Johnson declined. So, I started accumulating a short position in Johnson & Johnson by buying put options when the stock was trading at $97 a share. We began buying $95 put options over a three-day period. Over the next three months, the stock was down nearly $25 a share. Through that decline, we sold puts into the slide, taking profits and establishing put spreads to further profit from a continued slide.

At year-end, we typically look for stocks that might come under some pressure because of tax concerns. Investors might take a loss now for this tax year and then buy shares back 30 days later (to avoid the IRS's washed sale rule) for anticipated gains for next year. As we look for these opportunities, we might be short a particular stock in the last two weeks of the year, and then trade from the long-side for the first two to three months of the new year. With options, it takes a relatively small amount of risk and capital to get into these opportunistic positions.

Stocks in late 1999 that fit that description included Waste Management, Xerox, and BancOne. All of them were beat up and underperformed over the year, and as a result saw some aggressive selling for tax losses. As the year came to a close, we established an April call spread to own them on the cheap if the stock had a rebound. That worked two years ago in Apple and Oracle, which were both under $20 a share at the time. Apple went from about $16 a share to $150 in two years. Oracle, which was once $18, traded up to around $90.

In these instances, it all came down to having a plan and the discipline to carry it out. Further, if you are going to trade options, even as a retail investor using spreads, you must be able to deal with risk. With options, the best way to control risk is to buy options, because you then control your future. The option buyer can only lose the premium paid. Or, you use a spread, which also limits the risk potential.

Another key consideration for any trader or speculator is *capital preservation*. When you trade options, there will be times when the market goes against you. As a professional trader, for example, there are times when I sell an option and the market moves in the buyer's favor. Then the buyer exercises the option—something that I don't want to happen—and I have to either buy stock or deliver it. In fact, there can be times when, in a bad month, and using our massive leverage, a professional trader might lose hundreds of thousands of dollars. The saving grace in all this is discipline. If you can devise a plan, reassess it when necessary to enhance profits or cut losses, then you have a better chance of preserving your capital.

The problem is too many people make it appear that trading is easy. It's as simple as booting up the computer, picking up the phone, and throwing a dart at the stock tables. The truth is, you can lose money when you buy or sell a stock because the market can—and will—move against you at times. If you don't know why you are buying the latest dot.com, you might very well buy at the top, only to watch a fast and precipitous decline. When the music stops in Wall Street's version of musical chairs, things can get ugly in a hurry.

So before you trade anything, you want to practice, or *paper trade.* That means instead of executing the trades, you write down on paper what you would have done. You keep track of the buys and sells just as if they were real trades. You devise a plan and stick with it even though you are not executing any trades, because this dress rehearsal for the market is critical. The results of this paper trading will help you determine how well you pick stocks, and your simulated performance for choosing the entry and exit levels.

This then becomes like a journal, a recording of all your trades. All of your trades—both the winners and the losers—should be studied. In fact, how you handle losses is very important. Because when your money is really on the line, you must keep your discipline or else the losses will mount—and your capital will erode.

Remember, a really good trader is probably right 60 percent of the time. With that kind of a track record, what makes a trader successful is the ability to cut losses short and let the profits run. If you have half-point winners and two-point losers, you won't stay in the game for very long. In other words, you can't gobble losses and nibble for winners.

Regardless of the strategy that you use, the name of this game is discipline. It's the only way you'll be able to devise and stick to your plan—and preserve your capital to keep playing.

chapter 5

from the short side

The spread strategies we've discussed thus far focus on the long side of the market. But it's also possible to use spreads to play the short side when you're bearish on a stock, betting that the market will decline, or simply to protect your holdings, whether they are individual stocks or mutual funds. The next strategy we'll discuss is the *put spread.*

Let's say you've selected a stock after doing your homework, and you decide that the odds of the stock trading lower are greater than the odds of it trading higher. One way to play your hunch would be to buy a put spread. When buying a put spread, I lock both the maximum loss and the profit potential. For example, on a 10-point put spread, the most I can lose is the amount I paid for the put spread, but the profit potential, just as in the bull call spread, is the amount I paid subtracted from the strike price differential. For instance, if I paid $2.75 a share for a 10-point put spread, my maximum profit would be $10 minus $2.75, or $7.25 per spread. Ideally, I want to have at least a 2-to-1 ratio. That means for the times that I'm right, I'm going to be rewarded at least twice as much as the amount I'll lose when I'm wrong. Adhering to this kind of ratio is the essence of risk control and money management.

Here's an example of how a put spread works: Let's say eBay is trading at $150 a share. I decide to *buy the $150 put* and *sell the $140 put,* for a $10 spread. If I pay $9 for the $150 put and sell the $140 put for $6.50, I'll pay a net of $2.50 for a 10-point spread.

For one contract (equivalent to 100 shares), you would pay $250 per spread, which is also the maximum loss, and stand to reap a maximum profit of $750 per spread (Figure 5.1).

Now, even if eBay went to $200 a share—the exact opposite of what I wanted to happen—I would still lose only $250. Overall, I'm risking $250 to make $750 per spread—a three-to-one reward/risk ratio, which I consider to be great odds in my favor. And, I'm controlling the downside of what is otherwise a very volatile stock, which could be hard to borrow if I wanted to short it (as outlined in Chapter 3). At the same time, I would be in a position to profit handsomely if the stock trades the way I think it would and declines in price.

Put Spread

eBay trading at $150 a share

Buy $150 put and pay $9 premium

Sell $140 put and collect $6.50 premium

Maximum loss: $2.50 a share

Maximum profit: $7.50 a share

Figure 5.1 long 1 Oct 150 put, short 1 Oct 140 put

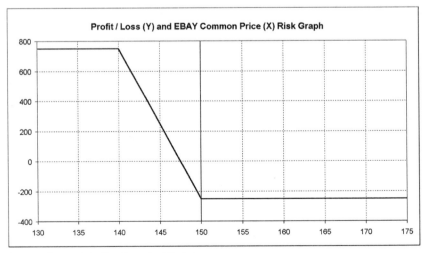

Source: Created by StockmarketWorkshop.com.

If eBay declines in price to $140 a share, profit on the $150 put is $10 a share, minus the $9 premium, for a net profit of $1.00 a share, or $100. However, since the $140 put expires worthless, I keep the $6.50 a share premium, for a total profit on the trade of $7.50 a share ($1.00 plus $6.50), or $750 per spread.

If eBay declines to $130 a share, I make a $20 profit on the $150 put, minus the $9 premium for a net profit of $11 a share. The $140 put I sold is exercised, requiring me to buy stock for $140 when the stock is trading $130. I lose $10 a share, which is partially offset by the $6.50 a share premium I collected, for a net loss on that trade of $3.50. My overall profit on such a spread trade is $7.50 ($11 minus $3.50), or $750 per spread.

If eBay rises to $160 a share, the $150 put I bought expires worthless and I lose the $9 premium. The $140 put I sold also expires worthless and I keep the $6.50 a share premium, for a total net loss of $2.50 a share, or $250 per spread.

For more sophisticated investors, there is another strategy that involves selling puts as a partial surrogate for owning the stock. Let's say you like Xerox, which has sold off rather sharply over the past few months, declining from $60 a share to around $25. As a result, you consider the options to be very undervalued, as the collapse pumped up volatility in both call and put options. One way to invest would be to buy the shares outright at today's price and wait for them to appreciate in value. Or you could sell the at-the-money puts that are a few months out and collect a premium of, say, $3 a share.

The buyer of those puts could be someone who wants to lock in downside price protection by buying put options. For example, the buyer could purchase April $25 put options, which would protect his or her investment if the stock declines below $25 a share.

You, on the other hand, are bullish on the stock. You believe there is little chance, if any, that Xerox will trade below $25 a share. By selling the $25 puts, you get to keep the $3 premium if the stock behaves as you anticipate and trades at least at or above $25 a share. Interestingly, in this scenario both you, as the seller of the put, and the buyer, looking for downside protection, are both bullish on the stock. The stock buyer probably has a long-term bullish bias for XRX, while the put seller is simply thinking the stock is oversold and the options overpriced.

A variation on this theme is *cash-secured put selling*. This is an immensely popular strategy that allows you to be the "house" or the "insurance company" to take on someone else's risk—for a payment reward, of course. The obvious benefit is that you get to collect the premium, just as a life insurance company or the casino does. And, especially in volatile times, you're rewarded very handsomely for taking on that risk. But you are taking on risk.

In the 20 years that I've been trading, I'd say that cash-secured put selling is a strategy that works wonderfully 90 percent of the time—that's as long as you have the cash and haven't leveraged yourself too much for the 10 percent of the time that it doesn't work—such as those infamous "downturns" in the stock market that we saw in 1987, 1989, 1991, 1998, and in early 2000.

Cash-secured puts work very well, although many investors don't understand this strategy. Those who do, however, often put it to good use. Consider my friend, whom we'll call Frank, a very successful entrepreneur. After his introductions to options, he started buying seats at the Chicago Board Options Exchange and leasing them out. There are a limited number of seats and they lease just like an apartment on a monthly basis. And, unlike an apartment, there is no need to paint them and you never get a call in the middle of the night that the pipes are broken. Returns on Exchange seats average about 18 percent, which is certainly an attractive return.

My friend Frank then graduated from just owning seats to figuring out some other way to make money with options. That's when he became familiar with selling cash-secured puts. He sells puts on stocks that he loves, the ones he really thinks have upside potential. When he's right, he collects the premium. And for the few times he's wrong, he's got the cash in his brokerage account to buy the stock that's "put" to him at an unfavorable price.

Here's an example of a typical "Frank trade." Let's say he's bullish on Intel (INTC), believing that the world's largest chipmaker is going to grow by 20 percent, come hell or high water. He knows the stock will have its share of ups and downs, but overall, this is a stock he wants to own. Now, let's assume that Intel is trading at $100, and the $95 puts that are two months out (which is the right to sell the stock at $95 a share) are trading for a $3.50 a share premium.

Frank would put up the cash at the brokerage firm to cover the stock, and sell these $95 puts, which are out of the money at the

moment. (Remember that by selling these puts, Frank would be obligated to buy Intel at $95 or lower if the buyer exercised that right.
In return for selling these puts, Frank collects $3.50 a share.)

Intel trading at $100 a share.

Sell $95 put (two months out). Collect $3.50 a share premium.

Keep $9,150 per contract (100 shares) in brokerage account to
secure puts in case the puts get exercised and he is
forced to buy the stock.

In this instance, Frank is really bullish on Intel; he thinks this
stock is heading higher. You, as the buyer of these puts, are also
bullish on the stock. But you also want a little insurance to help
you sleep at night, which is why you buy the puts. You already
own Intel shares, 100 of them, now trading at $100 a share. You
want to protect the value of your $10,000 investment, so you're
willing to pay $3.50 a share—or 3.5 percent—to protect a $100 a
share asset.

If you're correct and the stock price does rise, you will lose the
$3.50 a share premium you paid for the puts. But you may very well
make up for that loss—and then some—with the increase in the
value of the shares that you hold. In the meantime, if you have
$10,000 in Intel stock, you're happy that increased to $110 a share
from $100. But with that kind of investment, you may very well
want to "insure" it by buying puts that, as with insurance on your
home or car, you really hope you never have to use. Frank, the put
seller, meanwhile, is rewarded for providing the downside insurance by being able to keep the $3.50 a share premium.

Now, what happens if Intel shares do go down to say, $91.50?
With a $95 put option you paid $3.50 a share for, you put the stock
to him at $95, but the put protection cost you $3.50 a share. But if
Frank loves Intel at $100 a share—and is willing to own it at that
price—how much more will he love it at $91.50 a share! He's not
upset about taking the stock at that price and holding onto it until,
as he expects, it increases in value. With the cash in his brokerage
account (remember these are cash-secured puts) he can purchase
the shares when the put is exercised. The proceeds of that stock
sale, meanwhile, help to offset the losses on the value of the Intel
shares held by you, the put buyer.

For each time Frank did this trade, however, he would have to have $9,150 in his account to cover the 100 shares (at $91.50 a share) that could be "put" to him should the option be exercised. Assuming he does this trade 10 times, that amount increases to $91,500. The cash that secures the put can be in the form of a deposit at the brokerage firm, on which he can get interest. Or it can be in the form of a Treasury bill or a money-market fund, as long as it's a cash-secured holding that can be liquidated at a moment's notice.

Overall, from Frank's perspective, he's earning interest on the cash or cash-equivalent investment that secures the puts. And he's collecting $3.50 a share in premium for the puts he sells. If he's able to do that six times a year, that's $21 a share in premiums—or $21,000—plus interest on $91,500, which at 5 percent would amount to $4,000-plus. In total, Frank is making about $25,000 for six trades on a $91,000 investment, which is a pretty good rate of return for being the "house."

There's another reason why speculators like Frank love cash-secured put selling. Frank has owned an insurance company or two in his time. He knows that the actuarial tables used to predict occurrences (deaths in the case of life insurance) make similar assumptions as the option pricing models but with one rather glaring difference: Stocks rarely die! Oh sure, there have been a few, but overall, the occurrence that is final for the premium seller at the life insurance company, isn't nearly so final for the put option seller. In fact, a cash-secured put seller like Frank will tell you that stocks have many more lives than any cat!

The risk, which I must stress, is that this strategy is not just about collecting premiums to protect other people's stock holdings from downside risk—risk that you and the put buyer don't expect to materialize. You have to know that there will be times when you end up buying a lot of stock, potentially at very unfavorable prices.

It doesn't feel very good when the market makes a 10 percent or 20 percent correction and you know that you have $1 million worth of stock tumbling into your account because put buyers are exercising these options. And these situations do occur, such as during the crash of 1987, 1989, 1991, 1998, early 2000 . . . and the next time the market "corrects."

Many of you probably remember when Russia defaulted in 1998 on its domestic debt on the heels of economic crises in Asia and in some Latin American countries. I remember being in Paris with my wife, Brigid, in October 1998 when the market was down 400 points. There I was on vacation, and I had all these obligations out there in the form of puts that I had sold. Like other cash-secured put sellers, I had been riding along for months, collecting premiums every month. Suddenly, the stocks everybody had to have went from "must haves" to "don't wants." At times like this, the market doesn't look so good, but that's exactly the time you are buying big chunks of stocks.

The impact on you when that happens depends largely on how greedy you've been. Sometimes, instead of selling puts that are 5 to 10 percent out of the money—and collecting relatively small premiums—you start selling puts with strike prices that are a lot closer in and collecting larger premiums. The problem is, there is a far greater probability that these close-in puts will be exercised if the market makes a "dip," than the farther-out puts that won't be exercised except in the case of an all-out correction.

Just like the Bear Call Spread (discussed in Chapter 4), you have a limited amount you're going to win when you're right, a much greater percentage you're going to lose when you're wrong.

As a professional trader with leverage in my favor, I can execute trades that could, potentially, expose me to risk that would make most retail investors very nervous and probably sick to their stomachs, especially in 1998, or early 2000. I trade some major names among the tech stocks—Micron Technology, Sun Microsystems, Intel, Cisco, Microsoft, Oracle. And I've had puts on many of these stocks in spreads that have gone against me. As a result, I've probably had to buy $60 million worth of stock, due to the compounding effect of the professional leverage (sometimes as high as 100-to-1) that I can use, which is both a blessing and a curse.

In times of notable downturns such as in 1987, 1989, 1991, 1998, and early 2000, that leverage is a curse, and I've had stock put to me that far exceeds the cash value of my trading account. At any given time, my firm is carrying $150 million to $250 million worth of stock on the books. So you can see the impact if, in a two-day period, all of a sudden you end up with $60 million to $70 million worth of stock in your account in a falling market.

Luckily, we're able to limit our exposure on such adverse moves, sometimes through the use of stock index puts, other times by ownership of way out-of-the-money "disaster puts." So if I have a losing position in Sun Microsystems, Microsoft, Oracle, or Intel, I'll own Nasdaq Index options (NDX). If I end up having a lot of stock put to me at an unfavorable price, I'll make up at least some of the money in my index positions. And, as my friend Frank and I know, stocks don't just "die."

Cash-covered put spreads are a wonderful way to play the market from the bullish side, and you collect a premium for your efforts. It's like you're playing the "house" in Vegas, taking on the risk that someone else wants to offset, which is why they are appealing to so many knowledgeable investors.

In early 2000, I was asked to speak to an investment club whose members included several engineers and doctors who had amassed a multimillion-dollar account, which they had increased with cash-secured put selling. This strategy paid off handsomely, reaping a 42 percent return in the fourth quarter of 1999 alone. Anyone who remembers the December 1999 run in the Nasdaq and the Dow could see how they could post those returns by selling puts on the Nasdaq "names" among the tech stocks that tended to have a lot of volatility. Remember IBM may have 30 percent volatility, whereas eBay, Yahoo, and so forth may have volatility in the 100 percent range. When you sell an out-of-the-money IBM put, you may collect $2 a share. But when you sell an out-of-the-money Yahoo put, you may collect $20 a share. (Of course, the reason that premium is so high is there is a greater chance, with Yahoo's volatility, of a strike price being hit.) But when the market goes up and you've sold a Yahoo put, it's a very good day.

There are other put spreads that investors can use, such as *selling a put spread*. In this strategy, as in cash-secured put selling, we profit from the upside movement of the stock. (Since we are selling the put, our expectation is that the stock will not decline in value enough to hit the strike price.)

Again, let's assume that Intel is priced at $100 a share. To do this spread, we sell the $95 put—granting the buyer the right to put stock to us at $95 a share—and collect a $3.50 premium. Then we buy the $85 put for $1. In this example, we have sold a $10-point put spread for $2.50 (Figure 5.2).

If Intel is at $95 a share or higher at expiration, we keep the $2.50 per spread ($250). But if Intel is lower than $92.50 a share (the $95 strike price minus the $2.50 per spread credit), we're going to own stock at that price or we're going to have to trade out of that

Figure 5.2   long 1 Aug 85 put, short 1 Aug 95 put

Profit / Loss (Y) and INTC Common Price (X) Risk Graph

Source: Created by StockmarketWorkshop.com.

position. The advantage of this trade, however, is that you only have to invest $750 to make a one-contract trade—the difference between the $10-point spread and the $2.50 per spread you collected. Making this kind of trade for $750 is a far more economical strategy than cash-secured put selling, which requires you to have a large account—often in the hundreds of thousands of dollars—at your brokerage firm.

The drawback, however, is that the risk/reward ratio is out of balance. Your potential on this trade is $2.50 a share, or $250 per spread, but if you lose, at least your loss is capped at $7.50 a share, or $750. That means you risk $750 to make $250. On the other hand, $750 is not a large upfront investment to make, especially compared with cash-secured put selling, which required $9,150 per contract.

    Intel at $100 a share

    Sell $95 put and collect $3.50 premium

    Buy $85 put for $1

    Net profit on $10 spread would be $250 per contract

    Loss capped at maximum of $750 per contract

When you compare the $750 per contract the put spread seller has to put up versus the $9,150 the naked put seller has to have in his or her account, it's easy to see why put spread sales are popular with people who have less capital—or less risk tolerance—than those who do other forms of spread trades.

In options, spreads come in many varieties and in many forms, playing both the long and the short side. And they sometimes come under some very unusual names. (We all know about Bulls and Bears. But what about Butterflies and Condors?)

An *iron butterfly* is more than just a reference to the 1960s heavy rock group. An iron butterfly is a spread that allows you to profit from options on stocks or indexes that are trading in a range. When you buy a stock outright, you're speculating that the price will increase. If that stock stays in a range—trading a little higher and then a little lower and then a little higher again—it's tough to make a profit. But with specialized spreads such as the iron butterfly, you improve your chances greatly of making a profit, *especially* if that stock continues to trade in a range.

Say, for example, that I believe that during the month of April, which as we all know is the height of tax season, investors have significantly less capital to invest because they had to send money to Uncle Sam. Even if you file for an extension, you still owe Uncle Sam the cash on April 15. With less cash on hand, there is less cash to invest in the market, which then tends to stagnate in April. As a result, April is a time when the market normally trends in a narrow band, instead of rocketing up and down as it does in December and January (when it typically rallies) and October (when it usually sells off because of lingering fears of the crashes of 1929 and 1987).

In other words, times of the year that a given stock or index are likely to stagnate are perfect for doing iron butterfly spreads.

An iron butterfly is the simultaneous sale of a call spread and put spread, which result in a hedged short premium position that reaches its maximum profit potential if the equity or index stays in your predicted range. Let's use the S&P 500 Index as an example. Butterfly spreads are quite popular with index option trades. They'll see that among the S&P 500, 20 stocks are up, 20 stocks are down, and 440 are just about unchanged. That means the S&P index is going to trade in a band. Plus, the diversification within that index, across a spectrum of industries, tends to work in favor of the premium seller during times of low volatility.

Let's say the S&P 500 Index is trading at 1450. I believe it will trade between 1430 and 1470—up and down 20 points from where it is currently. I could sell the 1470 call for $8.00 and buy the 1480 call for $6.00 to protect it. In effect, I've sold a 10-point call spread (the differential between the strike prices) for a net of $200 per contract.

For the downside end of the range, I sell the 1430 put for $7.00, and I buy the 1420 put for $5.00. I've sold a 10-point put spread, again for $2.00. With these two spread trades, I have bracketed the market just above and just below where I think it will trade, and I've collected a net of $4 in premiums. The most I could lose on this butterfly spread is the difference between the net of $4 in premiums received and the $10 spread value, or $600 per contract (Figure 5.3).

Now, assume that the S&P fails to stay in my projected range and instead drops to 1400. The 1420 put that I bought is now worth $20. The 1430 put that I sold is now worth $30 to the buyer. My exposure on that trade is that I owe $10 per contract. But that's offset

Figure 5.3 long 1 Aug 1480 call, short 1 Aug 1470 call; long 1 Aug 1420 put, short 1 Aug 1430 put

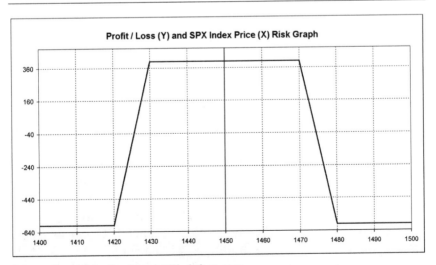

Source: Created by StockmarketWorkshop.com.

by the $4 in premiums that I collected, so my loss on that trade is cut to $6 per option.

Conversely, let's say the S&P rockets out of the range to the upside, reaching 1500. The 1470 that I sold is worth $30 and the 1480 that I bought is worth $20, leaving me with a net exposure of $10. But taking into account the $4 in premiums that I collected, my net loss on that trade is $6 a share.

But if the market stays in the range that I projected—in this instance between 1470 and 1430—then all the puts and calls expire worthless, and I'm able to keep my $4 in premiums. The maximum loss of $6 and potential profit of $4 is just under a 1:1 risk/reward ratio. While that's short of my optimal ratio of 2:1, it is not as skewed toward a higher loss than some other spread trades.

One reminder: S&P index options are European-style options, which means they are only exercisable at expiration, which makes them very popular.

S&P Index at 1450

Range projected to be 1430 to 1470

Sell 1470 call for $8.00 a share

Buy 1480 call for $6.00 a share

Sell 1430 put for $7.00 a share

Buy 1420 put for $5.00 a share

Net premiums collected: $4

Maximum loss is $6.00 a share ($10 spread value minus $4 in premiums collected)

Maximum profit is $4.00 in premiums collected

For stock options, which may be exercised any time up to and on the day of expiration, the iron butterfly is a strategy that I like to use when a stock is in a range, such as right after earnings. If Cisco Systems has just announced earnings and there is no big trade show or other potential news-making event, then I know most of the information—good or bad—is probably out about Cisco. That makes it a good time to look at establishing an iron butterfly spread. For example, let's say Cisco announced its earnings one week ago and the stock was trading at $100 a share. If I thought the prospects were good for it settling into a range, I might do a spread such as selling the $110 call and collecting $5 a share, while buying the $120 call and paying $2 for that protective leg. On the other side of the range, I'd sell the $90 puts for $3 and buy the $80 puts for $1. In total, I would collect $5 in premiums, and I'd have two 10-point spreads covered (Figure 5.4).

The most I could lose in this position would be $5, the difference between the $5 I collected and the $10 that either spread could hit at expiration. For example, if Cisco broke out of my projected trading range and went to $130 a share, I would face net exposure of $10 a share on the call spread, which would be partially offset by the $5 in premiums that I collected. If Cisco broke through the range on the downside and went to $70 a share, I would face a net exposure on the put spread of $10, which would again be offset by the $5 in premiums that I collected. Keep in mind that not only would CSCO have to trade up to $130, or down through $70, but it must stay above or below at expiration for either spread to go the maximum $10. The stock can rock and roll up and down, but as long as Cisco finishes at expiration between $115 and $85 (the strike prices with premiums collected taken into

Figure 5.4   long 1 Jan 120 call, short 1 Jan 110 call; long 1 Jan 80 put, short 1 Jan 90 put

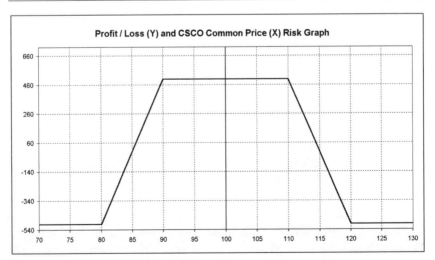

Source: Created by StockmarketWorkshop.com.

consideration) I would win. And with Cisco trading at $100 a share after earnings, when things tend to relax, I like my odds of winning on this trade.

Cisco trading at $100 a share

Sell $110 call and collect $5 a share premium

Buy $120 call and pay $2 a share premium

Sell $90 put and collect $3 a share premium

Buy $80 put and pay $1 a share

Picking the range for a stock is a combination of art and science. I try to use my own experience and gut instincts for what risk/reward ratio I'm comfortable with on a particular trade. This is also an area in which I like to employ some technical analysis to determine likely trading support and resistance areas. Additionally, I try not to do anything that is 3:1 against me. In other words, if all I can collect for selling two 10 point spreads is $2.50, or $3, I don't like my odds very much because I could lose $7 to $7.50 if I've misjudged the trading range. Another thing I look for is a stock that has moved around a lot, because then you have the luxury of picking among many strike prices. For example, if Apple Computer runs from $40 a share to $110 and is presently trading at $90, you'll have a myriad of strike prices to choose from above and below the market, which increases my choices of strategies.

Generally speaking, a static stock with low volatility, such as energy companies and utilities, just don't have enough strike prices above and below the market. So although they would be great candidates for a range trading strategy such as the iron butterfly, that lack of available strikes virtually rules out those sectors. The stock has to have had some movement in it to establish strike prices, which will most effectively allow you to plot your strategy.

That's one of the nice things about Internet stocks. By early February 2000, Yahoo had a run from $260 to $500 a share in one month, and then came back down after its earnings to $330 a share. With that kind of movement, Yahoo options have a lot of strike prices. Say that one month into the future I'm going to sell the 500 calls and buy the 520s—a 20-point spread—and collect $2 a share. With Yahoo at $330 a share, I could sell $250 puts and buy $230 puts, maybe for $3.

If I have enough strikes above and below the market, I could withstand a 25 percent to 30 percent move. That's a lot of market movement that I can withstand. I'd only get hurt if there was a 40 percent or 50 percent move on Yahoo. Of course, that 50 percent+ movement is exactly what happened to Yahoo and other members of the Internet sector in March and April of 2000, which shows why selling put and call spreads, with defined profits and losses, is much safer than the alternative of naked sales.

We call these spreads iron butterflies because they involve out-of-the-money puts and calls, which means they carry less risk (and therefore more protection) than butterflies of a different breed. But there are other butterflies that involve in-the-money calls and puts, which carry both a higher risk and a higher potential reward.

Let's say we're trading Apple Computer, and I think there's a good chance that Apple will finish right where it is at $110 a share.

I could then sell a *straddle*—meaning I would sell both the $110 call and the $110 put. Since these are both at-the-money, I sell the $110 call for $6 and the $110 put for $5.50. I'm taking in $11.50 a share ($1,150 per option spread), which means I could withstand a move of $11.50 in either direction. That's a good amount of premium to collect, but there is also a trade-off for that kind of reward. I have almost unlimited *risk* if Apple were to announce suddenly a new "iMac" computer that everybody just has to have, and the stock moves to $200 a share on the announcement. Then the $11.50 in premiums I collected pale by comparison to the upside risk I face.

To place a limit on the risk, I then do two other trades. Those other two trades become the wings, capping off the potential loss to either the upside or downside. The straddle we sold is the body of the butterfly. When you graph them out, they look like looping lines, resembling wings around a circular body. (Hence, the term butterfly.) I limit my upside loss by buying the $115 call for $4.00, and I put a floor on my downside risk by buying the $105 put for $3.50. Now, my net on the premiums is reduced from $11.50 to $4.00 a share (or $400 per option spread). But I have significantly reduced my exposure in case of a surprise, adverse move (Figure 5.5).

With this trade, we make money if Apple trades between $114 on the upside ($4 above the straddle we sold) to $106 on the downside

Figure 5.5   long 1 Aug 115 call, short 1 Aug 110 call; long 1 Aug 105 put, short 1 Aug 110 put

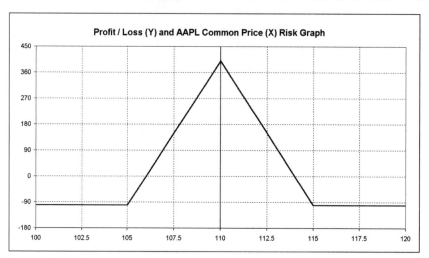

Source: Created by StockmarketWorkshop.com.

($4 below the straddle we sold). Outside of that spread, we could only lose a net of $1 a share as we have effectively sold the 110–115 call spread and 110–105 put spread for $4 and the most either side could hit at expiration is $5.

Apple trading at $110 a share

Sell $110 call and collect $6 a share premium

Sell $110 put and collect $5.50 a share premium

Buy $115 call and pay $4.00 a share premium

Buy $105 put and pay $3.50 share premium

With this kind of risk and reward, you would want to do this trade to an almost unlimited amount. On occasion you can find some butterfly trades with this kind of payout. But most of the time, a butterfly spread will net you $2 or $3 a share for $5 butterflies with a risk/reward ratio of roughly one-to-one.

The higher reward trades often occur when there is a big anomaly in the options pricing for some reason, placing a high value on both the calls and puts around the current price. Maybe the Wall Street analysts are divided over the prospects for a stock. In a classic analyst's tug-of-war, three analysts have downgraded it, and two have upgraded it. Now you have people betting on both the upside and the downside of the same stock. In this situation, you might be able to sell the body of the butterfly (the straddle portion, which involves the simultaneous selling of a call and put near or at the same price). Then you buy the wings to give yourself upside and downside protection, all of which puts you in a potentially very profitable position.

There are several factors that come up when you trade any of these multiple leg strategies. The iron butterfly has a greater range, but less profit potential, because it involves out-of-the money options and thus, you can withstand greater market movement. Butterflies, on the other hand, generally have more profit potential, but also more risk because the options are at-the-money, which means the stock has to stay in a tighter range to allow you to keep the premiums you've collected. Additionally, you should keep in mind that these strategies will be more expensive to execute due to the multiple legs involved. Both butterflies and iron butterflies are comprised of four options per complete spread, so commissions are a big factor. Also, finding a broker to execute butterflies can be more difficult than finding the actual spreads. Make sure your broker understands and has the capability of carrying out your wishes, as fewer and fewer brokers can execute such trades.

What we've discussed thus far are some very commonly used spread strategies for options trading. There are many varieties and variations of these trades, depending on your strategy, risk/reward profile, and the prevailing strike prices.

When you start out in options, you don't need to do all the butterflies and condors, which are a bigger version of the butterfly spreads. Rather, remember the KISS principle: Keep it simple, stupid. Simple works. Use simple strategies that you understand, particularly when it comes to the maximum profits and maximum losses. Don't get carried away by a complex trade that may look good or sound good when you describe it.

The people who lose are those who abuse options because they don't understand what they're doing or how these instruments work. For virtually any educated investor (or investor who is willing to learn), there are a myriad of ways to make money in options.

Among the strategies we've discussed thus far, the straddle—the simultaneous sale of a call and put—is among the most risky. (Remember a straddle is basically the body of a butterfly trade, without the wings to protect the upside and downside.)

Take Qualcomm (QCOM), for example. Let's say that it's trading at $140 a share after its four-for-one split, which was effective at year-end 1999. What was basically a $25 stock in January 1999 traded over $500 a share (on a presplit basis) that year. My firm trades Qualcomm (QCOM) as well as other high-tech stocks, which soar very high at times, but also carry a lot of risk. A $500 or $600 a share stock could easily move $50 or $60 in a day. Even on a post-split basis, Qualcomm could see a $15 move in a day.

This kind of movement illustrates the challenge to pick the projected range for these high-tech stocks. That's why it can be very risky to use a straddle, since these strategies require a stock to stay in a range to be profitable.

As we'll discuss in later chapters, Internet and other high-tech stocks have changed all the rules. Our marketplace has moved from having 20,000 to 40,000 professional traders who move the market—both on the floor and upstairs in trading offices—along with the large hedge funds, to a democratization of the markets with legions of retail traders. Online, discount brokerages have sparked not only an increase in stock trading, but also options trading. The Internet has leveled the playing field and widened the arena.

In today's marketplace, we could very well see 10,000 customers or more trading 100 to 500 shares in Qualcomm. Plus, you could have fund giants trading 200,000 shares.

Against that backdrop, let's say you're looking to play options in Qualcomm (QCOM), which at $140 a share, is extremely active and volatile—commanding a high premium in all of its options. That increases the profit potential—but also the risk—for doing a trade such as a one-month straddle, which is the simultaneous sale of a call and a put, both at the $140 strike price. You might collect as much as $50 a share, say, $27 for the call and $23 for the put. Then, as long as Qualcomm traded between $190 (the $140 strike price plus the $50 in premiums) on the upside and $90 on the down (the $140 premium minus the $50 in premiums), you'd win and be able to keep the entire premium you collected.

But if it trades outside of that range, you lose. And the chances of that happening increase along with the volatility. With the

March and April Nasdaq debacle fresh in investor's minds, its easy to see how being on the wrong side of a short straddle can be a life-changing event. Keep in mind that Qualcomm is a stock that has made $100 moves at times. I remember the news report about the trader who was asked to make a market for a $240 straddle when Qualcomm was trading at $260 and on its way to $600! He sold the spread for what the firm thought was an outrageous premium and in about two weeks the firm had lost somewhere between $8 and $20 million. I'd call that a life-changing event, wouldn't you! You can see the severity and volatility associated with options on this kind of stock.

The beauty is that by selling the straddle at $140 (after the split), you make money in a very wide range. In our example, the straddle seller would have made money between $190 and $90—a 100-point range. But the trade-off is: You have to have very high-risk tolerance, and be able to live with the battle scars from these kind of trades. With Qualcomm at $140 a share, it could easily rocket to $200. At $200, you could probably sell the straddle premium for $70 a share because of the volatility!

This is perhaps an extreme example of why selling a straddle is the most risky strategy for selling premiums. As we stated before, selling a straddle works best when you're convinced that a stock or an index is in a range. Remember, a straddle is basically the body of a butterfly trade, without the wings to protect you. In a high-flying, volatile stock you better have those wings!

Because of this risk, I never recommend that customers sell straddles—no matter how much money they have. It always is a good idea to buy some disaster-protection, even though this will cut down on your profit potential. (What price can you place on peace of mind?) Maybe you'll never need that risk-protection. But it's never wasted money to be able to sleep at night. I've tried to convince my friend Frank to buy some out-the-money puts against his cash-secured put sales, but to no avail. Unfortunately, it probably takes events like the Nasdaq calamity of 2000 to convince people that there are better ways to manage short premium.

A slightly less risky version of the straddle is its cousin, the *strangle*. Again, let's assume that Qualcomm is trading at $140 a share. But instead of selling the $140 call and the $140 put (as in the straddle), give yourself a wider spread. You sell the $150 call and the $130 put, which widens out the range for which you'll be able to keep the premium you collect. Let's say you sold the call and the put for about $15 and thus collected $30 a share ($3,000 per strangle). That means, between $180 on the upside and $100 on the downside you make money. But if you're wrong, it's still going to be painful. The farther out you spread the strangle, the more opportunity you'll have to keep the premium you collect.

As the options you choose move from at-the-money to out-of-the-money, the premium you receive will be reduced. For example, if Qualcomm is trading at $140, you could decide to sell the $180 call and the $100 put, collecting maybe a total of $15 in premiums ($1,500 per strangle). Your risk is spread over a wider price range, but you'd still be in for a lot of pain if Qualcomm skyrocketed to $250 a share.

Deciding upon the best strategy to take will depend mostly on your risk tolerance and your outlook for the stock—as well as your experience. Most people begin speculating in options with covered writes, because it is the most analogous to buying a stock outright. Then they typically graduate to bull call spreads because, like most retail investors, they speculate with a bullish bias.

But in time, investors want to make money when a stock is in a range or to take advantage of changes in volatility. That's when other spread trades come into play.

For example, consider the AOL-Time Warner merger. As an Internet stock, AOL used to have a Price/Equity (P/E) ratio of 400. More established Time Warner, with media holdings that include radio, television, and some high-speed digital cable, had a P/E of 90. After the deal, AOL will no longer be viewed by the street as the fast-growth, Internet high-flyer it once was because, in effect, it's becoming a more mature company, carrying the overhead that comes with the Time Warner properties. When the deal was announced, I expected we'd see a big drop in volatility in AOL, which used to trade around 80 percent. Now, a volatility of 50 percent or even 30 percent (which would put it more in line with stocks like IBM) is more likely.

To me, that means the pricing for AOL could also move down.

Still, there are plenty of options plans in AOL, although I must now take into account this change in fundamentals. If AOL begins to trade in a range, it's time to look at the spread trades, with the appropriate counter measures to guard against upside and downside risk.

Whatever the scenario, it's important you understand everything that's happening with a particular stock. You can't just buy a call tomorrow because you heard a stock mentioned on the television or in a chat room today. You need to do your homework and devise your plan. Then you go to your options toolbox, and select the best strategy.

chapter 6

playing the broad market

Individual stocks aren't the only way to participate in the options market. The most efficient way you can play in the broader market is through *index options.* Increasingly, index options, which used to be used mostly by institutions to hedge portfolios, present an opportunity for retail investors.

In 1983, 10 years after the founding of the CBOE, the Exchange launched options on broad-based stock indexes. The first was an index of 100 of the biggest capitalized stocks listed on the CBOE and dubbed the Options Exchange Index, called by some the Standard & Poor's 100 Index, which has the ticker symbol OEX. Seventeen years later, the OEX is still one of the most active index products on the market, trading an average of more than 130,000 contracts per day in 1999. The CBOE also trades options on the Standard & Poor's 500 index (SPX), which is based on the current or "cash" value of the S&P 500. (*Note:* This should not be confused with the options on S&P 500 *futures* contract, which trades at the Chicago Mercantile Exchange, where S&P futures are also traded.)

For years before the launch of these products, indexes had been tracked and traded by institutions. But most of that trade had occurred without a consolidated market. For instance, a customer would call an investment banking firm or trading company such as Goldman Sachs and ask for a "market" for cash value of the S&P

500. Goldman Sachs would quote a price at which it would buy the future price of the S&P 500 if the customer were selling, or the price it would sell the future price of the S&P 500 if the customer were buying. A transaction would be conducted which was *off-exchange* or *over-the-counter*.

But that kind of transaction, which still takes place in certain customized options and other off-the-exchange products, presented a large risk, known as *contra-party risk*. That means, by doing an over-the-counter trade, you have to bear the full credit risk of the person or party with whom you traded. Thus, if that other party had other obligations that caused losses, it might not be able to fulfill the obligation to you under terms of the trade you made. Likewise, that other party had to deal with your potential credit risks, in case the situation arose that you could not financially fulfill your obligations.

This credit risk posed by party-to-party, over-the-counter trades and the sheer size of the market for index options were the catalysts that prompted the creation of options exchanges in the first place. Before the exchanges were created, options on individual stocks had traded over-the-counter for years. Likewise, the catalyst for index options was partially the burgeoning OTC trading of index options, as well as the initial success of the index futures contracts listed first by the Kansas City Board of Trade, which brought out the Value Line Index and the Chicago Mercantile Exchange's subsequent listing of the S&P 500 futures contract. Since indexes are generally made up of anywhere from 10 to 1,000 stocks, over-the-counter trading of these options dwarfed the dollar-value—and, therefore, the potential risk—of equity options trading.

For example, let's say IBM is trading at $105 a share. The S&P 500 might be trading at $1,450 a share. That would be $1,450 times 250. (When the S&P Index contract was launched, the multiplier for the value of the overall S&P contract was 500. About two years ago, the size of the S&P contract was cut in half, reducing the multiplier to 250.) That means that a single contract for the S&P 500 would represent an underlying value of $1,450 times 250, or $362,500. By the same token, at $105 a share, a single contract trade in IBM would represent an underlying value of $105 times 100, or $10,500.

That difference—$362,500 for one S&P contract versus about $10,000 for one equity contract—underscores the need for contra-party credit risk protection for index options trading—the size gets pretty scary really fast. The need for protection from contra party risk was one of the reasons to list index options and the other was the oft-forgotten individual investor. The OTC index option market left the retail investor out in the cold, as virtually no retail customer was on the radar screens of the investment banks and trading houses that made markets in the OTC index options. The early successes and relative contract size of both the KC Value Line future and S&P 500 future at the CME indicated the retail investor was willing to invest in index futures. And if they were willing to trade futures, it was only a matter of time before index options took hold as well.

The institutions that called Goldman Sachs or any other major brokerage house to find a market in index options (in the days before they were listed on an exchange) were looking to offset portfolio risk. In other words, they were looking to protect the value of their stock portfolios and to obtain some downside "insurance" through the use of other financial instruments such as futures and options.

Thus, if they thought the market was going sideways or was in danger of declining, they would look to sell futures on the indexes. This way, the profit they'd made on the futures would partially or fully offset losses suffered in the stocks, themselves. (Conversely, if the market *did* rise, gains in the stock portfolio would offset losses on the futures.) But without listed derivative securities (as futures and options are considered since their value is *derived* from the underlying cash market) a customer could be at the mercy of whoever was quoting the market. In other words, if a customer with a large stock portfolio called to find out the market in S&P index options trading over-the-counter, it was a pretty good bet that customer was looking to buy puts or sell calls to guard against downside protection. Knowing that, the trading firm could conceivably quote a price that would guarantee the house a favorable deal at the expense of the customer. And since these options weren't listed by any exchange before 1983, there was no easy access to bids and offers. The only way would be to make dozens of phone calls to individual brokers and financial institutions who were willing to quote you a price and take on the contra-party risk.

In an open outcry, pit-trading environment, there is a constant stream of competitive bids and offers, consolidated in one place. From the customer's perspective, this is a huge improvement.

Open outcry provides instantaneous access to numerous bids and offers, all at competitive prices—without wearing out the speed dial on the phone to call a dozen brokerage houses for quotes.

Those competing, continuously quoted markets were why the OEX (options based on the CBOE's 100 stock index) quickly became popular with retail and institutional players. And as stated previously, the OEX is one of the few American-style index options that can be exercised at any time. SPX options, which are European-style, can only be exercised at expiration and are thus, even more popular with institutional users, who usually want to put on positions for portfolio insurance and not worry that the option would be exercised until expiration. On the other hand, since European-style options can't be exercised in the interim, the cost of holding the position has to be factored into the overall value. Thus, there's no way the options can trade at parity. For example, if the S&P index is trading at $1,450 a share, the $1,400 calls would normally have $50 worth of intrinsic value (the difference between the strike price and the market). But in reality, the cost of carrying the position until expiration would reduce the value of a $50 option, which, at 8 percent interest, might cost you $1 for 90 days, to $49, reflecting a $1 discount from its intrinsic value ($50 \times 8\% \times 90 / 360 = 1$) . And the further out the time (and therefore the longer the carrying value), the greater the discount to the intrinsic value.

The OEX, however, is an index option of a different flavor. Made to appeal to retail investors, and not just the hedgers who were trading over-the-counter products, the OEX is American-style, meaning it can be exercised at any time at the buyer's discretion. As retail customers quickly found out, the OEX allowed them to participate in the broader market and thus avoid the "right church, wrong pew" syndrome. As most active equity investors have experienced at one time or another, the overall market can be up strongly, but some individual equities will make a contrary move to the downside. On those days, you indeed feel like you're in the right church, but you've definitely sat in the wrong pew.

Trading an index, on the other hand, gives you exposure to numerous stocks; in the case of the OEX, you can trade the value of 100 of the biggest stocks as one unit. This is not only a cost effective way to gain this exposure (as opposed to trying to buy and sell options on 100 different equities), it also gives you instant diversification across several industry sectors. Trading the OEX, you're going to have exposure to the top financial stocks such as Merck (MRK) and CitiGroup (C); the top industrial shares Alcoa Inc. (AA), Boeing Co. (BA), or United Technologies (UTX); the top oil stocks such as Exxon (XOM); networking stocks such as Nortel Networks (NT) and Lucent Technologies (LU); chipmakers such as Micron Technology (MU) and Motorola (MOT); and so on for American-style options. And since American-style index options give the buyer the right to turn their call or put options into cash at each evening's settlement price, they carry their premiums virtually all the way until expiration, rather than trading at a discount to intrinsic value like their European cousins.

Going back to our example, let's say you own a $750 OEX call, and now the OEX is trading for $780 per share. Since it's an American-style option that may be exercised any time at the buyer's discretion, it has $30 a share in intrinsic value. Moreover, it would probably be trading for a premium above its intrinsic value, putting the price at $30.50 to $31 a share. If that OEX, American-style option did trade at a discount, you could simply buy that option and exercise it for cash (remember, equity-index options settle for cash, not the basket of stocks that underlie them), thus capturing the difference between the intrinsic value and the discounted price that you paid them. For this reason, American-style index products are not for everybody—especially large institutions that like to sell options against their portfolios and hold that insurance until expiration. They don't want to find themselves cashed out at a time when the option trades below parity before expiration.

early exercise

For American-style options, one of the most common times for this cashing out (technically known as an *early exercise*) is during the 15-minute window between the close of stock trading at 4 P.M. Eastern time and the time when index futures stop trading, which is 4:15 P.M. Eastern time.

Let's say an institution had sold 500 OEX call options several weeks before, and those options were trading slightly above parity going into the close. This would probably lead the institution to think its hedged position is relatively secure. But now let's say the stock index futures start dropping after the stocks stop trading. Maybe some key stock declared less than expected earnings and the S&P futures started freefalling. The customers (institutional or regular retail investors) who purchased those OEX options could exercise them for the closing cash value of the index—and buy the discounted futures to replace the exercised long position in the market. That would place the call option buyer back in the same position since they've simply replaced the long in-the-money call with a long position in the futures, which they purchased on the after-hours dip at a lower, more favorable price. The net effect is, they've taken the institution out of its short position by exercising these options. The institution is cashed-out of its short options on the closing price, despite the fact that the future is now trading at a significant discount to the cash value.

The same could occur on the short put side of the early exercise predicament. For instance, you could be short the 810 puts in an American-style index like the OEX, trading at $780. Those puts are $30 in-the-money. (Remember, a deep in-the-money short put makes the seller money when the market trades higher and loses the seller money when the market trades lower. The customer that sold these puts may have sold them as a bet the market would trade higher, or as a hedge against a short position in the market.) If the OEX cash closed at $780 at 4:00 P.M. and then the S&P 500 futures began to run to the upside after the cash closed, those short puts could come back and bite you. Here's how: the cash value of those puts is pegged at $30 (810 strike price minus $780—the closing price at 4:00 P.M.). If the futures began to run after the cash closes, the owner of those puts might infer that the market will open higher tomorrow and thus, his or her put would be worth less than the $30 they are trading for tonight. Therefore, the put owner might exercise the put for the cash value ($30 in this example) and either replace their short position in the market by selling the rallying futures contract, selling a call which should be rallying along with the futures, or buy a replacement put at a cheaper price.

If you're an institution wanting to hedge your portfolio, that's not the kind of scenario you want to face suddenly. For that reason, the institutions favor the S&P 500 and other European-style index options—not so much for speculation but for insurance.

The same goes for a customer. You don't have to be an institution to get hurt by this arbitrage, or the difference between the index options value and that of the underlying cash or futures market. If you were a customer who has sold five OEX index options as a hedge against your mutual fund holdings, you'd face a similar situation if there were a sell-off in the futures market between the close of the stock market and the end of the futures session. You could very well come in the next day to discover that you're without your short index calls because the buyer exercised them. You'd be long your mutual fund holdings, without a hedge, and you would have bought back your short index calls the night before at a higher price.

Yet, index options, when used in conjunction with an investment strategy (remember, you never want to sell a naked option—on an index or an individual stock—without some offsetting factor to reduce risk) can allow you to play the broader market. The exact strategies that can be employed in stocks (as discussed in previous chapters) can also be used in an index.

One important thing to keep in mind, however, is that an index tends to smooth the volatility of the component stocks, the same way that a mutual fund gives the diversity of many stocks. This diversity tends to flatten out the peaks and valleys of the volatility of the stocks in the index. This is why the OEX, which contains multiple sectors, has a smoothed volatility that normally trades in a range from 18 percent to 36 percent, although its components collectively probably average twice that.

If you look at a volatile sector like biotechnology or Internet, the stocks that make up that index might average 100 percent volatility. However, differing from the OEX, or SPX which contain multiple sectors, a single sector index will smooth the volatility, but not nearly so much as an index that can spread risk over a wider variety of stocks.

One indicator looked at by many people is the range of volatility for the index. The CBOE expresses this as the VIX—the Volatility Index. When the VIX is at its zenith, many of us are active sellers of index premium (Figure 6.1). When it's at its low point, we tend to buy index premium because the odds favor the buyer on the low end and the seller on the high end. Also, historically, low ebbs in volatility for the index have signaled a rapid movement forthcoming.

Options, like most commodities, are driven by supply and demand. When there is extremely large supply, they are cheaper. When they are in demand, the supply dries up and they are more

Figure 6.1   VIX weekly

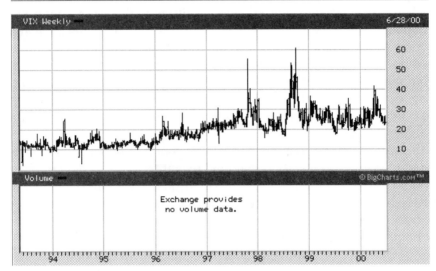

Source: BigCharts.com.

expensive. In the case of index options—which do not reflect a single stock but rather marketwide (or at least sectorwide) action—you can watch this market movement to help your trading.

Here's an example: When volatility (which, as you recall, is a gauge of risk) gets extremely low, I know the buyers of portfolio protection have not stepped into this market. That tells me the professionals and others in this market could be getting a little too comfortable, and very few people have come to the options market for protection. Perhaps instead of buying puts to protect against a fall in the price of shares they own, they have simply elected to sell calls. Thus we might see an oversupply of call sellers and, therefore, premiums are cheap. That's usually an opportunity for buyers since, in my mind, the market rarely makes an extraordinary move without some sort of short-supply or buying panic. So when the world, that has become overconfident, suddenly perceives a need for protection, the price and market volatility suddenly skyrocket. And if you've bought just before that panic materializes, you may be in for a nice market ride.

Conversely, when the VIX is on the high end, it reflects the demand from everyone who panicked and sought out protection from options. The buying frenzy pushes premiums for puts and calls higher as volatility increases. It's unlikely that this sort of panic-triggered accumulation will hold for a long period of time. Remember, with index options such as the OEX, the focus in on a basket of the largest capitalized stocks, as well as overall market sentiment. It's not dependent on an earnings announcement or Food & Drug Administration (FDA) approval for a company's new medical device. In an individual equity, there are considerable risks in selling premium, because you could face short squeezes, stock buybacks, or takeovers.

In indexes, there can't be any takeovers or short-squeezes. Even if one or two stocks in an index have an extraordinary event—like a takeover or a stock buyback—the overall basket of issues results in a smoothing effect. Put another way, Microsoft could decide to buy back 100 million shares of its stock, which would undoubtedly send the price of its shares soaring. But what would be the net effect on the other 99 stocks in the OEX? Most likely, it would be negligible, in particular because the MSFT move was an isolated event.

Another advantage of premium selling in index options is that there are usually many strikes above and below the market. So if you are a person who is comfortable with selling premium (understanding the risks and devising an offsetting strategy), you can pick a wide range in which your strategy will work and you can make money. This is a far better deal than the relatively narrow range of strike prices for an individual equity.

If I was looking for Dell and Cisco to make a breakout move and OEX volatility was low, perhaps I would use that information as one more factor that could help fuel a rally, as the lack of buyers may indicate premium levels could move quickly higher, benefiting the option buyer.

To find out more about the VIX and to get daily updates, go to the CBOE Web site (www.CBOE.com). The site displays a table that includes the current quote; net change; 52-week high and low; and the open, high, and low quotes.

Whether or not you choose to trade index options, consider these instruments—such as the VIX—to be one more tool in the toolbox to help you construct a profitable trade.

Now, consider spread trades, as discussed in previous chapters. When the range of strike prices is narrow, we have fewer strategies that we can effectively employ. This is rarely the case in index options, which normally have numerous strikes above and below the cash value of the index.

One example is the iron butterfly, with a body formed by a straddle trade, and wings that limit the upside and downside risk. This is one of the most popular spreads for selling premium with limited risk. Now, let's see how this trade would work with OEX options.

Let's say the OEX is trading at $850 a share. You might sell the $880 calls and sell the $820 puts. To protect the upside, you might buy the $885 calls and, similarly, you'd buy the $815 puts to insure the downside. Your maximum risk would then be the difference between each spread. We've basically sold a $5 call spread on the upside, and a $5 put spread on the downside. Our maximum exposure on both sides would be $5.00. Now let's say we only took in $1.75 in premiums. Our maximum risk would be the $5 spread minus the premium received, or $3.25.

Now that risk/reward ratio would probably not be attractive for an option on an individual equity. But in this instance, it might be a reasonable investment for the opportunity to profit over a reasonably wide range to the upside and the downside of the broader market. And since we're investing in an index option, we know that the risk is spread over a broad basket of stocks, which smoothes out the volatility and the price movement. That's what makes this strategy attractive. For example, in the 1990s and early 2000, it has been common to see sector rotation. If Wall Street likes e-commerce stocks, those shares go up, and dollars get pulled out of other sectors like drug stocks. These rotations mean that the broad market might only advance by a small percentage—which is great if you are playing a spread trade on the broader market.

The above strategy works in both the SPX (based on the S&P 500 cash market) and the OEX (based on the top 100 stocks on the CBOE). But most customers will choose the OEX because they can collect more premium in that index because it's American-style.

But there are far more indexes than just the OEX and the SPX—such as the Philadelphia Semi-Conductor Index (SOX) and Nasdaq 100 Index (QQQ). Plus, there are *spiders,* a kind of hybrid securitized equity that trades like a stock but is actually a depository receipt that trades at a fractional value of the S&P 500. Here's how spiders work: First, State Street Bank, which underwrites the spiders, buys all 500 stocks in the S&P 500 and deposits them into a trust. (In return for overseeing this S&P 500 Depository Receipt—which is how spiders are officially known—State Street Bank receives about 18 basis points in management fees. State Street Bank also collects interest on the dividends paid on the basket of stocks before the payouts are sent at the end of the quarter to the spider holders.)

State Street then issues shares, known as the spiders (AMEX symbol: SPY), that trade on the American Stock Exchange and track the dollar-for-dollar performance of the S&P 500. What makes spiders convenient is that they have one-tenth the value of the S&P, making it a more reasonable investment for retail investors. As of this writing, the S&P 500 is trading at 1450, so a $\frac{1}{10}$ value SPY trades for $145 per share. A great feature of spiders is that unlike normal stocks which represent corporate equity, you don't need an uptick to short shares. Additionally, these little beauties trade in increments as small as $\frac{1}{64}$th and trade multimillion shares per day, making them one of the most liquid securities in the world. Due to the success of spiders, the AMEX has listed depository receipts on the Dow Jones Industrial Average (DIA) and the Nasdaq (QQQ).

In our proprietary trading firm, PTI Capital Management LLC, a strategy that we might use for clients is basically an insured index portfolio using the spiders.

Here's how we'd make the trade: We buy 1,000 shares of SPY. Then we buy one long-term or LEAP put option on the S&P (we only purchase one LEAP put because unlike the SPY, which trades $\frac{1}{10}$ the value of the S&P 500, the LEAP represents 100 shares of the full value S&P). Finally, we sell one out-of-the-money short-term call against this position. A simple way to explain this is, we have bought the SPY to speculate on the upside, and we have downside protection by virtue of our purchase of a long-term put. We finance that long-term put by selling a short-term call. We normally sell a call that is 5 percent to 7 percent out-the-money, so although the upside is capped by the call sale, we participate fully up to that level.

Since July 1997, this strategy has successfully tracked the performance of the S&P 500 within 6 percent, but with less volatility and less downside risk. We also use this strategy for the QQQ and the Dow Jones 30 (Diamonds).

Many customers who come to us for this strategy are investing fresh money in the market. But, because the market is so volatile, they're not comfortable just buying it. Rather, they want some protection in case the market turns out to be driven to its lofty heights by the "greater fool theory": Every fool who buys from the next fool at a higher price becomes the greatest fool, until there is the greatest fool of all who buys at the peak.

This strategy can't be guaranteed, of course. But it has shown about a 16 percent annual return if the market does what it has historically. And, we believe it carries must less risk than just buying the S&P or the Vanguard 500 (which is a fund variation of the SPY).

We also believe that the SPY has greater benefits to the retail investor than just buying a mutual fund. For one thing, there is the question of fees when it comes to a mutual fund. Second, to get in or out of a mutual fund—even if you wire-transfer the money—you can't move the money in or out in a day. Let's say there is a market calamity in the morning, and the S&P index is down 2 percent in the first hour. If you wanted to invest—seeing this as a time to buy—by sending money to a mutual fund, you won't be able to get in until the next day when most of the opportunity is gone. But with the SPY, if you choose to buy, you're in today!

Additionally, since spiders are not corporate equities, there is no downtick rule. You don't have to wait until an uptick to short a spider, or another index such as the QQQ or the Dow 30 industrials. (To short a stock, you have to wait for an uptick in the market price.) From a hedging standpoint, this is fantastic, because if the market was in a freefall you could still hedge part of your exposure, while the person trying to short IBM, Hewlett-Packard or any other stock needs to wait for an uptick in order to sell the stock short. Spiders are also a very liquid market, trading some 6 million shares a day. For investors big and small, liquidity is your friend. It assures you that, when you need to make a trade, chances are there will be supply to meet your demand, and vice versa.

When you look at index options, it's interesting to see the approach of most big, successful firms. What many have done is to create a single portfolio, or global position for the firm. That portfolio or "book" reflects the sum total of all the trades and speculations and hedges that the firm takes on. That enables them to get a fix on their overall market exposure. They may be buying option premium in the S&P 500, and selling premium in the Nasdaq 100 as a hedge.

For example, one index arbitrage firm that I know, employs seven in-house traders that may account for nearly 15 percent of the volume in the SPX (the S&P index options at the CBOE). Simultaneously, in the OEX, they have another six traders who account for just under 12 percent of the average daily volume. Similarly, in the Dow 30, two traders account for 30 percent of daily volume. Computer networks link the trades done by one group to the offsetting trades done by another.

So when a large buy order comes into, say, the Dow Jones Index Options pit, those traders don't just look at where they can hedge in that market. Their computers help them determine the best hedge, whether it's to sell something in the S&P 500 (SPX), go into the OEX, or go to the Nasdaq. A computer can do that calculation in a microsecond and alerts the traders in that pit to make the offsetting trade.

When they buy SPX, they'll mainly sell the Nasdaq 100 or the Dow 30, or S&P futures, or Nasdaq futures, or futures options against it, capturing the divergence between the markets. Ripples go through the market in seconds—not hours or even minutes. In other words, one large trade affects all three major indexes within seconds as the computer starts the hedging process, which is carried out by the firm's minions.

Now, let's take a look at this strategy in light of the zero-sum theory, which states that for every winner that has to be a loser. That doesn't work in options. For one thing, a professional trader has the use of margin that the customer doesn't. With my specialist margin, I can trade a huge position for a fraction of the upfront cost. Moreover, it's possible (remember the cash-covered put selling in Chapter 5) for us to either make money or lose money, depending upon the individual option that we trade.

An increasingly competitive and ultra-sophisticated marketplace is index arbitrage. This, by no means, is a strategy for retail investors. In fact, most of the firms engaged in this strategy have both a multimillion-dollar capitalization and direct computer links to each of the U.S. options exchanges and futures exchanges. But it's interesting to look at the way these firms play arbitrage in the index futures and options markets.

A basic arbitrage trade would be to take the S&P 500 and determine what the fair value is for S&P 500 future, using a formula that any options trader would understand. You take the value of the S&P and assume that if it were deposited in a risk-free account for 90 days, how much interest would it earn. That would give you an indication of the risk-free rate of return. (You could also use U.S. Treasury bills to approximate that rate.) That rate of return is then applied to the value of the S&P over 90 days, which is the length of one futures contract, and then divided by 360 or

$$\frac{\text{S\&P value} \times \text{Interest rate} \times 90 \text{ days}}{360}$$

The result is a dollar value, which then must be adjusted for the dividends that are paid on the actual stocks in the S&P 500 basket. (The dividend equivalent amount is added to the contract if you're long, and subtracted if you're short.) The dividend equivalency is published every day, including on the Standard & Poor's Web site. The bottom line of all the calculations is *fair value,* or the difference that a futures contract should have versus the cash market.

As people became more sophisticated, they began to take another factor into account in their fair value calculations—*slippage.* Slippage is best and most easily described as the difference between the price you see on the quote screen and the price at which your order is executed. Particularly if you're executing a big order off the trading floor, you may not be able to buy, for example, 500 options contracts at the price you see displayed at the moment you place an order. Rather, it's likely that you're going to buy a little higher than you anticipated and sell a little lower.

Traders who use sophisticated computerized trading programs would often factor in slippage of one-half point. (So if fair value was deemed to be $3, they'd add on another $0.50, meaning the difference between futures and cash would have to be more than $3.50 before they'd consider making a program trade.)

Once fair value was determined, traders would look for opportunities to trade the imbalance between the cash and futures markets, which is commonly known as *arbitrage*. When a disparity exists, the goal is to buy one market and sell another, and then exit the position when the correlation comes back in line. So if you determined that the fair value of S&P futures ought to be $3 ($3.50 accounting for slippage), and instead they were trading at $5 over the cash market, as an arbitrageur you would sell the S&P futures $5 over fair value and buy the underlying securities. The selling pressure would start to bring the futures market back in line, while buying the cash would raise the value of that market. When the gap between the two came back to $3.50 or so, you'd see the buy program come to a screaming halt. When the futures drifted lower than fair value, you would seek to reverse out of the trade by buying back your short futures and selling out the underlying stocks.

But what happens if the future market is undervalued compared with cash, say, trading at a $5 discount? Ideally, you'd want to buy the undervalued futures and sell underlying securities. But you need to have the ammunition to make that trade in the form of stock on hand. Because of the downtick rule (you can't short a stock on a downtick, but must wait for an uptick), you can't short a stock you don't already own. But if you own the physical stock, you can sell it at any time. Assuming you're long stock, you can buy the futures and sell your shares until the market returns to equilibrium.

It should also be noted that there are curbs or limits that were enacted voluntarily at the Nasdaq, New York Stock Exchange, and the Chicago Mercantile Exchange, where S&P futures trade. The purpose of these curbs, which were put on the market following the crash of 1987, is to act as a brake to slow down rapid market movement.

The kind of arbitrage trade I just described was far more common in the late 1980s and the early 1990s than today. For one thing, with the increase in participants, the markets are more efficient and discrepancies are far more rare. Rather, today very sophisticated arbitrageurs do cross-index arbitrage, taking advantage of what they determine to be discrepancies in the value of one index—such as the Dow Jones—and another—such as the S&P 500. Or, they may make arbitrage plays in a sector index, for example Internet stocks, versus the Nasdaq.

But this is a game for professionals. The capitalization it takes and the margin requirements of this kind of trade would be extreme for a retail investor, who couldn't simply buy the Nasdaq and short an index as a hedge. Rather each component trade would be considered a separate transaction, meaning you'd be naked long the Nasdaq and naked short the index. As a professional trader, however, I am allowed to consolidate all these trades into one hedged transaction, thanks to margin relief from the participating exchanges.

While that's an obvious advantage for the professional trader, the retail customer also benefits. When the professional arbitrageurs play the spreads between the markets, they help to bring the price relationships back in line. If it weren't for these arbitrageurs, then the one-way stampede by retail customers (who tend to want to buy and sell the same things at the same time) would create imbalance in the markets, which would trade at extreme discounts or premiums to each other. The more efficient the market, the less time the futures stay out of line versus fair value.

Just because retail traders shouldn't do arbitrage, it doesn't mean they are shut out from complex index trades. Rather, there is an opportunity for a sophisticated retail trader to hedge using index options. Let's say you're long a portfolio of stocks and you decide to lock in some gains by selling options against your position. In this case, say you had Microsoft, Intel, and IBM in your portfolio, and to lock in profits in these equities you wrote options—or sold calls—against them. You have hedged yourself somewhat against an adverse move in the individual stocks. But you still have exposure to a major market correction.

One way to protect yourself from this kind of move might be to buy puts or put spreads in S&P 500 options, which closely tracks Microsoft, Intel, and IBM. Let's say you held 1,000 shares each of the three stocks. To lock in profits, you sold at-the-money calls (a 10-contract position for each security) in each stock. You sold 10 IBM $115 calls for $5 a share, 10 Microsoft $100 calls for $6, and 10 Intel calls for $5.50. And you'd reap $5,000 in IBM call premiums, $6,000 in Microsoft call premiums, and $5,500 in Intel call premiums for a total of $16,500. While that looks like a hefty premium sum at first glance, remember you have $320,000 in total market exposure through our stock ownership. Obviously $16,500 is only a small percentage of that.

To protect against a sharp market decline, you might buy put spreads in S&P index options—say, an out-of-the-money put spread in S&Ps, which might cost a total of $4,000. With the S&P at 1440, you would buy the 1430 puts for $7 a share and sell the 1410 puts for $3, for a net cost of $4 a share or a total position cost of $4,000.

Combined with the proceeds from the sale of the in-the-money calls, our net profit thus far is $12,500.

Putting this all together, if the market had a 10 percent correction, the S&P would decline 140 points, and our put spread that we paid $4 a share for would now be worth $20 a share, for an overall profit of $16 a share or $16,000. But we have a total of about $30,000 to offset if Microsoft, Intel, or IBM decline 10 percent a piece, each losing around $10 a share. With the $12,500 in net options profits from the hedge, we've basically neutralized this loss. We have a net profit on our hedge position of $28,500, and a loss in our stocks of $30,000, for a net loss of $1,500. For a hedge, that's not bad.

Keep in mind that the person who owned the stocks outright lost $30,000, or 10 percent of the portfolio's value. By taking in some options premium on the stocks that you own and investing some of the proceeds in index options, you provided yourself with some substantial protection against an adverse move.

Let's recap that hedge trade: You own 1,000 shares each of Microsoft, Intel, and IBM for $320,000 stock portfolio value. You are seeking to guard against a 10 percent correction, or a loss of $32,000 in stock value. To lock in profits, sell at-the-money calls in each security as follows:

Microsoft $100 calls for $6 a share in premium

Intel $100 calls for $5.50 a share

IBM $115 calls for $5 a share in premium

Total premium received: $16,500

Buy 1430 S&P Index puts for $7 a share

Sell 1410 S&P Index puts for $3

Total net cost $4,000

Market declines 10 percent. S&P put spread increases from $4 a share to $20 a share for a profit of $16 a share, or $16,000. Combined with $12,500 in premiums received (profit on equity call options minus $4,000 in net S&P put costs), total profit on hedge is $28,500. The loss on your equity portfolio is $30,000.

Large investors routinely use index options to hedge overall portfolio risk. These investors include family trusts, professional money managers, and large customers with multimillion-dollar portfolio exposure. But smaller accounts are also recognizing the value of hedging their holdings.

Maybe you have $50,000 in Vanguard or some other index fund. A 10 percent correction could hurt you just as badly, proportionately speaking, as the guys with the multimillion-dollar portfolios. To hedge your position, you might use the same strategy that I just described here, locking in profits on your portfolio by protecting yourself from an adverse, downward move.

Beyond the protection offered by index options as hedges, frequently there are attractive opportunities to speculate using these types of instruments. One reason is that it's often easier to pick a trend—upward or downward or even a sideways holding pattern—in an index such as Nasdaq versus picking a trend in an individual stock.

Right now you think Nasdaq is probably going to stay "up." But what about Cisco? You say you like this stock for the long term, but you're not sure if it's going up or down in the meantime. Like I said, picking trends in individual stocks can be very tricky. When you do have strong feelings and convictions about a stock, that's the time to invest that individual equity option, rather than the index. For the rest of the time, you might consider focusing on the indexes because with one transaction you can get exposure to a broad range of stocks. As money flows into and out of the market (and these stocks), the indexes will move up or down.

Here's how an index trade for a retail investor might look. Remember, a stock index settles for cash. If you buy an OEX call option and exercise it, you'll receive the difference in the index value in cash; you won't receive any shares of stock comprising the index.

So let's say you buy OEX $750 calls for $6 a share. If the OEX fails to rise, you lose your premium—but that's all you lose. Now let's say, the OEX runs up to $870 a share. If it were expiration, you would receive $20 cash per share ($2,000 per option) into your account. Your net profit would then be $14 a share, taking into account the $6 a share you paid for the option. If you decided to take a profit, perhaps because the index value ran up farther and faster than you expected, and you wanted to take a profit, you could exercise your $650 call and cash out for that same $20 gross profit, $14 net. But remember, you can't exercise early with most indexes, only the OEX or the SOX. Most of the rest, like the SPX, must be held until expiration.

For beginners, one of the best things about index products is that they offer an extremely liquid market. Despite all the hoopla over the Internet stocks, many of these have less-than-desirable liquidity in their options. But the indexes are always quite liquid because there are so many firms doing cross-market arbitrage, as described earlier. But which index to look at and possibly invest in?

I think it's best to look at what else is in your portfolio, particularly any stock holdings that you might have. One important thing to consider when you invest in a stock is its *beta*. (Beta information can be obtained in a variety of sources, including Multex and Hoovers online.) A beta is a measurement of how much that stock moves relative to an index, usually the S&P 500. So if a beta is relatively high, that means the stock is comparatively more volatile than the S&P; if the beta is low, the stock is less volatile than the S&P. So, for example, if you saw that a stock had a beta of 3, you would expect it to move 3 points for every 1-point that the S&P moved. That 3-beta stock would probably be a technology stock and a Nasdaq issue. A stock with a beta of 1 would move lockstep with the S&P, and would generally be a listed stock such as IBM or GM.

If you have a portfolio of stocks with large betas (meaning stocks that are more volatile than the S&P), you're going to need protection offered by the QQQ index or the Nasdaq 100, rather than the OEX or the SPX. Why? Because the large betas indicate that your portfolio tracks the more aggressive indexes such as those dominated by technology stocks.

As a retail investor, most likely you're trading the indexes because you think you need the protection for your overall portfolio (hedging your holdings in a comparable index), or because you believe an index is likely to move in your direction and you are more comfortable picking overall market direction than that of an individual stock. As discussed previously, there are times when an index is more likely to make a big move. One time is when volatility is low (as measured by the VIX) and the world is looking overconfident.

When it comes to investing in the indexes, you're not going to be limited to just one or two choices—the OEX, the SPX, or the

QQQ, for example. There are dozens of indexes on everything from biotech to utilities to durable goods to Internet stocks. (Of course, some will have more liquidity than others, and some will fade from sight.) In addition, Standard & Poor's, Dow Jones, Goldman Sachs, Morgan Stanley, Salomon Smith Barney, and other large financial institutions create proprietary indexes for their customers. Still, very few of these indexes have garnered a large enough following to be a successfully listed product.

Generally speaking, the most successful indexes among the newest listings have been the more volatile ones, including Internet, e-commerce, and biotech (which is seeing a resurgence due to human genome mapping). Those three indexes also are increasing in popularity. Plus, being in a volatile index, they can avoid the "right church, wrong pew" syndrome. They're playing in the whole sector, instead of just one stock out of the whole sector, which could potentially be the one that underperforms all the rest!

You can't discuss indexes without looking at the Nasdaq, and its volatile, skyrocketing performance in 1999 and early 2000. In early March 2000, the Nasdaq Composite broke 5,000. Like the 10,000-level in the Dow Jones Industrial Average, the Nasdaq 5,000 was a psychological level that had transfixed the market place. At the same time, amid great debate about the Old Economy versus the New Economy (see Chapter 10), the Dow Jones Industrial Average was selling lower (although it experienced several volatile up and down days), while the Nasdaq's general direction was ever-higher.

On Friday, March 3, 2000, the Dow rose 300 points, largely on a U.S. Employment Report that showed 43,000 new jobs had been created—far less than the 300,000 new jobs that Wall Street had expected. The huge decrease in the number of new jobs created quelled inflation fears in the marketplace and, with that, a belief that the Federal Reserve would be less likely to raise interest rates further to cool down the economy that was growing too rapidly. That led to euphoric buying in the stock market, which was particularly evidenced in the Dow, which had been beaten up so badly. The Dow was trading around 9700, down from its previous 11,800 high.

On the following Monday and Tuesday, March 6 and 7, we had a big "cooling off" in the market amid some intense volatility. The Nasdaq Composite traded above 5000 points for the first time in history on March 7, then sold off 100 points within an hour. Then on Wednesday, the Nasdaq was back above 5000, and it closed above that level on Thursday, March 9.

The Dow, meanwhile, traded back above 10,000, and then sold back to 9700 on Tuesday, March 7. It finished the week around 9800, some 500 points below the previous weeks' high.

During this time, my firm, Mercury Trading, was playing the Nasdaq stocks and the indexes. Among the individual equities we were trading was CMGI Inc., which, as of early March 2000, had a 52-week range of 33⅛ to 163½ a share! As I mentioned previously, one of the most volatile times for a stock is just prior to earnings. CMGI was no exception. The stock was trading at about $145 a share prior to its earnings announcement, and its volatility had increased from about the mid-80s to about 110 percent to 120 percent. The higher the volatility, the wider the stock's anticipated price range. As a result of that volatility pump, CMGI options that should have been trading at $5 a share, were trading around $8.

Based on the opportunity we saw, here's the option play we made: We bought CMGI shares and LEAP call options that were one- or two-years out. Then we sold calls in March and April with strike prices around $150, $155, and $160. Even if the buyer exercised these calls, the worse that could happen, we knew, was that we'd have stock taken away from us at $150, $155, or $160 a share and we owned the underlying stock and LEAP options against those shorts. At the same time, we were collecting premiums on options that were higher than normal.

CMGI's earnings were relatively good, and the stock did trade up about $5. But the next day, the stock opened a little lower, around $148 a share. We sold out of our stock position, netting about $3 a share. Call options we had sold, collecting premiums of $8, $9, and $13 a share, were down to around $5, $7, and $10, adding to our profits—and reducing the risk that the call options would be exercised by the buyers.

At the same time, we were looking at opportunities in the indexes. For the week ended March 3, the Dow had rallied more than 5 percent. We considered the rise in the market to be a knee-jerk rally that could quickly reverse. So we looked for put spreads to play in the S&Ps, OEX, and Dow Jones because we believed there was a good chance of profit-taking affecting these market indices.

Let's say OEX was trading around $850 a share. We bought the $830 puts and sold the $815 puts, locking in a 15-point spread and paying about $4.50 a share ($450 per option). With the market correction, OEX fell to $810 a share. We sold out of our put spread for a nice profit.

Such index trades allow you to play the direction of the broader market such as when you believe a rally is likely because it's oversold, or you're looking for a correction after a strong rally. In other words, the indexes are a great way to play the extremes— whether the market is basking in the euphoria or in the midst of white-knuckle panic.

chapter 7

when to do
what—and why!

Once you've got the basic mechanics of the strategies, the issue then becomes, when—and how—do you employ them. The strategy you pick reflects your market opinion. For example, let's take the simplest case—a Bull Spread. If you opt for this strategy, it's because you have a bullish bias. You're buying calls because you believe a particular stock or index is going higher.

But there is another reason to employ a bullish spread: It smoothes out the volatility, particularly when a stock has been bid strongly higher. Ideally, you buy the lower volatility option (which carries a lower premium) and sell the higher volatility one (which has a higher premium). When you have a bullish bias, however, it's important to realize that you are not the only one who is bullish in the marketplace. And with a prevailing bullish opinion, you could end up buying an option with high volatility and, as a result, an unusually high premium. Cisco, Qualcomm, and Intel are all great stocks that have had a wonderful performance for much of the 1990s and through the first quarter of 2000. If you are bullish on those stocks, chances are the volatility will reflect the demand for those call options, especially ahead of industry events such as Comdex or companies' quarterly earnings reports. With all the people betting on the upside of those stocks, if you're trying to buy a call option, chances are you aren't alone, and the excess demand has already pumped up volatility above the normal range. In other words, you're buying expensive options that reflect the market's higher expectations for the company.

If you were bullish on any of those three stocks and blindly went out and bought at-the-money or slightly out-of-the-money calls, chances are you would have to pay up because of the high volatility. This is especially true ahead of earnings or stock splits when people want to speculate wildly that earnings will be much better than Wall Street expects, or that the stock will rise because of the pending split. As a result, going ahead and wildly buying call options may be the wrong thing to do. Why? Because you could end up buying options with a high price that reflects the high volatility. An alternative would be to consider buying a *bull call spread,* which will help you to neutralize volatility and time decay.

Let's say Cisco is trading for $77 a share. You buy the $80 call three months out and sell the $90 call three months out, thus creating a bull call spread. What we've also done is neutralize the volatility, because we've sold one option for every option that we've purchased. Thus, if the volatility suddenly drops in Cisco—because the stock price is going down or the Street's perception of growth diminishes—the call options that you've purchased are going to lose money as the volatility is reduced. Similarly, the out-of-the-money calls that you've sold are going to decline in value, lessening the impact of volatility to your overall position.

For instance, let's say you bought the July $80 call for 7¾ and sold the July 90 for 4¼, for a net cost of $3.50 a share ($350 per spread). At the same time, you've locked in a $10 spread. The profit potential is $6.50 while the most you could lose is $3.50. That's nearly a two-to-one ratio of the potential reward versus the risk, which is ideal (Figure 7.1).

Bull Call Spread

Bought Cisco July $80 call, paid 7¾ a share

Sold Cisco July $90 call, collecting 4¼

Net cost of $10 spread, 3½

Now, let's assume the volatility declined from 46 percent to 40 percent because of a drop in demand for options. As a result, the $80 calls would experience a drop in premium from 7¾ to 6⅝ while

Figure 7.1   long 1 July 80 call, short 1 July 90 call

Profit / Loss (Y) and CSCO Common Price (X) Risk Graph

Source: Created by StockmarketWorkshop.com.

the premium on the July $90 calls dropped from 4 ¼ to 3⅜. You've lost 1⅛ on the calls that you bought, while the calls you sold lost ⅞—which you keep. The net position is now worth $3.25, down $0.25 from $3.50. But if you had just bought the calls—without doing a bull call spread—you would have faced a decline of more than $1 a share on the volatility contraction. If you did the spread 10 times, you'd be risking a grand total of $3,500. Rather, somebody who just bought the call 10 times is risking $7,500.

What was the reasoning behind this trade? For one thing, you had a bullish opinion on the stock. At the same time, you were worried about your exposure to comparatively high volatility. If there was suddenly a 10 percent correction in one week, the risk of buying call positions without a hedge might be more than you wanted to handle. True, when you buy a call option, the most you could lose is the premium that you paid. But when volatility is high you may have paid more premium than you intended. By buying a bull call spread instead, you can reduce that risk by neutralizing the effects of volatility and time decay, and still maintain a bullish stance.

Using this options model, if you move out 30 days, the call that you bought for 7¾ declines by 1⅜ to 6⅜ due to time decay. Now, say the stock goes up from $77 to $95. The $80 calls that you bought are worth $15 at expiration, compared with the $7.75 you paid. If you bought only the $80 calls, the net profit on that position would be $7.25 a share. The person who did the spread trade, however, would have captured the $10 difference, minus the $3.50 a share net cost, for a profit of $6.50 or $6,500 on a 10-lot spread. That's some 90 percent of the profit potential from buying naked calls with only half the investment and a fraction of the downside risk due to volatility and time decay.

That's why big players, the brokerage houses such as Goldman Sachs and Morgan Stanley, execute these kinds of strategies. But it's not a strategy that's limited to institutions and market makers. Retail customers frequently make this kind of spread trade when market conditions make sense.

By the same token, a *bear put spread* is employed when you're bearish on a stock for whatever reason. Maybe you think an "old economy" stock is out of favor, or you're expecting a massive correction in a "new economy" issue.

Here's another example: MicroStrategy Inc. (MSTR) traded up to $333 on March 10, 2000. By comparison, in early 1999 it was a $15 stock. Even though many people thought MicroStrategy was a great company, the stock fell from the $333-range to 85¾ in six trading days. There was no stock split to account for such a massive stock price drop—just a market sentiment change after the company announced it was going to restate their earnings for the previous years.

Now with the benefit of hindsight, when MicroStrategy was trading in excess of $300 a share at the beginning of March 2000, you could have decided to buy an out-of-the-money put spread to guard against a correction. For example, you could have bought the July $250 put for $38 and sold the $200 puts for $19, for a net cost of $19 a share ($1,900 per spread). Again, the reasoning behind this trade is that you have a short-term bearish opinion on the stock and you are worried about a decline in the extreme volatility. If you bought the puts naked—without a put spread—you would be risking a defined amount of money, in this case $38 a share or $3,800. But by doing the put spread, you would have to make only half the investment and you can lessen the impact of time decay and volatility erosion (Figure 7.2).

Figure 7.2   long 1 July 250 put, short 1 July 200 put

Profit / Loss (Y) and MSTR Common Price (X) Risk Graph

Source: Created by StockmarketWorkshop.com.

Bear Put Spread

Buy MSTR July $250 put for $38

Sell MSTR July $200 put for $19

Net cost of position, $19 a share

Now, suppose the volatility declines about 10 percent. The $250 puts that you bought would fall from $38 a share to $33 a share, a loss of $5. The $200 puts that you sold would decline from $19 to $15, a $4 move in your favor. The net effect is that the value of the spread trade declined by only $1 ($100 per spread), whereas if you had just bought the puts naked, you would face the $5 a share ($500) loss.

The downside of doing a spread trade is that, while it decreases the potential risk, it also reduces the profit potential. So when MSTR fell from around $300 a share to $121, those $250 puts that you bought are worth $135—a gain of $97 a share. At the same time, the $200 puts that you sold for $19 are trading at $89, a $70 move against you. The net effect, is a profit of $27 a share. Granted, that's less than the $97 a share you would have made by simply buying the puts. But you had far less money on the line.

At this point, another issue comes up. Once you've realized a profit on a trade, what comes next? I always advise our traders and retail customers alike that I think it is important to take some of the money off the table. You don't wait until the last possible minute, hoping to squeeze the dime out of a trade. Because time decay and decreases in volatility can change the nature of even a simple bull call or bear put spread and cause the trade to move swiftly against you.

One possible strategy is to take a profit on this particular spread trade, and then put on a new position. After the decline to $121 a share on MSTR, you reassess your outlook. Let's say you decide to switch sides and become bullish on MSTR. If you think it is likely to recover, you could put on a bull call spread three months out. Or, you could establish a more sophisticated version of this strategy with a relative of the bull call spread known as the *diagonal call spread,* buying a July call, for example, and selling the April call against it. (Time decay, after all, favors the seller not the buyer, and the July option will decay significantly more slowly than the near-term April option.)

If, on the other hand, you maintain your bearish outlook for MSTR, you could establish another bear put spread. You could also diagonalize the bear put spread by buying the further out in time July puts and selling the pumped up April puts against it. As it turns out, this would have been the winning strategy as MSTR continued to sink, falling to $20 a share in early May 2000.

Bull spreads and bears spreads are particularly good strategies when there has been some sort of disaster that results in a stock being oversold, or a swift rise that indicates the stock is overbought. One important thing to keep in mind is that when the market makes a dramatic move one way or another, it usually reflects a panic move. Perhaps there was some sort of disaster (rumored or otherwise) that took the stock price down sharply. Or, maybe there was a short-squeeze in the stock and short sellers had to cover their positions, driving the price dramatically higher. Whatever the reason for the panic, there is often an opportunity to take advantage of the imbalance that follows these wide swings in price.

But how do you know that a stock is overbought or oversold? There are a few rules to keep in mind: Most stocks will have trouble maintaining a rate of growth (when charted) that's greater than a 45-degree angle. Trees don't grow to the sky; if they grow too tall, they will collapse under their own weight. By the same token, if a stock rises in price at a sharper angle—70, 80, or 90 degrees (as did MSTR)—it is virtually unsustainable.

In these situations, it's time for you to act like a card counter in Las Vegas. Let's say you've recognized an overbought situation, so now you need to think, how can I move the odds further in my favor? Perhaps, instead of selling calls naked—which could expose you to virtually unlimited loss—or even buying a put, you increase your chances of establishing a winning trade by creating a spread trade. So if you don't believe that the performance in a stock such as MSTR is sustainable, you can put on a spread. Just like the card counter who knows there are a lot of face cards left in the deck, you can improve your odds of making a play by knowing that a stock rarely can maintain an 80 percent rate of growth in its share price. When you see that kind of increase in the share price, it's a good indication that this stock is overbought and ripe for at least a short-term correction.

A person who speculates on, say, that downside potential with a spread trade is further decreasing the risk that must be shouldered. Those who trade this way are going to stay in the game far longer than those who speculate that a high-flying stock is overvalued and is going to decline in price tomorrow.

Remember, the goal of trading is not to make a huge profit on a single trade. Rather, the aim is to have a limited amount of risk on the table, which will help you to control potential losses while, hopefully, making a realistic profit. That's exactly what you want to do. You want to manage your capital to be a long-term winner in this game.

Let's consider another strategy—the *iron Butterfly*. As we discussed previously, an iron butterfly is a strategy that's often employed when a stock or an index is trading in a range. A butterfly allows you to lock in a profit potential if a stock (or index) stays within a specified range, while offering protection from unexpected upward or downward moves.

For example, if you expect the S&P cash market to stay in a range, say between 1350 and 1450, you might decide to put on a butterfly trade to capture the value of selling premium based on this outlook. But first, you would have come to that conclusion by tracking the performance of the index over time. You would see that, despite the momentary upward and downward gyrations—remember a diversified index such as the S&P 500 rarely moves in a straight line—the index tends to trend within a defined range. And remember, since S&P 500 options, or SPX, are European-style, the only time they can be exercised is at expiration. Moves within the life of that option don't amount to much, and should not cause too much concern. Further, since you're dealing with an index with multiple stocks, there is a smoothing effect compared with the volatility of the individual issues.

Plus, there are certain times of the year that are more prone than others for the market to trade in a range. There is tax time, when many individual investors have to commit their capital to paying Uncle Sam instead of the market. During the summer, a lot of fund managers, individual investors, and yes, even market makers go on vacation, which keeps portfolio adjustments—including massive flows into and out of certain stocks and sectors—to a minimum. Individual investors are also less likely to be active during vacation time, which leads to the general expectation that the market will be duller in the summer. On the other hand, the most volatile times in the market are typically December, January, and February. Late in the year, there are expectations of the "January effect" when a new year means new optimism, and, often, a bullish tone to the market. In January, you also have the funding of 401(k)s and individual retirement accounts (IRAs), which continues into February.

For some undefined reason, which may be put down as mass psychology, there is the October panic factor. People have a fear of the market going down in October and so, volatility usually picks up steam going into that cycle. Of course these fears aren't totally unfounded: there have been plenty of October crashes—1929, 1987, 1989, and so forth. The market has a long memory when it comes to bad events. There is another factor that may have a fundamental effect on the October dynamics. Fund managers who want to preserve their good performance through the first nine or so months during the year may want to reposition their portfolios to lock in gains and remain market neutral for the balance of the year.

Whatever the reason, there are times when the market is more likely to trade in a range and times when its apt to move up or down sharply. Knowing these dynamics helps you determine if it's a good time to place a particular trade; it's all about moving the odds of success into your favor.

Now, say you're looking at the indexes: The Dow Jones, if you look at 1999 performance, traded from 10,000 up to 11,000 and back to 10,000 and then up to 11,000. Early in the first quarter of 2000, it broke through 10,000 to the downside, and then had a knee jerk rise to 11,000 in short order. So if I were putting on a trade based on that range, I might target the upper end of an established range, say, 11,050, and a downside of the range around 10,000. When you're putting on a range-trade, the wider the spread the more protection you have. Remember though, where there is less risk there is less reward. But since the main goal of trading is always to stay in the game, make sure you pick a spread that is wide enough to offer protection, while still offering a decent profit potential. Also, if you are trading small amounts, the commissions can eat up a substantial part of your profits, which is all the more reason to widen the upside and the downside price points.

Let's say that, for the next month, I pick a range for the Dow Jones and, for this trade, I'm going to use the "Diamonds" (DIA is the underlying symbol for the security which trades on the Amex) or DJX (the options traded at the CBOE), which trades at one-tenth the value of the Dow Jones Industrial Average. So I sell the 116 calls (equivalent to 11,600 in the DJIA) for 1⅝ and buy the 118 calls (equivalent to 11,800) for ⅞. That results in a net credit of ¾ ($75 per spread). For the downside, I sell the 106 puts (equivalent to 10,600) for 1¾ and I buy the 104 puts (equivalent to 10,400) for 1, again taking a ¾ net profit (also $75 per spread). (See Figure 7.3.)

Spread Trade

Sell DJX (based on DJIA) 116 call for 1⅝

Buy DJX 118 call for ⅞

Net Position Credit ¾

Sell DJX 106 put for 1¾

Buy DJX 104 put for 1

Net Position Credit, ¾

In both of these trades, I covered a $2 spread (116 to 118 and 106 to 104). Plus, I took in a total of $1.50 in net premiums. That

Figure 7.3   long 1 July 118 call, short 1 July 116 call; long 1 July 104 put, short 10 July 106 put

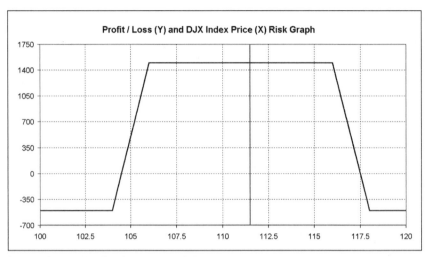

Source: Created by StockmarketWorkshop.com.

means, the most I can lose is $0.50, and I've got 75 percent odds in my favor.

If it trades between 106 where I sold puts and 116 where I sold calls, I keep all the premium, collecting $150 per spread. If the market goes completely against us in either direction, all we can lose is $0.50 ($50 per spread), thanks to the protective wings I've put on my butterfly by buying calls above that spread and puts below it. In the process, I locked in a livable spread trade that allowed me to sleep at night. Remember you never want to put yourself in trades that cause you to panic.

And in the interim, we know that Diamonds (DJX) are European-style options that can only be exercised at expiration. So during the course of the month, the index could break down to 10,000 or shoot up to 11,200 and there would be no cause for alarm. I believe this market is going to be in a range for whatever timeframe and I think it's likely to come back to that regardless of how much it fluctuates in price. A price chart would tell me that I had good history on my side with a trade that was on either side of 10,500.

As was all too apparent in early 2000, volatility in the markets is on the rise. Moves of 200 or 300 points in a market (DJIA or

Nasdaq), which would have been "stop-the-presses," news-making events, are more and more commonplace. What does this mean for an options investor? Volatility impacts you two ways: If you're an options buyer, increased volatility means you'll have to pay up for both puts and calls. And if you're selling options, you may expose yourself to more risk than you intend. Hence, one possible solution is to do a spread trade to neutralize the volatility and reduce the impact of time decay.

Some people might shy away from spread trades simply because they don't understand them well enough. That will severely limit the times in which you can participate in the options market to merely when you believe an overvalued stock is going to fall (and you buy a put) or an undervalued one is going to rise (and you buy a call). But when the price is bouncing around, you may be on the sidelines with nowhere to go. Or, if you buy puts and calls blindly, you may be taken advantage of when volatility is high. Why? Because as a buyer, a sudden reduction in volatility will cause a sharp decline in the premium (or value) of the option you just bought, and the acceleration of time decay will put a nail in your financial coffin.

Rather, high volatility can be a great time to be a cash-secured put seller. As we discussed in Chapter 5, to be a cash-secured put seller you must be bullish on the stock. So, if the market does decline and the stock is put to you, you own it at what you see as a favorable price. (Remember the example of Frank, who sold cash-secured puts for Intel, which he believed would be a good stock over time. And if he liked Intel at $100 a share, he would really love it if the stock were put to him at $90, at least that's what he thought going into the trade. Remember, if your outlook changes, you can always dump the stock or sell some covered options against it.)

But when your favorite stock has become volatile—or in the case of Internet issues *more* volatile—you might consider cash-secured put selling. This strategy will enable you to (1) collect a higher than normal premium due to the increased volatility, and (2) if stock is put to you, you'll end up with shares that you believe have good upside potential.

For instance, you may decide that eBay is a great stock. For the past few years, Wall Street and the investing public have loved eBay. But there are some days when Wall Street doesn't like it so much. Because of the great performance it's had for the last few years, volatility tends to be sky-high. So if I were bullish on eBay and I wanted to buy options, I'd have to pay a hefty premium for calls.

But what if I took a look at a cash-secured put sale? As the options seller, the ensuing time decay will work in my favor because with every passing day there is less time for the option I sold to become in-the-money and be exercised. If I sold the eBay 210 puts I could collect $18 in premium. As long as eBay is above $210 at expiration, I keep the $18 premium ($1,800 per contract). If the price drops suddenly, I'm essentially buying the stock at $192 a share (the strike price of $210 minus the premium paid of $18). And if I'm bullish on eBay at $240 a share, how much better do I feel about the stock at $192?

Again, the most important things to remember in this trade are that you *must* be bullish on the stock and you must believe the option premiums are moderately to substantially above normal.

When you're trading and using cash-secured put selling, a lot of people use technical analysis to help them determine when and at what price to get in. For example, looking at a chart of eBay (as of March 27, 2000), it appears there is good support around the $140 a share level and tremendous support at the $120 level. Therefore, if I wanted to be more conservative (which reduces both my risk and my potential reward) I might want to sell the $130 puts or the $120s, and so forth.

As outlined in Chapter 5, to do cash-secured put selling you must have the money in your account to pay for the shares should the stock be put to you. However, you could also take advantage of high premiums on a stock that you like with a less risky strategy. In this case, you could sell a very wide put spread, which essentially gives you a floor in case of a catastrophic price drop.

For example, you could sell the three-month-out 150 puts and collect the $18 premium, and buy the $100 puts for $3. Essentially, you sold a $50 spread for $15. Your maximum loss is $45 a share, and your potential profit is $15 ($1,500 per spread). While that risk-reward ratio is not favorable on its own, it is a viable means to take advantage of the volatility of a stock while reducing the amount of capital you have to put up. To illustrate, if you sold 10 eBay three-month-out 150 puts, you would need to have $132 a share (the 150 strike price minus the $18 premium you collected) in cash in your account in case you had to buy the stock. To do this 10-contract trade, you would need $132,000 in your account.

But if you're not that aggressive, and want to reduce both your risk and the money you have to invest, the put spread is a better way to go. Selling the $150 puts and buying the $100 puts would require $50,000 for 10 contracts (as opposed to $132,000 for cash-secured put selling). And in the case of cash-secured put selling, the most I could make on 10 contracts is $18,000 (the premium I collected). For the put spread, my maximum profit potential is $15,000 for 10 contracts. That's not a bad play to make—about 83 percent of the profit potential with about one-quarter of the up-front cost.

As I've said repeatedly, our goal is to move the odds in our favor. And by doing the put spread, your potential reward is $15,000 on a $35,000 investment, a 42 percent return with limited risk! As for the cash-secured put selling, your potential reward is only $18,000 on a $132,000 investment, or a return of a more pedestrian 13 percent.

From a money-management and a risk/reward perspective, the spread makes more sense. Selling a put to collect a high premium while buying a put to provide a floor under your potential losses gives you disaster protection to keep you from getting wiped out should there be a catastrophic event like the one that happened to MSTR.

There is a lot of homework and study to do before you place a trade. You need to determine what strategy will work the best, and how to improve both your money management and risk reward. But the work doesn't end there. You must also know when to exit a trade. This may be especially important with winning trades. There comes a point when it's better to exit rather than try to squeeze out one more point or two. Time decay, after all, is a buyer's worst enemy.

For example, say you've been buying LEAP calls in a favorite stock and selling near-term calls. This is a good strategy when you have an overall bullish bias for a stock. But there will come a point when the risk/reward ratio for your trade will stop making sense. At that point, it's time to close the trade.

Every day, I look at the risk/reward of all my ongoing trades. The question I must continually ask myself is *would I buy or sell this option today.* It doesn't matter if I've already doubled or tripled my money as the stock rose and took the call premium with it. There will come a time when the existing trade I have no longer has a good risk/reward balance. The near-term calls that I've sold, for example, may not have sufficient premium to offset the appreciated value of the LEAP calls that I've bought. That's when it's time to adjust or close out the trade.

As a professional trader, I want to have a very short memory when it comes to what I paid for something. If I bought a LEAP for $15 or $20 or $12 or whatever, I want to forget about that investment as quickly as possible. Why? Because I need to address the overall value of the trade, and not focus on the amount of money I have invested. Put another way, once I place a trade, it has to stand on its own merit. As time goes on, I need to ask myself if this particular trade still makes sense, given the price of the stock at the time and the value of the options I have bought and sold. If the trade still makes sense, I keep it; if it doesn't, I close it.

Now, as a retail investor you have a slightly different motivation. For one thing, I'm trading for pennies, in terms of commissions, which enables me to make thousands of trades a day for a relatively small amount of money. An active retail investor probably trades several times a week or several times a month, and he or she is trading for dollars and not pennies. In addition to commissions, the tax-implications of capital gains are more of a concern for an investor than for the professional trader. But there are definite similarities when it comes to concerns over existing trades. Both the professional trader and the retail investor must monitor their positions to ensure their risk/reward balance is intact, and that the value of what they've bought or sold still makes sense for what they're trying to accomplish—whether it's offsetting portfolio risk or riding the upside of a stock.

Let's say you've bought a one-year LEAP call for $10, against which you've sold a short-term call option, collecting a $2.50 premium. Now, as time decay takes the value out of the premium, the options that you've sold three weeks ago are worth $0.50. That doesn't mean you've made a bad trade. On the contrary, $2.00 of the $2.50 a share in premium you collected when you first sold those calls is already in your pocket. But as these call options are nearing the time at which they will expire worthless (which for you, the seller, is a good thing!), it's time to examine this trade.

Have you wrung out all the profit you can from this particular trade? Do those short-term calls—10 days from expiration and worth $0.50—offer adequate protection for the LEAP that's now maybe worth $11 or $12?

I'd say you've squeezed everything out of that particular trade that you can. Rather than hang on for the last $0.50 in value, why not buy back those short calls and sell something else with a higher premium, which can better offset the LEAP that you're holding?

As you evaluate an existing position, however, you can't just look at the premium prices. A strategy will continue to work for you only if your basic premise hasn't changed. Simply put, if you're still bullish about a particular stock, for example, then it makes sense to hold a LEAP. But if your opinion has changed, it's time to close that position and formulate a new plan.

How often should you evaluate your positions? Personally, I monitor my positions at least daily and often more than once a day. At the moment, I have positions in 80 to 100 stocks. At least once a day, I look at my positions and decide, with computer printouts of analysis in hand, if I still like these positions.

For example, I saw in late March 2000 that Oracle (ORCL) had run straight up. During this run, I've sold a lot of near-term puts, expiring in April and May. By late March, some of these puts were worth only $0.25. I had squeezed all the premium out of these puts, leaving me with no real reason to hold these positions any longer. If I were still bullish on Oracle, I could roll out of this position by buying back the puts and selling other near-term puts that still carry a higher premium. Or, I could close out the position altogether and pick a different stock. Granted that's easier for me than for a retail investor, most retail investors don't have more than 10 stocks to worry about, and most are probably going to have only five or so stocks that they have option positions in. That's a great deal easier than keeping track of hedged options positions in 100 or more stocks.

But regardless of how many stocks you hold positions in, the process is the same. Every morning, I look at the positions I hold. I see where I'm long and where I'm short, and I evaluate whether these positions still make sense, again not based on what I paid to enter the positions but rather on the current economics. You can't be married to any one position. You can't say, "I paid $3.50 for these options so I've got to sell them for $4.00." That's a bad way to evaluate a trade. Know why you placed the trade, and see if that reasoning still holds. If not, get out and move on to the next position. Keep in mind that you don't have a gun to your head to make trades constantly. If you don't see an opportunity to enter at prices that seem attractive, stay on the sidelines. Professional traders don't have that luxury. We have to trade, either through obligations to quote two-sided markets constantly or to keep the phone ringing with solicitations from brokers. You don't have to trade all the time.

As I said in Chapter 1, this sort of cut-your-losses attitude has served me well in life. Why else did my college career span so many different schools? I wanted, above all, to play college football and then move onto the professional ranks. If that wasn't going to happen at one university, I had to find a place where it would. I became unemotional about my evaluation, not only of my opportunities, but also of my abilities and circumstances. It's the same way with trading. I can't get caught up with the concept that I'm suddenly "wrong," and I need to prove myself "right" by holding onto a position that no longer serves my needs. When it's time to cut a trade loose, I have the discipline and the emotional distance to do that.

Retail traders, who aren't going to be moving in and out of a position as rapidly or frequently, have to adopt some of the same attitude. Look at the positions you're holding. Would you make the same trade today? Either at that price, or with that market outlook? If not, it's time for an adjustment.

Again, this is just as important for a "winning" position as it is for one that has suddenly moved against you. If I own a $10 LEAP call and I sell a $2 option against it, I have 20 percent downside protection. But if that near-term call that I sold erodes due to time decay to being worth $0.50, it's not providing much protection for my LEAP, which may be valued at $11 by now. There is no value to wait the last three weeks until expiration for the sake of the last $0.50 in that option value. It's far better, in this scenario, to buy back the calls that I've sold for $0.50, and sell some $2 calls that are a little further out in time.

But maybe as I'm evaluating my position I discover that not only did my opinion of this stock change, my whole opinion of the market shifted. Maybe I don't want to be exposed to an "Old Economy" stock. Maybe I only want Internet-related issues. Maybe I think everyone is running for the relative safety of high-dividend stocks, while we decide if the market is in a correction or just resting.

If that's the case, I don't want to say to myself, "well, I'll get out of this in three months because then I'm dealing with long-term capital gains instead of short-term trading profits." That's a horrible way to trade because it undermines your analysis of stocks and the overall market. The primary driver in any trade that I make is my risk/reward balance. If a trade suddenly becomes too risky, or if the rewards are too small, then it's time to exit the position.

Similarly, if I put on a trade to make money on volatility—such as with a spread or a butterfly position—and the volatility suddenly diminishes, then the reasoning for my trade no longer exists. Chances are the risk/reward scenario also has to be altered. Granted, if I have a spread such as an iron butterfly trade on—locking in my upside and downside range—the stock or index might very well hang in there within the range I've targeted. But if my primary purpose was to capture a volatility edge that no longer exists, then the backdrop has changed.

The question ultimately becomes one of judgment, which only you—the professional trader or the customer at the brokerage firm—can answer. How much is enough? If you've sold a straddle, a strangle, or an iron butterfly, and you've reaped half the profits—taking half of your money off the table—and the position still has a month-and-a-half to go, do you want to stay in? Do you know there is a risk that you could give back what you've made if the stock suddenly starts to move, or the index that you've pegged to be in range suddenly breaks out of those parameters? That's a question that every trader and speculator has to address.

Here's an example, say you've sold a straddle at $3, and the value has collapsed down to $1. There is a month-and-a-half left to go. Or you've sold an iron butterfly for $5, and you only have $1 left to make on it. If the market explodes out of your range, you could lose $4. It's your $4. You are not playing with the house's money; it's your money! Better to get out of the trade once you've made a reasonable profit (and only you can determine what that is based on your risk/reward goals) than to hang in there too long. Remember, pigs get fat, hogs get slaughtered.

This is especially true for beginning traders and speculators. It's better to sell "too soon" as you get your feet wet than to make the mistake of staying in a trade too long and risking more than you should—or losing it all.

Among all the options strategies, there are others that, by their very nature, require ongoing analysis and maintenance. After all, that's what they are designed for. One example is the *collar,* which is a defensive or protective strategy to guard a large, single-stock position.

Curiously, collar trades are probably one of the most popular and in-demand strategies out there, but most of the investing public never hears about them. Undoubtedly, that's because collars are used to protect large, single-stock holdings that we may associate with being a top executive of a Fortune 500 company. But in truth, there could be lots of reasons why you could end up with a large holding of a single stock that, due to its weight in your portfolio, you want to take extra measures to protect. Perhaps you were lucky enough to be part of a dot.com start-up, which made you a paper millionaire after the company went public. But you don't want to sell and with such a large portion of your net worth tied up in a single stock, you don't have a diversified portfolio. Or perhaps, as a long-time company employee, you've amassed $100,000 or $200,000 in company stock, which you want to hang onto to avoid the capital gains and because you are ultimately sold on the growth prospects of your employer.

A collar trade basically involves the purchase of a protective put, to insure the down side, which is financed (at least partially) with the sale of a covered call.

Here's how a collar trade works: Say a stock that you hold is trading at $70 a share. But since you were a long-time company employee (or a company co-founder) you were lucky enough to have gotten in at $1 a share. You don't want to sell the stock. But you know that the fortune you've amassed in this single share is vulnerable to the whims of the market. To protect your treasure, you purchase a 65 put and finance the put purchase by selling the 80 call.

So, on 1,000 shares, you'd be obligated to sell the stock at $80 a share (which you could conceivably buy on the open market or deliver from your shares, whichever suits your situation). The $65 put that you bought protects you on the downside. If the stock falls to $55, the $65 put is worth $10, which helps to offset the $15 loss on the value of the stock.

The protective put that you purchase can have a strike price based on whatever comfort level you need. You can put it farther down and pay less of a premium. And you can design a collar strategy that not only pays for itself (the difference between the call you sell and the put you buy), but also actually makes money, in and of itself.

Granted, a lot of these collar trades are done off the exchange floor because of the huge size involved. Perhaps you're looking to protect 200,000 shares. As a single stock millionaire, you can do this trade to protect your holdings and sleep at night. You can design a trade that gives you only $5 a share of downside risk even if the stock drops as much as $20 a share. Through my brokerage firm, PTI Securities & Futures, we have dozens of high net worth investors that have employed the collar strategy.

There's another financial trick that single-stock millionaires can take advantage of, which—even if it doesn't apply to you right now—is good to know about. You have all this money tied up in a stock and, on paper, you've amassed a small or large fortune. But that's on paper. You're still living in the house or apartment you've had since before your ship came in. You want to upgrade, say, to a $2 million property, but everything you have is tied up in your stock, and you don't want to face the capital gains if you liquidate part of your position. Many brokerage firms and investment banks will loan you up to 95 percent of the value of your stock at competitive rates (usually tied to prime or broker loan), which is usually far less than you'd pay for a mortgage. While you face interest charges, it's one way you can enjoy the fruits of your stock holdings without having to sell what you hope will continue to appreciate in value.

When it comes to collar trades, this doesn't apply only to the ultra-wealthy. As a long-term employee, you could have 1,000 shares of a stock, such as Hewlett-Packard (which as of this writing was trading around $146 a share). That's $146,000 in one stock that you'd undoubtedly want to protect, and a collar trade is one way of accomplishing that.

Here's how it might work: You could sell the $155 call, using the $3 premium to help purchase a $140 put for $4. If the stock makes a large downside move, you're protected from 140 down to zero. And if it spikes suddenly in one month, the worse that could happen is you have to sell some stock at $155, locking in a nice profit. You could adjust the parameters of that collar—by rolling your short 155 calls up to the 160 or 165 calls if you thought the stock was poised for an upward run or a lower put to keep more of the premium profit in return for a bit more downward risk.

Now, as time goes by, let's say it's two weeks to expiration, and Hewlett-Packard is trading at $150 a share, having bounced around to both the upside and the downside. The $150 call that you sold has slipped in value to $0.75, but you've pocketed the other $2.25. The put that you purchased for $4 is trading down to $0.50. It's time to re-establish another position, out one month or maybe three into the future. So you buy back the call and sell another one further out, and you sell the put and buy another one, again adjusting the strike prices to fit your needs. Maybe I want to buy the July $150 puts and sell the July $160 calls. This is a position that must be managed going forward. The purpose is to protect a large stock asset, whether it's 1,000-plus shares of a high-priced issue in your 401(k) or the founder stock you have from the latest dot.com IPO. If you wouldn't drive a Ferrari off the showroom without insurance, why would you let $140,000 in stock go unprotected?

There are other options positions that can, and must, be managed going forward to offset a stock holding. These strategies fall under the umbrella of "stock repair." Let's say you received what you thought was a hot tip for a stock that was selling at $70 a share. You rushed out to buy 1,000 shares—without doing your homework—believing this was going to the proverbial moon! Now, the stock has declined to $57 a share, and you're out $13 a share or $13,000 on your position.

What do you do? Options may be the answer. The stock has ample strike prices available, given its recent activity. Here are a few examples: The $55 calls are quoted at $9\frac{3}{4}$, the $60 at $7\frac{5}{8}$, the $65 at $5\frac{1}{2}$ and the $70 at $4\frac{3}{8}$.

Now with the stock at $57, you could sell the $60 calls against it, collecting $7\frac{5}{8}$. (Remember as a call seller, you'd be obligated to deliver stock if the call is exercised by the buyer.) Now, let's assume the stock finishes above $60 at expiration. The call I sold is exercised and I deliver stock (which I originally purchased for $70 a share) for $67\frac{5}{8}$, before commissions.

Or, I could have opted to sell the $65 calls, which would obligate me to deliver stock at $70\frac{1}{2}$ (taking into account the premium collected). Or, I could sell the $70 calls, and deliver stock at 74⅜. Granted, none of these are great solutions. But they do offer some repair to a damaged stock holding.

repair strategy

My preference would be to establish a stock repair strategy in the following way: I would buy 10 July $55 calls, paying 9¾, and sell 20 July $70 calls at 4⅜ each, or a total of 8¾. That means your net cost on this position would be $1. On a 10-lot trade, that would involve a net cost of $1,000 in additional cash outlay for this position.

At expiration, if the stock rose from $57 to just $65 a share, my long calls would be worth a total of $10 or $10,000 on my 10-lot purchase. Plus, the stock would have risen $8 a share from its lows, recovering $8,000 of the $13,000 decline in value. With total gains of $18,000 on the options and stock price recovery, you'd be back in the black by $5,000 on the overall position—even though the stock was still trading below the price at which you purchased it! And all it cost to put on this position was $1 a share on a net basis. If the stock rallied to $70, my stock would have recovered 13 points, or $13,000, and my 55 calls would be worth $15 or $15,000 at expiration. The short 70 calls would be worthless at $70, but at any price above 70, the 20 short 70 calls would max out our potential profit as 10 of the 70s are against my 55s and the other 10 are against my stock. Thus, we get the upside performance of owning 2,000 shares of stock until we cross the 70 strike, with an additional outlay of just $1,000 for 10 contracts.

Note the relatively small percentage move necessary to get back the initial investment versus waiting and hoping and praying that the stock rallies back to where I bought it.

I could have picked the 60–70 repair and established it for a credit. For instance: I could buy 10 of the 60 calls for 7⅝ and sell 20 of the 70 calls for 4¼. Again, the extra 10 short 70 calls are not naked; they are written against the stock we already purchased. This 60–70 1 × 2 spread is established for a credit of ⅞ ($875 on a 10-lot spread).

If the stock rallied to 60, we recover $3 on the stock, but both our long and our short option finish worthless at expiration. However, we keep the $875 credit we collected for the spread. As a result, we recovered $3,875 less commissions. At $65, the stock is up

$8 (from $57), and our 60 calls are worth $5 ($5,000). Our short 70 calls finish worthless. Result: We recovered our original investment ($13,000), less commissions. We're back to breakeven!

At $70, the stock is up $13 (from $57) and our 60 calls are worth $10 ($10,000). Our short 70 calls are still worthless. Result: We recovered our investment, and we are now up $10,000 less commissions!

At $75, the stock is up $18 (from $57) and our 60 calls are worth $15 ($15,000), and our short 70 are each worth $5, or a loss of $10,000 ($5 × 100 shares × 20 contracts). We recovered the investment plus $10,000. (Any price higher than $75 would be the same result, as the short 70 cap the stock and long 55 call potential.)

Additionally, there are times when this trade (based on strike prices and premiums) can be executed for a net credit. As a rule of thumb, these are not quick-turnaround strategies. Normally, you must go out two or three months for these to be most effective.

Regardless of the strategy that you use, remember that a position must be managed. With the possible exception of European-style options like SPX, you can't buy a call and then forget about it until expiration. Your market research is an ongoing process. You must constantly ask yourself the key question: Would I buy this option today? If the answer is yes, then you can maintain the position. But if the answer is no, then it's time to rethink the strategy.

chapter 8

building a team— the day-trading firm

I always wanted to build something. In college, when I wasn't con-templating a career in the NFL, I planned to go to architectural school. I wanted to design and construct buildings or at least put "something" together. For me, that dream has been fulfilled in put-ting together a trading firm. Even when I was a trader on the floor— a one-man entrepreneur with no one to worry about, or depend upon, but myself—I wanted to have a company with employees. For some, that might seem like a nightmare. But for me, that was a won-derful prospect.

When you work only for and by yourself, you may enjoy suc-cess, but in a sort of vacuum. To me, success is all about building on your own skills to train, teach, and empower other people. With that comes greater success, which is shared by all. (All of our traders at Mercury Trading Group share in the profits that we make as a firm.) My motivation was not just altruistic or socialistic. Building and running a firm makes good business sense. Directing your energy at the management level can be a far more profitable endeavor than going it alone. With the right people, you can dupli-cate your efforts and thus, your successes. Then you can reap far greater rewards (even if they are shared) than you could have on your own.

Building a company—whether you're trading puts and calls or putting soles on shoes—has some basic requirements. You have to have an idea that can be replicated and you have to have the right people. In a business such as trading, having the "right" people is essential. Trading is not for everybody, particularly in the high-stress, emotional, and high-risk world of day-trading options. That's the bread-and-butter of Mercury Trading, which has traders both on the floor and in the upstairs offices at three locations— New York, Chicago, and San Francisco.

When I think about the people I've brought into the Mercury fold over the years, I've had some wonderful successes and some spectacular failures. Overall, it's been a very interesting adventure. For those who contemplate trading professionally, it's essential to know what it's like in a firm such as mine, where you're given responsibility and, at the same time, required to follow instructions from a senior trader or principal of the firm. And for those of you who are retail investors, knowing what it takes to be a professional can give you insight into this marketplace. Even if you buy a call and hold it for weeks, you need to know the dynamic of the day-to-day market, in which volatility can shrink or expand the option that you're holding. There are lessons to be gleaned about discipline, about cutting your losers before they eat away your capital, and about having a plan—always—for the options that you hold.

With the headlines filled with stories about day-trading firms, it's important to discuss the kind of operation that Mercury is. Ours is a firm in which we employ traders who make a salary and get a discretionary bonus that is based on the profits made trading our capital. Opportunities for young traders vary from straight salaried positions to percentage deals. As we discussed in earlier chapters, some firms don't require much in the way of trading skills, as they employ a "Fat Brain" concept of an upstairs person (or persons) who determines appropriate hedges and manages the global portfolio. Other firms give traders wide latitude in establishing and managing their positions. You can probably imagine that the more independence the firm gives the trader, the greater the possibility the trader will not only be salaried, but share in the profits of his or her account.

Because of the wide divergence between what the traders are required to do (buy when the screen turns green, sell when it turns red, versus employ your judgment to initiate and hedge trades), the salary range is also quite varied. Some traders get a job with a trading firm and a salary of, say, $50,000 a year, and 30 percent of the profits they make the first year, 40 percent the second, and 50 percent or 60 percent the third year. Most firms will provide some form of training and that firm will also provide capital for their trading. We employ a slight variation on that theme, as we pay our traders a salary, back them with capital, and coach them through the learning curve, watching how they develop and then put them to work in one of our option specialist trading areas. Our firm acts as a kind of incubator for traders, who will, in time, be fast, decisive, and, above all, disciplined. We want our traders to make profitable trades for the house. Period.

That's different from the so-called day-trading firms that capture negative headline attention, the trading rooms that let wanna-be millionaires plunk down their $50,000 nest egg to point and click their way to becoming a stock day-trader. These traders are often trading on margin, sometimes excessively. The blow-out stories can be frighteningly sensational.

swimming with the sharks

In our seminars, we encounter a lot of aggressive retail investors, who want to make options their new vocation. When the bull market was percolating along and almost any reasonable option (or stock) strategy was working, it may have been tempting to chuck your job and become a trader. Before you give up your day job, it would be prudent to remember you have to walk before you run. I hear hundreds, perhaps thousands, of stories about folks that made that bold move long before they should have. Why not hone your skills as a customer before you jump into these shark infested waters? (The joke about traders goes something like this: An options trader falls into a shark tank, but emerges unscathed. Do you know why the sharks didn't eat him? Professional courtesy.)

The best way to walk before you run is to get some quality trade execution and/or strategy counseling from a knowledgeable broker. Our firm, PTI Securities & Futures, is staffed with former market makers with a wealth of options experience. Thus, I think we offer an attractive, but not the only, solution. I know great brokers at both full service and discount brokerages, so it really comes down to finding someone who will work hard for and with you.

If you are ready to venture into the day-trading arena, you may consider an Internet-based trading firm such as iTradem.com (see Chapter 10). Trading professionally, to be candid, is a job that is suitable for only a special kind of individual. There is great opportunity being a retail investor (and if you hold any position longer than about 10 seconds, I consider you to be an investor and not a trader). Still, there are those whose aggressive nature and demeanor makes them a natural for a career as a trader, but those individuals are a rare and valuable find.

With the kind of professional trading operation that we have at Mercury, the right people are as essential as the right information. We can have every online quote, chart service, and options analysis program available. But if we don't have the kind of traders a firm needs, we're doomed to suffer a poor performance, if not worse.

Trust in the traders I have working at my firm is invaluable on days like we've seen through the month of April 2000, when volatility has been greater than normal—or more specifically on a week like April 10 to 14 when the Nasdaq lost 25 percent of its value. That's when you need to know, beyond a doubt, that the traders on staff will follow your instructions to the letter. You have to know they will not exceed risk parameters by taking on positions that are too large, or hold onto unhedged positions. That kind of trust can save a firm from losses that you'd rather not even contemplate.

The Mercury Trading Group, which I founded in 1989 with three traders, now has three offices and between 60 and 70 employees. Mercury's traders work primarily on the floor, but we have about five traders upstairs. Our ratio tends to average one trader upstairs for every five we have on the floor, but that ratio is likely to change as all electronic exchanges draw our trading talent upstairs. Mercury's business is proprietary trading, meaning we are trading for the house, and not executing customer orders (which is the job of the brokers at my brokerage operations, PTI Securities & Futures and iTradem.com).

When I started Mercury, I looked primarily for traders with some experience who needed capital to back them. Today, I look for energetic people with an upbeat attitude. (If you're a mope, I can't be around you! The market throws enough challenges at us each day without having to deal with people who have a perpetually negative attitude.) In fact, the majority of successful traders at our firm and our competitors' on the trading floor(s) are those who are the most upbeat and outgoing. Not surprisingly, I find that traders recognize this and, even if they are not sociable by nature, they push themselves to be more gregarious and affable. To that point, we have a trader who, by nature, barely says two words when he's off the floor. But on the floor, you'd think he's the most convivial guy around. When he hits that trading floor—where he makes his living by shouting out bids and offers and dealing with a host of brokers—he turns on his personality.

Another case in point is my brother, Peter, who is a very successful trader. By nature he is a comedian and has a very imposing physical presence (6′3″ and 235 lbs.), having been a pro football player for seven years. When he stands on the trading floor, he doesn't look like anybody else in that pit. I'd say his commanding presence and outgoing personality are definite assets when he's competing to get the best bids and offers on the floor. His success is evident from the $20 million of stock he buys and sells every day, working in the AOL pit—one of the most active in the world.

Peter, like other good traders, can turn that presence on and off. You have to. When you trade, you want a presence that's larger than life, but you better check your ego at the door. You don't want your ego to dictate your trading position. When you're wrong and you're holding a losing position, you have to be able to get out. If the blinders go on and you can't see clearly, you won't last as a trader.

The traders who do well on the floor have what I consider to be the three big attributes: discipline, aggressiveness, and some sociability. You need the balance that comes with all three. You may be personable. You may be extremely aggressive. But if you lack the discipline, then chances are you'll blow out after the first year. At the same time, you also must be aggressive enough to be the first to respond when a broker wants to know the market for whatever options you're trading. Traders on the floor are competing with each other, not colluding to make a market. When options are bid at 4¼ and offered at 4½ and nobody's buying, you have to be the first to lower your selling price to 4⅜, or 4¼. Then you get that trade. You can't just sit back and raise your hand. To quote J. Paul Getty, "The meek shall inherit the earth, but not the mineral rights."

Over the years of hiring and training traders, I've encountered many who are enchanted by the market, who believe they will make this their "life." But the problem is after a month or so, too many begin to give up. Perhaps they succumb to the feeling that this is all over their heads and they'll never "get it." Or else they came in a little too cocky, believing they were just that much smarter than everyone else and, therefore, immune to the rules that govern the rest of us. The market can be a humbling experience. Just when you think you cannot only outsmart your fellow traders but also outsmart *The Market,* you're in for a lesson—and most likely a painful and costly one.

fire in the belly

Whether someone is an experienced trader or a college-student intern, those who are successful in the business have one common trait: They have fire in their bellies. They have the passion and the commitment to go the distance, to weather the inevitable stormy times, and to stay disciplined. As someone who has traded on and off the floor for 20 years, I know that the only way to survive is to have a passion for this business. Money, alone, won't do it. You can only water ski behind one boat at a time, only drive one Porsche, or Ferrari at a time. And if you don't love this business, there aren't enough zeros on the check to make up for the pressure and headaches.

Given the changes in the options industry, those who want to become traders must be comfortable at the computer. As I stated earlier, those who have gone on to trade on the floor over the years had certain qualities, including a physical presence; you have to be both visible and audible in a crowded, noisy trading pit. And you have to have a high energy level. At The Mercury Trading Group, we're not recruiting floor traders. Those whom we bring onboard may initially assist our floor operations, but they will ultimately be trading upstairs, where the market is increasingly moving.

Today, we are building for a future that will be determined by electronic trading. I hope the trading floor and open outcry trading survives, but I believe the jury is still out on this issue. As I discuss in Chapter 10, I believe that the trading floor will become increasingly electronic, with the expanded presence of and roles for electronic communications networks (ECNs) that handle trades electronically. True, the traditional exchanges have the advantage of liquidity at the moment. But that edge could be taken away rather quickly if—or when—volume builds to a critical mass on these alternative, electronic exchanges. Without a brick-and-mortar presence and related overhead, ECNs and other electronic competitors can operate at slim margins.

These electronic competitors will challenge traders to become increasingly technologically savvy and at-home on the computer, pointing and clicking rather than waving and shouting. But certain traits will still remain essential—on and off the floor—especially discipline. That's one of the reasons I like athletes, because most had to have discipline to survive. And, I like to hire traders who have played a team sport, whether it's football, basketball, or hockey. Because on a team, you have to make sacrifices and act in concert with others. You have to give up the personal flourish, sometimes, for the sake of the team victory. In a trading room, that's vital. You can't have one player taking on too much risk in the pursuit of personal glory.

If you're backing a trader, meaning you're putting up the capital they trade in return for a share of the profits they make, you must have confidence in your trader's ability to execute trades according to a plan (especially your plan). You have to know that your traders will do what they say they'll do, that they'll trade within specified parameters of risk and position size. They have to be self-starters, always looking for opportunities in the market. They have to want to read or surf the Web, looking for information on a particular company, industry, or sector of the market. Information is disseminated immediately, thanks to the Internet, narrowing the time advantage. If you can learn something a few seconds before the rest of the crowd, you may have an edge.

In the old days, some of the traditional brokerage firms touted an edge of having the best information, analysis, and so forth on the stocks that they traded. They knew about earnings, special dividends, conference calls, and special events. Today, even the whisper numbers on a company's projected earnings—which differ from the widely published earnings estimates—can be found on the Web (WhisperNumber.com). What used to be so incredibly secret on Wall Street is now incredibly public, and that's a very good thing. If there is any advantage to be gained, it will go to the swiftest and the most aggressive.

But the challenge to the upstairs, professional trader (and by extension to the aggressive retail speculator) is to gather information as quickly as the so-called insiders. You can find the latest stock upgrades and downgrades by analysts. And, you might be able to do well trading on that information. But the people who undoubtedly make the bigger killings are those special customers whom the broker told yesterday that he was going to make a stock recommendation, or upgrade today. (Early dissemination of that information is legal since it's not considered inside information because the firm making the upgrade or downgrade is just an interested third party, not the stock itself.)

the information edge

Information dominates this market. If you want to trade professionally or invest aggressively you must have an overriding passion for the market. Do you read the *Wall Street Journal* for fun, or is it work? Do you jump past the business pages of your newspaper and dive into sports? If you don't read the financial pages then this is not your business, it's as simple as that. When I look for traders, I must see that intense interest in the market. (Unfortunately, some of the best traders can be some of the biggest bores because they turn every dinner conversation into a market discussion. Personally, I can't even plan for a vacation without looking at airfares, seeing if they're rising or falling, figuring in fuel costs, and then wondering if my market position ought to be in airlines or the energy sector. If they don't have a similar obsession with news, they probably won't make it as a trader.)

I should draw a clear distinction between a professional trading firm like The Mercury Trading Group, which backs traders who trade the house account, and day-trading firms that let virtually anyone with enough capital trade. Those retail day-trading firms have come under a lot of scrutiny lately, particularly from the Securities and Exchange Commission (SEC). (SEC Chairman Arthur Levitt, in recent testimony before a U.S. Senate subcommittee, has stated: "I am concerned that some day traders don't fully understand the level of risk they are assuming. I am concerned that some people may be lured into the false belief that day trading is a surefire strategy to make them rich.") There is even continued debate over whether or not day-trading firms should be subject to stricter regulation, especially when it comes to trading on margin, which would allow an unsophisticated trader to put on larger trades with bigger risk than is prudent.

Luckily, we're not in that category. Our traders are professionals who are hired by the firm to trade the house's money. Our traders didn't quit their day jobs, take their life's savings, and spin trades at a computer like it was a video poker machine. Our traders are employees, members of a team I've put together. Because we day-trade options, we're already heavily scrutinized. As a specialist firm, we are audited every year by our self-regulated organization and the CBOE, to ensure, among other things, that we have the adequate capital minimum and that we are adhering to our responsibilities as an options specialist. Our first line of defense is always the clearing firm, which watches both our risk exposure and our capital, then the exchange and, ultimately, the SEC.

There is also another key issue between traders at my firm and aggressive speculators out there. It comes down to a clear and strict definition of the term *day trader*. Some people say that if you're in and out of a position within one day, you're a day trader. I narrow that definition further. I say that if you rarely hold a position for longer than a few seconds, then you're a day trader. Otherwise, you're an investor. That's a clear-cut distinction that anyone in this business—whether you're a professional trader or an active speculator—must ponder. Regardless of what you might want to be, you must know what you are. And if you're an investor, you must trade like one, and have realistic expectations of what your performance can be.

If you're going to be an investor and generate returns of 40 percent, 60 percent, or 100 percent, you must be very aggressive. You have to be picking a lot of stocks that are performing just as you have projected, to manage a four-fold increase from the average performance of the stock market. [According to Chicago-based Ibbotson (www.ibbotson.com) the stock market has averaged a return of 10.8 percent annually since 1929.] But if you're going to be a day trader and make 40 percent, you are setting your sights way too low. Your goal must be to make 100 percent or 200 percent, otherwise you're kidding yourself. First of all, most day traders are not opening an account with $200,000 or $500,000. They open with $25,000 to $50,000 and use guts and leverage to make it trade like $100,000. But people frequently ask me, is it possible to open a day-trading account with $50,000 and make 100 percent? The answer is yes, but you've got to be lucky, good, and have discipline. But it's imperative that you cut your losses fast and move on with the profitable trades. You have to be glued to the screen to do this. There are those who can and make it—taking that $50,000 all the way up to $1 million.

That requires a 100 percent return day trading, turning $50,000 into $100,000, then $100,000 into $200,000, and so forth. As anyone who has done it can tell you, it's easier to turn that $50,000 into $1 million, than $1 million into $2 million. To make $50,000, you only need a profit of $200 a day, which is not unreasonable. To turn $500,000 into $1 million, however, you have to make $2,000 a day. That's a lot of trading, both more often and bigger size. Eventually the returns begin to drop as the market impact created by multi-thousand share stock scalps, or multihundred option trades begins to become an issue.

Whether you're an aggressive day trader or a cautious investor, you must know yourself and your pain threshold. There will be days when, mentally, you're carrying that day's market action home with you—and into the night when you're lying awake with gritted teeth. If that happens too often, I'd say you're in the wrong position. It may be the first sign that instead of being an aggressive trader, you're really an investor. And for an investor, 40 percent is a good, healthy return, which is entirely possible. But as an investor, you must have many of the same attributes as the most aggressive traders at my firm. You must have a passion for the market, you must do your homework and you must have discipline. An investor can suffer big losses, too, if you get in a stock for the wrong reasons or without an adequate plan.

At Mercury Trading, that "plan" will depend largely upon whether a trader is on the floor or at the screen. The guys on the floor are really more like the catcher on the baseball team. They are very defensive, reacting to retail and institutional buyers and sellers who are willing to trade on our posted markets. They are required to make a market, which means they may be buying when they'd rather sell, and vice versa. But the people upstairs are more offensive and strategic. They are plotting their market moves like a chess player, knowing when and where they'll make a play—and for what reason. They're studying the various catalysts in the market—earnings, new products, lawsuits settlements, sector rotation. Then they plan their moves in the various stocks that they trade. The market maker on the floor understands those same dynamics, but has to trade in this defensive manor to justify our preferential margins.

We don't just look at the price of stocks that we're trading. We also look closely at volatility, which we treat like a rubber band that stretches from one extreme (fear) to the other (greed). Let's say that Micron's volatility is 50 percent normally, but selling pressure could take that volatility down to 35 percent. Maybe some institutional trading company thinks the market will be rangebound and is looking to milk some premium out of what is expected to be a dull market. Or perhaps some concern in the marketplace (the fear factor) has brought droves of buyers into the market seeking protection, bidding up the volatility to, say, 80 percent. When these out-of-balance situations occur, there is an opportunity to act, but timing is everything. And in these times, you need to know that your traders are following not only the trading plan for the day, but the risk parameters that will keep them out of trouble.

For example, we knew that April 14, 2000—the day that Nasdaq closed down 9.7 percent, dropping by 356.74 points—was going to be a tricky kind of a day. There was already a lot of fear in the market, resulting in high premium for issues such as Sun Microsystems, Micron, and AOL. Stocks like these normally have volatility in the range of 60 percent or 70 percent. But the fear factor had pushed the volatility on these stocks to 150 percent or 200 percent. The challenge for us was to determine if this was a good place to sell the premium, or would fear push it even higher. You don't want to sell too soon and have to buy your position back in a rising market. Or, conversely, you don't want to buy too soon and have to sell in a falling market.

back and front spreads

Ideally, you'd like to have a *back-spread trade* whereby you buy more contracts than you sell. Let's say you've bought 10 $50 at-the-money calls that have about a 50 delta. That delta means that for every $1 the stock moves, the calls will move by $0.50. Therefore, with 10 call contracts I'm 500 delta long [10×100 shares (per option) $\times .50 = 500$] equivalent to being long 500 shares of stock (even though, without taking the delta into consideration, 10 options contracts are equivalent to 1,000 shares). As a hedge against this call position, I would sell 500 shares of stock. That's a classic back spread, because I own 10 call contracts, which is 5 contracts more than I've sold (500 shares of stock).

If the stock were to move up to $60 a share, you'd face a $10 a share loss on the 500 shares of stock, or a loss of $5,000. The options, however, have increased both in value and delta, moving from a 50-delta to a 70-delta or more (meaning that for every $1 move in the stock the option moves about $0.70). The call options that I may have paid $3.50 for when they were at the money at $50 have risen by $7 and are now trading at $10.50 a share. That's a profit on the call options of some $7,500. On a net basis taking into account the $5,000 loss on the stock position, I'm still up $2,500.

To show how well hedged this position is, if the stock fell to $40 a share, the stock position makes $10 a share for a total profit of $5,000. My call options that I bought for $3.50 are worth about a $1, for a loss of $2,500. My net profit on the overall position is still $2,500. I make money either way, although time decay as expiration approaches will eat away at the value of the call options.

But there are times when market conditions—particularly high volatility that pushes premium to lofty levels—dictates a different, and far riskier, kind of trade—*a front spread.* In this trade, you're short more contracts than you're long, which increases your exposure to potential losses as market gyrations are not the front spreader's ideal situation. At Mercury, when we're putting on front spreads, which may involve thousands to millions of shares of stock and hundreds and even thousands of options contracts, you want to make sure that everyone is following the same play book. You can't afford to have a trader decide to break rank and go his or her own way. When the risk is high, trust becomes crucial.

Let's say Sun Microsystems is trading at $90 a share. With normal volatility, the stock might trade in a daily range of $87 to $93 a share. But when volatility increases—as we saw in April 2000—it's going to trade in a wider range. Instead of its usual 3-point range, let's say the price is fluctuating by 15 points. This increased volatility also pushes up the premium on options. (Increased volatility, after all, means that the stock is moving in a wider range, improving the chances that a particular strike price will be hit.)

As I've said, times like these favor the seller since it's assumed that abnormally high volatility cannot be sustained. Thus, when the volatility is on the high end, we favor front spreads in which you sell more than you buy. In this example, we'd sell 1,000 Sun Microsystems $90 at-the-money calls, which have a delta of 50. So even though those 1,000 calls are equivalent to 100,000 shares, with a delta of 50 it's more like being short 50,000 shares of Sun Microsystems at $90. To hedge the trade, we'd buy 50,000 shares at $90. If the stock price doesn't move a dime, we're completely neutral. But our hope is that volatility will decline and we, as the call sellers, will be able to keep much of the premium we've collected.

Let's say that the stock falls from $90 to $80 a share. We lose $10 a share on our 50,000 shares of stock, for a loss of $500,000. (Remember, as a proprietary trading firm we have the advantage of no Reg. T requirement which exempts us from the 50 percent margin customers must pay.) The options we sold decline somewhat, but volatility remains high. So the premium on those call options is now $8, down from $10, and at this point, as the seller of the calls, we have pocketed the $2 difference. We make $2 times the 1,000 calls, or a $200,000 profit. But taking into consideration the $500,000 we lost on the stock, we're out $300,000. The only hope is for the volatility to decline further to more than make up for the decline in the stock holding.

When market conditions dictate, we may do dozens of trades like that—some winners and some losers (and, of course, we hope for more profitable ones than unprofitable positions). So as we review the trades on the books, we want to see that the traders have executed according to our plan, based on our analysis of volatility and pricing models. You don't want to find out, at the end of an adverse move, that you suddenly have a negative surprise to deal with, which you weren't anticipating.

As we tell our traders, both on and off the floor (and retail speculators could learn a lesson from this), you can't let the market tell you what to do. You have to have a plan and stick to it. Of course, conditions that affect that plan may change. But you must follow the plan to keep from getting sidetracked. For example, you may be a buyer—whether of stock or options. Then a massive sell-off hits, and everything around you indicates that you should be a seller.

Maybe Nasdaq is down 400 points and you're long stock. To cut your losses, maybe you'd sell the stock. If you were a floor trader, you could easily become swept-up in the emotional panic selling on a day like that. In such circumstances, you need to brace not just for the continued selling, but in the back of your mind, you must anticipate some profit taking, which may lead to a rebound. This anticipation causes you to ask yourself: Could the Nasdaq sustain being down 400 points? Or would it likely recover. Conversely, if the market is up 200 or 300 points and you're short, everything in the market says that you need to buy. But can you afford to buy knowing that the market could come back down just as quickly in the afternoon? This, admittedly, puts a lot of stress on traders who are handling these big positions, especially on days when an adverse market move could cost the firm $1 million or more in losses. It takes discipline to withstand moves like that and keep a clear head. But that's exactly what successful traders do every day.

Granted, I monitor the positions of the traders at the firm. But mostly I rely on them to follow instructions and keep disciplined. That's so critical in these times when volatility can expand to 120 percent at the end of one week and, by the end of the following Monday, collapse back to 80 percent and then 60 percent a day later.

The challenge is different for traders on and off the floor. Floor traders often can't see the forest for the proverbial trees. They are up to their eyes in trading. They're surrounded by the emotions of the pit. In the frenzy, they can't gauge the shift in sentiment. They can't see that the selling is exhausting itself at some level and the market has reached a point at which they could buy with some degree of confidence.

Traders will tell you that there are many days when they go to the floor with a very bullish bias. And even if you disagree with (or despise) every other trader in that pit, it's hard to keep your perspective when you hold a view that's opposite of the prevailing emotion on the floor. So even if you're bullish and you want to buy this stock, you can easily become swept up in the sentiment and turn seller.

To give an example of what it's like, think of being at a sporting event and becoming swept up in the emotion of the crowd. Even if you're a tepid fan at best, you find yourself screaming your lungs out or cursing the opposing team, even though, in reality, the game is not that important to you. Now imagine that the game is the market, and you're trying to keep your head while everyone else is losing theirs.

That's why a lot of trading firms have senior traders on the desks who call the biggest shots. They direct the other traders on the desk to buy and sell. By no means am I belittling the talents of any trader. But there are times when it's better for someone more senior and experienced to pick the levels at which a stock or an option should be bought or sold, and then a more junior trader executes that trade. The senior trader who is calling the shots wants to see discipline among the ranks, and not some less experienced trader trying to "please" by taking initiative when they shouldn't.

the disciplined broker

Discipline is also essential for a broker, who must know when it's more important to execute a customer's trade quickly at the prevailing market price, rather than to "fight" for a better deal. A good broker will do everything reasonable to make the most money for the customer. Sometimes that means that calls were offered at 4½, but we were aggressive and got them at 4¼. It's great when that happens, and you can brag to the customer that you fight for every "teeny" on a trade. But brokers need to keep a disciplined mind to know the danger of being the proverbial penny-wise and dollar-foolish. If a customer needs to buy something, you can't try to save a teeny or an eighth by trying to get a better deal. The problem is that delay in filling the order, while you try to get a better price, can mean you miss the opportunity entirely. For example, if a customer needs to buy 50 options, the difference of an eighth is $625. But if you miss that opportunity to buy at the prevailing price and the stock moves $2, then those 50 options could cost an additional $10,000! Generally speaking, it's okay to fight for a better price in a static market, but when things are moving—you'd better be alert and agile.

Here's an example: On April 19, 2000, Bristol-Myers Squibb Co. announced it was withdrawing its request for U.S. marketing approval of the hypertension drug Vanlev (Reuters, April 19, 2000, "Bristol-Myers Says Vanlev Users Needed Breathing Help"). Trading in the stock was halted on the New York Stock Exchange, but shares plummeted in third-market trading. In cases like this, you know there is going to be a strong reaction when the stock does resume trading. You have to make your decision fast. In this case, I wanted to be a buyer and it was more important for me to get in at what I expected to be a dramatically lower quote when the stock resumed trading. I wasn't going to worry about a quarter or an eighth. I wanted to take advantage of the opportunity created by the panic.

I knew the stock was going to open under $50 a share, so I put in a market order even if that meant I didn't get the "best" price. Why? Because I wanted in. I knew that if I hesitated and said, "Let's see where it opens," then I could very well miss the opportunity. I didn't want to commit the sin of being "penny-wise and dollar-foolish." By that time, Bristol-Myers had lost some $30 billion in market capitalization. The drug was allegedly a $1 billion loss. So didn't that $30 billion drop in capitalization seem like an over-reaction? I thought so. I was a buyer at what I expected to be bargain prices. I wasn't going to quibble about a quarter or an eighth. In the end, when the stock reopened, I bought the stock at 48¼.

The point I want to make is I wasn't worried about an eighth—which is equivalent to 12.5 cents per share. I wasn't scalping for quarters and eighths in this scenario like a typical day trader. I was buying the stock because it was down $12, which I considered to be an extreme move, on bad, but not earth-shattering news.

The same goes for our customers when the market is moving and they say, "Buy this." It doesn't serve our customers if they miss a buying opportunity and the stock is $2 higher, because a broker was trying to do better than the prevailing offer. There are times when a broker wants to impress a customer by doing better on an order, by showing their skill as a trader. What the market demands, however, is for brokers to execute. That takes a kind of ego-less discipline, to put the customer's need to get a fill over the sense to prove yourself. But as we say in football, you don't want a player trying to be his own quarterback on the field, instead of following the coach's game plan.

Luckily for my partner, Tom Haugh, and me, all of our brokers are former floor traders. They have experience on the frontlines and now they don't mind getting out of the trenches. At the risk of painting with too broad a brush, perhaps they came upstairs to the brokerage firm because their backs were shot from standing or their voice gave out from yelling bids and offers. They could still grind it out in the pits, but why pound their knee cartilage to mush and further ruin their vocal cords? Being brokers doesn't mean they're out to pasture. They're still part of the market, but in their present roles they are the liaison between the customer and the floor broker who will execute the trade. As trading becomes more electronic and ECNs—including iTradem.com, which we're developing—become more dominant, our brokers will work in conjunction with an electronic order-routing system.

When I started PTI with Tom, his brother Dan, and a handful of brokers, we had a great idea of offering quality trade executions and great customer service. But we had one problem: We didn't have any customers. We knew there were customers out there who wanted to trade options, retail clients whose stock brokers didn't understand options. Whenever we'd lecture at a seminar, we'd heard countless times from retail customers that their broker actually tried to discourage them from speculating with options or even use options as an insurance against a stock portfolio. We knew there was an opportunity, we just had to build it. It took two years for PTI to be profitable, but we knew it was worth the wait.

Looking back, I suppose we should have built the firm with brokers who had existing clients. Instead, we built the firm from scratch, believing that excellent service and word-of-mouth would provide us with a loyal customer base. That's paying off. We've got experienced, former traders on staff, who wanted to come off the floor to have somewhat of a slower pace. Granted, options can help you limit your risk. But then you add in the leverage that professional traders have, the kind that can take $50,000 and turn it into $100,000 or $250,000. That can get pretty exhausting.

To get away from that hyperactive risk, some traders would gladly become brokers, working in more of an investing atmosphere. They're still part of the game, and in fact are integral players in a market that is seeing increased retail participation. The skills they bring upstairs—how to read the tape, how to listen to what the market is telling you at earnings time, when the market is worried and when it is complacent—are valuable to a brokerage firm and its clients. And as we'll discuss in the next chapter, there are times when you want a broker who will do more than pass along your buy and sell order, and give you advice on a trade. Additionally, the trade off for the freedom of independent market makers is that they don't build anything permanent. Specialists and DPMs build businesses that can be sold for millions of dollars, but independent market makers don't have such hard assets as a book of great stocks. This was a factor that compelled us to build our

172 how I trade options

brokerage and helps us attract former market makers to staff our trading desk.

At the risk of sounding too self-satisfied, I'm pleased with the firms I helped to build, both Mercury Trading and PTI Securities & Futures. Looking back, I remember what it was like to step on that trading floor for the first time, to be so clueless about what was going on that I never thought I would catch on. Now, I'm training others to trade, both the traders who come onboard at Mercury and the retail customers who come to our seminars. Trading is a way of life, which is not for everyone. But investing is an activity that can be adopted by a far wider population, from the cautious or casual player to the super-aggressive speculator. Regardless of what group you fall in, there is a commonalty among them—discipline. You have to devise and stick to a plan, and not let fear and greed sway you from your resolve.

That's easier said (or written) than done, sometimes, but the profits to be reaped are their own reward.

chapter 9

getting the right tools

In options trading, as in many endeavors, you must have the right tools. If you're not equipped you will severely handicap yourself or make it virtually impossible to be able to do the job. For options trading, we divide these tools into five categories: quotes, software, advisors, brokers, education. We'll discuss them one at a time.

quotes

How can you trade if you don't know the price of whatever you want to buy or sell? While that may seem oversimplistic, it really is the essence of this issue. When it comes to price quotes for options, the information you're receiving must be timely and accurate. For a buy-and-hold stock investor, it might be adequate to look at yesterday's New York Stock Exchange or Nasdaq settlement prices in this morning's newspaper. That newspaper won't tell you where the stock opened this morning or where it's currently trading. But if a day-old settlement price lets you keep track of your holdings, that's probably adequate. Generally speaking, the longer your investment timeframe, the more "dated" the information you can use.

If you are a little more active, or the next notch up on the vigilance scale, you might tune into the radio for market updates or watch CNBC, which has streaming quotes on the screen. Those up-to-date prices on the television screen may look like a good deal considering they're free. But that information isn't without its drawbacks, including the fact that you have to sit and watch for your stock picks to scroll by. Then you have to be able to interpret what you see. For instance, if 50 IBM 17¼ scrolls by and the price is in green, do you know that means 5,000 IBM shares traded on the offer at 117¼? (If it were red, that may reflect that the last trade occurred at the bid.) And when it's a fast market, the "50" goes away as does the change on the day.

Then there are the Web sites—Smart Money.com, ClearStation. com, BigCharts.com, SmallCapCenter.com, DBC.com—that offer free quotes services. Just type in the quote symbol you want, and up pops a price and the change from the previous night's settlement. Typically, these quotes are delayed 20 minutes from the current market, which may be okay if you are just keeping track of your holdings. But in a fast-moving market, a lot can happen in 20 minutes.

Similarly, option quotes can be obtained on a variety of Web sites, including CBOE.com, Amex.com, and my Web site, 1010WallStreet.com. If you typed in a stock symbol, such as IBM, you would receive the entire options chain with various strike prices and months, including the one-year and two-year LEAPS. These are snapshot quotes, meaning I must hit "refresh" each time to receive an update. That might be sufficient if I'm actively trading and tracking one or two stocks. But if I have a dozen different stocks to keep track of at any given time, this kind of service may be more of a hindrance than a bargain.

If you require up-to-the-second information, particularly on multiple stocks, you need live, streaming quotes. For the active investor and retail speculator, this is essential. Given the competition in the marketplace and the ease of online dissemination, live quotes are a fairly reasonable proposition, starting at about $60 a month. That quote service would pay for itself each month if it enabled you to make a small profit, even a teeny (one-sixteenth) on a 10-lot (10 × 100 shares per option × 0.0625 = $62.50).

Plus, the minute you include options analysis software in the picture, your quote information needs change. Software packages often demand a certain type of live quote, usually streaming quotes for option scans and real-time profit-and-loss updates. Again, these packages may not be necessary if you are only buying covered calls for stocks for which you have a bullish outlook. But if you are, or anticipate becoming, an active retail investor employing a variety of strategies, you must consider software—and the quote services that they require.

Before we launch into software, the next "tool" category, it's important to know that there are several different delivery methods for live quotes. The most popular means is the Internet, which is appealing to many traders and speculators who are used to an online venue. In fact, a number of quote services saw rapid appreciation of their share prices as the world began to realize that the Internet would free quote vendors from satellite and "hard-wired" delivery solutions. But there are potential drawbacks to using the Internet for quote delivery, including the speed and capability of your own Internet connection. If you have a 28.8 modem and you're trying to pull down quotes for 3,000 stocks that have options on them, well, good luck . . . that's going to be about as easy as trying to suck motor oil through a straw—at 30 degrees below zero!

If you have a cable modem or DSL connection to the Internet, that will speed up the process considerably. In a perfect world, cable and DSL access should allow you get quotes nearly as quickly as with a direct connection. But, of course, there is no such thing as a perfect world. The speed of cable access depends on how many other users are trying to access data at the same time. The more people who are on the Internet via the same cable service that you use, the slower it will pull quotes, and the longer it will take for the vendor to push quotes out to its subscribers. Many of the paid Internet sites can only pull through 500 symbols at a time because of limitations in bandwidth.

DSL is fast, but the service does have some geographic limitations. You cannot access this service from every location because proximity to the DSL source is a limiting factor. That's why many serious traders have satellite dishes to receive their quotes directly from the vendor. Most of us consider that to be the most reliable service when you absolutely, positively must have live quotes any moment that the markets are open.

Being a premium distribution method, satellite dish is also the most expensive. But it's what you'd expect an extremely active retail investor to have. No office, no trading room on Wall Street depends on quotes via the Internet. If a brokerage had only Internet-based quotes, it would lose a majority of its customers pretty fast. And the bigger the brokerage, the more they know that their clients are a sophisticated group, including hedge funds and institutional traders, who have their own direct connections. Thus they have to have the same direct market information as the most sophisticated of their customers.

There is a long list of quote providers who offer direct or "hard-wired" connections, including Thompson Financial, Track-Data, ILX, Bloomberg, Reuters, S&P Comstock, and others. Many professional trading firms have multiple services. At Mercury Trading, we have at least two at any given time. Given the expense, I wish we didn't have to use multiple services. But for the volume of trades that we do, it's imperative that we have a depth of price quotes and that is impossible to receive with only one service. In addition, having multiple services allows us to compare what the prevailing quotes are and see if one service is falling victim to bandwidth constraints that cause it to throttle-back its quotes. Since we are competing against other professionals both to price and to hedge our option positions, a stale quote could cost us hundreds of thousands of dollars in a matter of seconds.

For every stock on which options are written, premiums are quoted for calls and puts at various strike price and various months. The more active, or volatile, a stock, the more quotes will be available. And each strike price has two different quotes; one for the call and one for the put. Take a stock like Rambus (RMBS) that has moved from $57 to nearly $500 (52-week high 471, 52-week low 57). There would be options quoted at prices within that vast range, each with its own quote, according to expiration month. That results in a gibberish of potentially confusing, multiple-letter quotes like RMQAA (the January $5 strike) and RQMAA (the January $105 strike). Stocks like RMBS choke the Options Price Reporting Authority (OPRA—no relation to the talk-show host!) as RMBS may have 300 strike prices, each with a call and put, for a total of 600 potential price changes each time RMBS ticks up or down an eighth!

Or take the SPX, the options based on the S&P 500 cash market, which may have strikes between 1200 and 1650, in $5 increments all the way up. As the index moves, the underlying call and put quotes also change, say, from 127⅛ bid and 127⅝ offered, to 127¼ bid and 127¾ offered, each time the S&P 500 future ticks up. There could be 400 strike price changes, both calls and puts, each time the underlying security changes in value. This also illustrates the bandwidth problem for Internet-based quotes, and also shows why you need multiple quote services, particularly these days when there are 3,000 stocks with options compared to the 80 stocks when I began.

software

Now that you've decided that you're an active-enough trader to have a premium quote service, you must take a look at the kind of help that is available to you to analyze the options market. That's one of the reasons I believe database mining will be an important field in the future. Given the breadth of raw data, be it prices or volatility, there is a need to study and manipulate this information in a meaningful way. For example, you could look at a database of stocks and (if you were a value-oriented investor such as Warren Buffett) you might want to see companies that have a price-to-earnings (P/E) ratio of less than 20. Or you may be posing more sophisticated database queries such as scans based on price, volatility, time to expiration, increases or decreases in volume or volatility, and so on. The more you ask a program to do, the more sophisticated the software must be.

Plus, you may be analyzing both stocks and options, which often require separate programs. For stock analysis, such as based on price momentum, break-outs, and so forth, you may choose a software system such as TradeStation, MetaStock, or OmniTrader. For options, you might choose a program such as OptionVue 5, OptionStation, or OptionOracle. Each of these has various programs to assist you in technical analysis according to your trading methodology and criteria. Whatever system you choose, the most important consideration is the accuracy of the models behind the software. Simply put, you must choose a program that is based on good, solid mathematics, and not a lot of programming short-cuts that can result in erroneous, inaccurate analysis.

Again, this goes back to the key question of what kind of trader or speculator are you? If you're the casual investor who is looking to buy a call now and again, you may not need the high-priced, luxury model among options analysis. But the more serious you are about trading options, the more programming firepower you must have at your disposal. The key difference comes in with *iterations,* which in simplest terms is the way computers count. If you're using a basic program, perhaps a simple tool that's available online, the program may use one or two iterations to come up with an approximate valuation for an option. Thus, a program using only two iterations may determine that a particular option should be valued at 6.75. Now, another program, using four iterations, might further refine that valuation to, say, 6.70. With six iterations, you could get to 6.65, and so forth. The difference may not mean much to you, if you're trading two or three stocks with a one-year timeframe. But if you're an active option investor or professional trader, that one-eighth or one-sixteenth difference in valuation can, indeed, be costly. The big options programs that I use, for example, have 17 iterations.

In addition, there are at least a half-dozen options pricing models that use different pricing models, whether its Black-Scholes, Cox Ross, Gastineau, or Binominal. Most of those theories will result in calculations within a nickel of each other. But, again, the more sophisticated your needs, the more sophisticated your tools must be. Put another way, the more accurate you must be because of your short timeframe or the amount of risk (leverage) that you're carrying as a professional, the more demanding you must be of the tools at your disposal. As you can imagine, when options move to decimal pricing, the accuracy of the models will carry greater importance because, as of this writing, we still trade most options in minimum ticks of an eighth. So if I think an option is worth 5.50 and you think it's worth 5.61, there isn't any way for either of us to capture that difference. But with penny increments, disparities as small as a cent may be exploited.

Again, an investor with a one-year timeframe is probably not going to care if the software program he or she is using has mispriced an option by an eighth or quarter. But when it comes to me or one of my traders on the floor, we must have the utmost of confidence in the models that we're using. Particularly when trading activity on the floor is fast and furious, floor traders must rely on the integrity of the options-pricing model that they're using to make a market. Otherwise, it's like sailing into a rock-strewn harbor without out a map and channel markers.

But you can't let the software alone, make your decisions. As I tell my traders and the customers of my brokerage firm and as I teach in my seminars, before you place a trade, you should be able to graph what your trade looks like before you establish it. You must be able to give a pictorial representation of the risks you face.

For example, if you're buying a call, you have to know that your risk looks like an inverted hockey stick (Figure 9.1).

The call purchase means you have a defined risk upon entering the trade, which is the premium you paid for the call. Your option should start appreciating in value once the stock or index trades above the strike price. The upside is virtually unlimited.

Or, a back-spread trade, in which you are long more options than you are short, looks like a "V" when you chart the risk scenario (Figure 9.2).

With a graph, you can visualize and interpret various "what if" scenarios. You can see, clearly, how changes in volatility will impact the options position, or you'll see if time decay hurts or helps your position. You'll be able to see where your risk is, and whether your risk is adequately offset by your potential reward. Then, you can overlay all of your positions in the same graph, which gives you a clearer picture of the impact of market moves on your entire portfolio.

It's helpful that a computer can do that for you, and that there is software that will enable you to construct a graph of a trade with only a few keystrokes. But if you can't tell me, given five minutes

---

Figure 9.1   long call

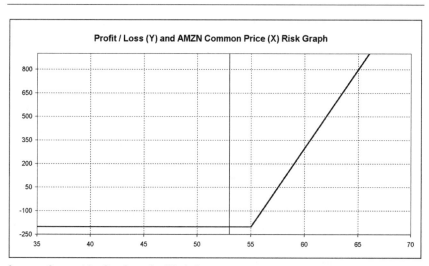

Source: Created by StockmarketWorkshop.com.

Figure 9.2   backspread

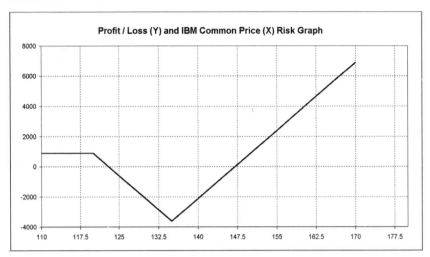

Source: Created by StockmarketWorkshop.com.

and a bunch of price points, where the risk is in a particular trade, then you don't fully understand what you're doing. If you don't know that if you sell a call spread, the risk is the difference between the two strike prices—the one you're selling and the one you're buying—then you shouldn't do that trade. Why? Because you can't rely on any computer program or software to make your decision for you.

You need to be able to show (yourself, at least) that the call you sold would make money until a certain price point, at which you begin to lose money—but not indefinitely because a protective call that you've purchased will flatten out your risk at another price point. Unless you're dealing with many complicated strategies, you should be able to show what your trades looks like. Otherwise, the risk is too dangerous, because you don't understand what you're getting into. Options, like any speculation, require that you do your homework. It's wonderful that your software program can generate a chart in three-dimensions with the colors of your choice. But if you haven't a clue as to how it arrived at that conclusion, then you're not ready to trade.

advisors

I decided to address advisors and brokers separately, even though the best brokers serve both functions. I'll address the brokerage services in a moment. So first, let's look at the independent advisory services that are available. They include well-known names in the options industry such as Bernie Shaffer, Larry McMillan, TheStreet.com, and 1010WallStreet.com, a Web site that I founded but no longer own. First, let's address the issue of why you would pay someone a fee for specific advice on the market. The only feasible answer is you believe their advice is valuable enough to spend money on.

In this field, there are registered investment advisors (RIAs). One example is Fidelity Insight, which is operated by former Fidelity fund manager Eric M. Kobren. This service tracks the performance of various Fidelity fund managers and, for a fee, will assist clients in jumping from fund to fund in hopes of capturing the best returns. Most RIAs will charge a fee that is normally a small percentage (such as 1 percent) of your assets for their services. The RIA designation is not an automatic endorsement of the value of their advice, but rather shows that they are subject to the oversight of the SEC and the NASD.

Other investment services are not RIAs, but rather publish market information and insight, either in a newsletter or on a Web site. Of these, advisors such as Bernie Shaffer, Larry McMillan, and 1010WallStreet.com operate under an interpretation of freedom of speech guaranteed by the First Amendment. As long as these advisors do not take commissions, they can print their opinions and analysis about broad market trends. The credentials of any advisor must include both intelligence and expertise in whatever is being analyzed. You have to have both. I certainly think of myself as a smart guy, but would you want me to tell you about airplane wings? I could read up on the subject, but I could never tell you enough about airplane wings to be considered an expert. But when it comes to options, my 20-year career as a trader should speak for itself.

Beyond that, you must ask yourself if this advisor's investment outlook, theory, and general style matches your own. If an advisor is too aggressive or too conservative for you, then chances are this is not the right fit for you. If you are interested in tech stocks and an advisor specializes in the financial sector, again, this is not the right advisor for you.

When you're trading or investing, give yourself as many tools as you can afford, but make sure you are going to use the services that you pay hard-earned money for. Just as software is going to help you, especially if you're watching multiple markets, so will one or more advisors. An expert advisor can give you insight into broad market trends or a particular sector that you're watching. But none of these advisors is going to enter a trade for you. Most of the Web-based advisory services will not buy and sell for your account. That's up to you. What a good advisor will do is give you insight into the market, and point out a few things that you may not have considered before. At 1010WallStreet.com, they remind you of key industry conferences, new product introductions, possible takeover targets based on unusual options activity, and in other words, expand your knowledge base and investment opportunities.

brokers

There was a time when your broker was next to your mother or your significant other on your telephone speed-dial. You talked to your broker as much as (if not more than) you talked with your best friend. Your broker kept you informed and, if you were a good customer, made sure you heard first. But that kind of service came at a price in the form of high commissions. Then came online brokerage and discounted commissions. Then brokerage commissions declined and at most firms, the services dwindled. If you're a sophisticated investor, you may not need hand-holding to place a trade. But there may be other services that you do need. Investors do not live by discount commissions alone.

There is a variety of brokerage services out there, to fit your particular investment demands. In some cases, you may want to have a broker act like an advisor, to assist you with your trades and, in some cases, to have the authority to execute a trade or adjust a position with your permission if you're not available. Having that watchdog for your position can be invaluable. What if you're a doctor in surgery when the market moves 300 points? Or you're a real estate agent who's in a million-dollar closing and you can't watch your position during the trading day.

Maybe you don't need help constructing a trade. But you might very well need someone to watch your position for you and alert you by pager or even adjust your position for you. Our goal when we established our brokerage firm, PTI Securities & Futures, was to give customers access to experienced floor traders who understand option strategies and how to execute spread transactions and deliver full service at discount prices. Services offered by us and other good full-service brokers is invaluable, especially when you're trading index options, such as OEX.

As American-style options, OEX can be exercised at any time. But unlike an equity option that involves the purchase or delivery of stock, OEX is exercised for cash. That's an important consideration if you're out of touch with the market or out of contact with your broker. Say you're on a plane. You're short OEX options and the calls that you sold are going to be exercised against you into cash. A bigger problem is if these OEX were used to cover stock holdings. Without the protection of the OEX options, you're suddenly naked long the stock in a market that could be opening down the next day.

For example, let's say I did an OEX bull call spread, buying the 870 calls and selling the 890 calls. On Monday of expiration week, we'll say the index is at 875. On Tuesday, it's up to 880 and on Wednesday it's at 890. That's great for me because now my spread is in-the-money. On Thursday, it's at 910, and the 890 calls that I sold are also in-the-money. While the 870 calls I bought are doing very well, I do face the very real possibility of the buyers of the 890 calls exercising their option.

Now comes the tricky part, at least for American-style options like the OEX. Every day, there is a 15-minute gap when stocks stop trading but the stock index futures pit is still open. This gap is between 3 P.M. and 3:15 P.M. Central. On the close, the OEX traders, who all hedge their positions throughout the day with S&P 500 futures, pay even closer attention to the futures. Now, let's say that at 3 P.M. the S&P cash market is at 1501 and futures are at 1505. Then the cash market closes. At this point, OEX and S&P 500 cash have all closed higher on the day.

But this 15-minute window is a time of unpredictability. At 3:05 P.M. Central, S&P futures are up to 1507. Then at 3:08 P.M., disappointing earnings are reported for some large S&P stocks. S&P

futures begin to decline, and by 3:10 are at 1498 and at 3:11 are at 1495. Let's take a look at this scenario: OEX options rose and S&P cash was higher, but S&P futures traded lower after the cash price of the OEX was pegged at 3:00. And just before the close of the CBOE, the buyer of your 890 OEX options had exercised the calls for $20 per contract in cash.

Meanwhile, you were long OEX options from 870. Without exercising them, you are naked long these calls the next day, when the decline in the S&P futures market could foreshadow a drop in the overall market and, of course, the OEX. Maybe OEX calls will be down from 910 to 900 or below. With a discount broker, you would have been on your own to monitor that trade. But with a full-service broker, you may have had the backup to watch your position if you were unavailable.

My obvious bias toward full-service brokers aside, it's important for retail customers to understand what they're getting with any broker they pick, either a discount firm or a traditional, full-service house. One consideration is how your trade is executed. A full-service broker may have its own brokers on the floors of the four major options exchanges. Or it may use a network of independent brokers across the various trading floors, as PTI does. However, some of the largest full-service brokerages have little or no representation on any of the trading floors. Unfortunately, the unwitting investor is being charged full price for a lower level of service than many discounters offer. In other words, just like the cheapest discount brokers, some firms farm out their option execution to one or more firms, which can affect the time and price at which your trades are executed.

Let's take an example of a discount firm we'll call "Gee-Whiz Trade," which clears through New York Brokerage House. But New York Brokerage House doesn't have its own options brokers on the floor. Instead, they farm it out to somebody else. That firm could then, in turn, pass it on to yet another party for execution.

With that kind of chain, is there any wonder why the customer who is used to the instant-gratification of trading stock on the phone is frustrated by the execution in options? The customer sees the option he or she wants is bid at $4\frac{1}{4}$ and offered at $4\frac{1}{2}$. But by the time the order hits the trading pit, the price has moved, and their brokerage blames the market makers. Let me assure you, my peers at the CBOE, AMEX, PCX, and PHLX would like nothing more than to trade with you. We aren't dodging your orders when they hit the pit. With seat leases at $5,000 to $16,000 per month, you can bet we seize every opportunity to trade. If your broker can't get you fills you are happy with, try someone else. You will probably find that the firm you were dealing with was the problem, not the market makers.

Professionals always want to trade against the public. Think about it. I'm standing in the pit where a broker is offering options, and the market is 4¼ bid and 4½ offered. In a split second I can yell, "Buy 'em," and execute the trade at the market. The public investor can never keep up with that pace. At best, the retail investor's order takes 10 to 15 seconds to travel from the broker to the trading pit. Any time longer than my quick, twitch response means speed is on the side of the professional, at least for the first few seconds, which is all we need. Multiply that by thousands of public orders per day, and you can see why brokerages are willing to pay for order flow just for the chance to trade against it.

On the floor, the market is incredibly fast. We're watching the buyers and the sellers in the market. All the trades are visible; it's no secret where the market is trading.

At home, retail customers are looking at delayed quotes, which is a snapshot of where the market was 20 minutes ago. Even with live quotes, it's still a slow-motion scenario. By the time a customer keys in an order to buy 10 Micron January 140 calls for 3½, the market could have moved. I may be able to buy those calls for a fraction lower, say 3¼. Now the market is 3¼ bid and offered at 3½. Now when that customer order to buy at 3½ reaches the floor, everybody wants to sell at that price. If you're the most aggressive, you'll get that trade.

The professional trader who is buying order flow wants to sell on the offer and buy on the bid, but he doesn't want to have the cost of exchange seats and other overhead to deal with. He'll do his trading electronically, with a computer to offset his trades or hedge with stock. He's not obligated to make a market. Rather, he'll match the National Best Bid and Offer (NBBO) quote. To play that game, though, you need to have thousands of trades to make a teeny here, an eighth there, and the occasional quarter, to replicate the scalping that we do on the floor. That's only possible if you buy customer order flow.

Trading against someone who has a different timeframe from you can be profitable and is how payment for order flow came into being. Simply put, payment for order flow began on the stock side of the world when smart folks figured out that if you could filter out the professionals and just trade against the investing public, your number of winning trades and potential profits were larger. Firms began looking to pay for this advantage by selecting the most likely retail outlets, such as most discount brokers, and paying $0.01 to $0.02 per share for the opportunity to trade against this uninformed order flow. If the average spread is ⅛ ($0.12 per share) between the bid and the offer, the firm buying the order flow would expect to capture part of that differential on a majority of its trades. As you can imagine, paying $0.01 for something you could make even $0.0625 (¹⁄₁₆) can be a very nice business indeed. In fact, Knight Trimark (NITE) built a multibillion-dollar business around the concept.

As of this writing, payment for order flow is just becoming a reality in the options world. Like most of my competitors, I loathe the idea, but realize it is coming whether I endorse it or not. Therefore, we have engaged in a soft-dollar exchange of our massive stock trades for option order flow, but I know the next step for us will be outright buying of option orders from brokerage houses. As you can imagine, the customer rarely benefits from schemes such as payment for order flow, but as long as firms are looking for additional ways to squeeze more profit from their customers, it will continue. What the customer must ask, therefore, when choosing a broker, is how are trades executed? Does your brokerage sell the orders? Does it have its own brokers or a network of brokers? Does your order get passed on to one or more firms before it's executed?

Most importantly, does your broker know about options? So many times we hear in seminars from retail investors who say their brokers are great with stocks, but are either not knowledgeable about options or try to talk them out of using options.

There is room for all types of brokers in this marketplace, the discount firms and the full-service houses. And there may be room for both types of brokers to handle your portfolio, the discount firms for the easy trades that you're the most comfortable with and the full-service firms for the trades that require assistance or extra monitoring.

education

As with every other tool we've discussed in this chapter, the amount of education that you need depends on how active and sophisticated an investor you are or intend to be. One place to start is the options exchanges, themselves, which have outreach programs for retail investors. The CBOE, for example, has educational information on its Web site and also offers periodic seminars on options. In fact, the CBOE's programs are the crème de la crème, which is not just my hometown bias. Ask anybody who has gone to an options seminar, and they'll tell you that the CBOE has some of the best offerings. Although they are free, they cram a ton of useful information into their two-and-a-half-hour programs.

In addition, many brokerage houses host seminars for their customers. So if you have a large account at Schwab, Smith Barney, or Fidelity, you might inquire about upcoming options programs. Our firm, PTI, holds several seminars a year in conjunction with the CBOE.

Those free, introductory option seminars are a great place to start. Then you enter the realm of the paid seminars, which may cost several thousand dollars in tuition. One word of advice, you should be very serious about trading options before you plunk down thousands of dollars for a course. Among the various course offerings are seminars through 1010WallStreet.com or StockmarketWorkshop.com.

At our seminars, one of the most frequent comments heard is, "If I knew this six months ago, I'd be a lot richer today!" (Or, "I'd be a lot less poor if I knew this six months ago.")

The first step on the education trail does not have to be a $3,000 seminar. You can certainly begin with a book (like this one!) and a free seminar to serve as an introduction. But the more you invest in your education, the more you will learn. And, the better prepared you are going into that $3,000 seminar, the more you will absorb. Consider too that the $3,000 you'll pay for a two-day seminar will yield far more useable material at a far less cost than, say, going back to school for a specialized graduate degree in derivatives and trading. Many courses also include videos, audio cassettes, and other support materials to help you long after the seminar is over. Some courses also allow you to retake the course for no addition cost.

Remember, if you eschew the seminar route, you'll still be paying for your education in the form of trial-and-error mistakes and commissions on unprofitable or low-profit trades.

Many of those who come to our seminars are already investing, and some have high net worth, often tied up in one or two stocks. If they're what we've described previously as "single-stock millionaires," they may be afraid to diversify their holdings because of capital-gain considerations or because they are so emotionally tied to the stock they can't possibly sell. Or perhaps they just believe so firmly in the prospects of the company that they want to hold on. With this scenario, they want to use options to protect their single-stock holdings, or to begin speculating in other issues.

These retail investors may be a customer of a large brokerage firm, but their broker may not be knowledgeable about options. Thus, the customer is left on his or her own when it comes to options education. Luckily, there are plenty of alternatives out there, starting with the exchanges themselves.

Whatever seminar you choose, make sure that you are a discerning consumer. What is the background of the instructors? Are they market practitioners, or are they just on the speaking circuit? How long have they been trading? What kinds of materials are included in the course? Will you receive a big, thick manual, or just some photocopied graphs and charts? Does the course include video and audiotapes that you can use as a refresher?

You don't need to jump into options as a novice by signing up for every service and enrolling in every course. But if you're going to be a serious investor, able to employ a variety of strategies to protect your stock portfolio and make profitable trades, you have to make sure you have ample resources at your disposal.

In every profession, there are the proverbial tools of the trade. Options are no different. And the more you know how to use the tools, the more skilled you'll be.

chapter 10

what changes,
what stays the same

The debate still rages about the New Economy versus the Old Economy. At one moment, the high-tech New Economy reigns, leaving the Old Economy to languish with price-to-earnings (P/E) ratios that are as low as its perceived growth prospects. In the next moment, the New Economy is deflating as quickly as a ruptured balloon, while investors seek refuge in company names that are more familiar and tested by time. But for all the talk about a new paradigm, there is one thing that hasn't changed. The markets are very much the same today as they were when I first came to the trading floor nearly 20 years ago.

Fund managers, institutions, and the public alike, still react the same way to various market stimuli. In other words, the herd mentality prevails.

When the herd is scared, there is panic. When the herd is confident, there is euphoria. These polar-opposite attitudes tend to accentuate the market moves, from oversold to overbought, and back again. When a few members of the herd go in a new direction (and get publicity in the process) you can expect a stampede to follow.

The aspects of the herd mentality—and the opportunities and the challenges it presents—still dominate today's market place. What is different, and will become increasingly so, is the impact of technology. Whether you're talking about the world economy or the trading floor, technology continues to make inroads, changing the pace, the dynamics, and the participation. I have seen a lifetime of change in my 20-year career as a trader. We have gone from the dark ages of paper and pencil to the new age of hand-held computers that can send an order to the New York Stock Exchange via an infrared communications signal.

Knowing what stays the same and what changes dramatically will help traders like me and investors like you to navigate the terrain ahead. Who knows what comes next! In late 1999 and early 2000, we have seen virtually unprecedented market gyrations. There is no indication that at least for the short-term this is going to ease. The market, once enamored with the Internet, is now running from anything dot.com and wringing its collective hands about its old foe, inflation. Is the sky falling or just getting cloudy?

It's times like these that call for perspective. As we said in previous chapters, nothing goes up continuously. Remember trees don't grow to the sky. Corrections are to be expected and, by and large, they are healthy for the market. But in between the corrections and the rallies there are going to be uncertain times.

That's when it's important to remember that the market does, indeed, move like a herd. (Think of a cattle drive from some old Western movie, with a few thousand longhorns on the move . . .) In first-quarter 2000, there was an incredible fertile valley for the herd to graze in called Nasdaq. And there was this Death Valley called Dow Jones. Every week you could track the money flowing into the high-tech, Internet, and mid-cap Nasdaq stocks. A significant portion of this money was flowing out of more traditional value stocks.

There were various explanations for these phenomena: A company like Gillette can come up with only so many varieties of razor blades (amazingly, they even followed an old Saturday Night Live skit and produced a "triple-trac" razor). Shares of consumer-product titan Procter & Gamble (P&G) dropped by more than a third—falling by $27\frac{7}{16}$ to 60—when it said on March 7, 2000, its growth would not be what Wall Street had expected.

P&G is a classic Old Economy stock, and can sell just so much shampoo and deodorant given its market penetration, a maturing marketplace, and a slow-growing population. P&G fell out of favor (at least for the moment), and Wall Street took its money and went elsewhere to play.

For a while in 1999 and early 2000, the world turned its back on these kinds of companies, the type that Warren Buffett would buy—Coca-Cola, Disney, consumer durable manufacturers, and insurance companies, just to name a few. Illustrating this trend, Warren Buffett said in his annual letter to shareholders of Berkshire Hathaway (his firm that invests in a variety of other companies) that 1999 was "the worst absolute performance of my tenure . . . and compared to the S&P, the worst relative performance as well" (The Motley Fool.Com—Fool Plate Special, Buffett's Worst Year at Berkshire).

At the same time, the Nasdaq rose some 380 percent in the 18 months from October 1998 through early March 2000.

Then the bottom dropped out.

The herd that has been gorging itself on the green pasture of Nasdaq stocks, developed a severe case of indigestion. And, at the risk of stretching a metaphor too far, the purge began. Nasdaq sold off hard. The Nasdaq Composite on April 14 had its largest-ever point loss—dropping by 356.74 to 3,320.04, down 9.7 percent. This followed a 286.27-point (7.1 percent) drop on April 12, a 258.25-point (5.8 percent) decline on April 10, and a 349.15-point (7.6 percent) fall on April 3.

The Dow Industrials, meanwhile, fell 616.23 points, or 5.6 percent, to 10,307.32 on April 14. Wall Street pundits said the market collapse was the worst ever since the 1987 Crash. But the effects could be more catastrophic because more Americans own stock today—an estimated four or five out of 10, compared with two out of 10 in 1987 (*LA Times:* Dow Suffers Worst-Ever Point Drop of 616; Nasdaq Falls 355).

The reason for the decline was the specter of inflation in the closely watched economic reports. That triggered panicked selling across the market, but most acutely in the high-flying NASDAQ market, which lost 25 percent or 1,125 points in one week.

The investment scene changes—dramatically. In late 1999 and early 2000, I watched the flow of money—and not just speculative capital—into Nasdaq stocks. More individual 401(k) plans had been allocating capital to Nasdaq stocks with the hope that strong double-digit percent gains would continue, outperforming the S&P 500 Index-type stocks. The market was hungry to the point of being insatiable for any stock that has at least four letters in its symbol. (Nasdaq stocks have four or more letters in their symbols, while New York Stock Exchange issues have one, two, or three letters.)

Fund managers were following suit, knowing that their investors would be looking for those same kinds of returns. It's like going to a tailor and saying that you don't want cuffs on your pants. If the tailor keeps coming out with cuffs, he's going out of business—and you'll be going to a new tailor. It was the same consumer-is-right attitude seen among retail investors, which was prompting money managers to shift out of value and into growth by the droves. If they didn't, they feared being abandoned by individual investors.

The herd had been on a feeding frenzy when it came to a variety of Nasdaq stocks. Rather than just dot.coms, investors were looking for companies that will provide information for the Internet, particularly in business-to-business applications. Just consider the hoopla surrounding 3Com's Palm Computing spin-off. Shares of Palm, which is the world leader in personal digital assistants or hand-held devices, were priced at $38 a share, then opened at $145 and ran up to a high of $165 on the first day of trading, before closing up 57$\frac{1}{16}$ at 95$\frac{1}{16}$. (TheStreet.Com: Palm's Stock Soars on First Day, while 3Com Dives, March 2, 2000).

Then came April 2000, and the Nasdaq rocket ship appeared to run out of fuel. On April 14, the biggest losses were seen in sectors such as Internet, wireless and biotechnology which had been the darlings of Wall Street's beauty queen contest and had posted the strongest gains in 1999. Even blue chips like General Electric and IBM and widely held stocks like Wal-Mart were not immune from the April 14 sell-off.

That purge forced mutual-fund managers to switch into the selling mode, as they had to raise cash for anticipated redemptions from their own panicked fund investors. That, in turn, created an opportunity for bottom-fishers to snap up some under-priced stocks. But keep in mind the trader's adage: bottom pickers get stinky fingers.

While the technology sector was, at least on April 14, 2000, out of favor, there is no doubt that technology will lead this economy. And while inflation fears may induce the Federal Reserve to raise Interest rates to slow down the U.S. economy, there is no denying the inextricability of the Internet in our businesses and in our lives.

Thus, even when the herd makes panic moves, these sudden changes in direction will produce opportunities for the more clear-headed. For example, on January 6, 2000, Lucent Technologies, which makes telecom and networking equipment, said it expected to report fiscal first-quarter earnings of between 36 and 39 cents a share, compared with previous analyst expectations of 54 cents. The stock fell 3⅜ to $69 a share on that day, then fell more than $16 a share more in after-hours trading (ZDNet Inter@ctive Investor, "Lucent Sees 1Q Shortfall," January 6, 2000).

When I saw this stock, which had been trading at $80 a share, decline to $50 a share, I bought some for my daughter, Tristen (now a year-old investor!). Why? Because I like buying stocks on panics and being a contrarian investor. When the market panics, the result is usually overselling. Lucent's price recovered to around $70 before the technology purge on Nasdaq. Not a bad return on a buying opportunity created by Wall Street's herd mentality. But panics, as we've seen time and time again (and will undoubtedly see countless more times) bring opportunities for buyers willing to withstand some near-term volatility.

For me, a trader who thrives on volatility, I know that a market panic is like 6,000 people trying to get out of one exit door when someone screams, "FIRE!" It's going to get ugly. When those fund managers, trying to hold the loyalty of a fickle investing public, see an earnings shortfall, they don't want that company's stock in their portfolios. Prices drop 20 percent or 30 percent as sellers rush to unload their holdings. That's a time when a buyer like me considers getting involved. Granted, I might bet on the upside with options. But Lucent, to me, was a different situation that enticed me to be a buyer, particularly on behalf of my daughter who has a lifetime of investing ahead of her. As a computer networking stock, Lucent is still in a growth sector of the market as far as I'm concerned. Buying in on a drop like this was like being at the blackjack tables and knowing there is an abundance of face cards in the deck. I may lose some hands, but the odds have moved solidly in my favor and now is the time to increase the size of my bets.

There will be more opportunities in the future for companies with technologies like flat-screen picture tubes and smaller, more powerful semiconductors, than those companies that make products for a mature consumer market. And in a global economy, there are worldwide opportunities in technology that are just being realized. In a rugged terrain like Finland or remote locations like some areas of Mexico, Africa, South America, and China, wireless communication will be easier to employ than the hard-wired variety, presenting a lucrative market to some technology companies (MOT, NOK, ERICY, QCOM, etc.). On the other hand, just how much soap can the world buy?

That's why when P&G took its plunge earlier in 2000, people like me were not diving into a great value. Rather, I considered this stock to have growth prospects that were less than the overall market just because of its product niche. That scenario still favors the technology sector. Technology, I am convinced, is not just the proverbial wave of the future. It is the backbone of the present. I don't have to look any farther than the trading floor to see the evidence.

When I began trading there were about 80 stocks on the CBOE floor and no indexes. I had to get in about six o'clock in the morning to do two-and-a-half hours worth of analysis because our computers were so slow. I would go to the floor with stacks of computer printouts showing the price matrixes of the stock options I was trading. If IBM was at $80 a share, I'd flip through the pages to see the $75 calls were worth 7⅛ and had an 80 delta, or that the $80 calls were worth $5/18$ and had a 52 delta.

With every ⅛ or ¼ move in the stock, I would have a column to find values on my printout on a piece of paper. If the stock moved $3, I'd have to sort through a stack of paper a few inches think. As I traded more and more stocks, adding issues like Starbucks to my usual activity in IBM, the stack got bigger.

At that time, it was against the rules of the exchange to have a computer in the trading pit. The only device that was allowed was a calculator. This, the exchange felt, would make the marketplace a level playing field. The only advantage you had then, presumably, was your own wits. But upstairs, traders had as much computer power at their disposal as they could get—although in those early days it was a far cry from the fast, agile technology of today. What finally brought the computer to the trading floor was the indisputable fact that there were more stocks than traders to efficiently handle them.

The CBOE went from 80 to 500 to 1,000 stocks and then to 2,900, but the number of memberships did not increase. In fact, the number of memberships on U.S. options exchanges has been reduced significantly while the number of issues has grown geometrically. In the late 1970s, the CBOE bought the Midwest Options Exchange during the first round of consolidation. The CBOE negotiated to absorb is cross-town rival with the caveat that the memberships would expire 10 years later.

The next round of exchange consolidation occurred when I was on the board of directors of the CBOE. The New York Stock Exchange (NYSE) decided it no longer needed to support its fledgling options exchange, as the threat of side-by-side trading of stocks was no longer the biggest threat to the world's largest marketplace; electronic communications networks (ECNs) were. So, the NYSE put its options exchange, the smallest of the then five exchanges, up for bid. The CBOE won the right to absorb the 165 option classes, which included the likes of Chase Manhattan Bank, Maytag, Campbell's Soup, and Quantum Hard Drive. The CBOE paid $5 million in cash, and created a stream of payments to the NYSE members that would run seven years, until April 30, 2004. The CBOE also built the newest, most modern home for the NYSE directly under its main trading floor. True to their options roots, when the clock strikes midnight on April 30, 2004, the 75 memberships on the CBOE/NYSE option floor will expire. Thus, the net effect in the overall options market place is a reduction in the number of market makers, although the number of stocks with listed options continues to build at an astonishing rate.

What does that mean? You don't need computer analysis and theoretical values to figure that out. More option classes and fewer traders meant traders had to become active in more issues. If you used to handle two or three stocks, you were then trading five or ten, if you were really a great trader. Today, I think our average trader handles 20 or 30 stocks because of the assistance of the computer. Gone are the days of the stacks of computer printouts and largely manual analysis. The average trader goes to the floor with handheld Pentium-powered workstations with either infrared communication capabilities or a connection to a wireless LAN. It's got a stylus for its touchscreen. These handheld computers with touchscreens allow traders to report their transactions almost instantaneously, with just a few taps of the stylus. Further, these handheld computers also allow traders to send a stock order directly to the New York Stock Exchange, Nasdaq, or a myriad of ECNs. With one tap on my screen, I can hedge almost instantaneously while keeping track of my options positions.

What has made this possible are the wireless LAN and infrared communication devices that the CBOE has not only allowed but pioneered. All around the trading floor are little black discs—miniature satellite receivers that these handheld devices can "talk" to throughout the day. Plus, we have the ability to access the NYSE's SuperDot, InstiNet, Island, Archipelago, BRUT, or the electronic Nasdaq marketplace via SelectNet.

So when our traders are standing in the middle of an options trading pit, one part of their job is completely different from what I experienced in the old days of the early 1980s. And part is exactly the same. They are still standing in the pit, staring at the price screens and contemplating "what if" scenarios in their heads. They remember from our morning meeting sessions that, for example, we think it's better to be a seller of CMGI options and a buyer of AOL (or whatever the analysis, depending upon the day). And, just as when I began trading, the SEC demands that we not only trade our opinions but also make a two-sided market. You may want to be a seller of a particular option ahead of a company's earnings. But if someone comes into that pit with a sell order, you're suddenly a buyer.

"What's the market for March 150 calls?" somebody yells out.

"3¼ . . . 3⅜," the market-maker replies, giving the requisite bid and ask prices, respectively.

"Sold," the broker says. The price moves based upon the supply and demand for those options, just as prices have been moving on the whims and actions of buyers and sellers since the birth of commerce.

As a market maker on the floor, you're hedging your position a fraction of a second later. And good traders will remember (just as they did when I started out and before that too) what the major players around them have been doing. They may recall, for example, that the Merrill Lynch broker was bidding just below the market price for a call some 20 minutes ago, or that a Schwab broker was offering puts above the market an hour ago. A good floor trader has a mind like a good computer, able to multitask, trading and hedging his or her own position while keeping track of what's happening around the pit. Those resting bids and offers may be the quickest, safest hedge once the market starts to move and the trader that remembers that those orders are there is in a better position to lock in profits, or limit losses when the stuff hits the fan!

Speed is just as important as it was 20 years ago. When a broker is looking for a market, you had better be the one to make the best market first. Remember from our earlier chapter that the broker is obligated to trade with the trader that makes the best market, highest bid and lowest offer, first. Brokers still don't disclose how many options they want to buy or sell, but anybody worth his salt has to know that a big institutional house like Goldman Sachs won't be doing a 10-lot trade.

Those are the same skills and nuances that I dealt with 20 years ago, when I first put on a trading jacket. What has changed the game, though, is the computer. This transition in floor trading, I believe, isn't completed yet. The final outcome, I believe, will be an electronic market place, ultimately replacing or at least replicating the trading floor as we now know it. That will demand some major changes at a brick-and-mortar exchange such as the CBOE.

Before that transition is complete, however, there will be other moves toward electronic trading. One is a new exchange, the International Securities Exchange (ISE) which, as I'll discuss later in this chapter, may present enough of a competitive challenge to prompt a change in the CBOE's own structure. Additionally, there is a rise of electronic communications networks, which act like an electronic order-matching system. That's where I hope my latest product—a computerized trading tool known as iTradem—fits in.

Phil Barnett, Craig Hellman, Tom Haugh, and I initially created the handheld iTradem to make the floor trader's job easier. On the floor, it acts as a robotic assistant, keeping track of positions and movements of other options, reporting trades to the exchange, and even facilitating automatic hedging. iTradem processes each option trade and, if the trader has set the device on auto-hedge®, iTradem will generate a marketable buy or sell order to the NYSE or Nasdaq market to hedge the delta exposure the trader just took on. On the Internet, iTradem.com offers electronic access to the options market.

Here's how iTradem works on the floor. Let's say I'm trading Sun MicroSystems (SUNW), AOL, and CMGI—very active issues that might trade 100,000 or 120,000 contracts a day. At the same time, I'm trading another technology issue, say, Spyglass, which might trade only 1,000 contracts a day. Stocks that are trading smaller volume may be more difficult to keep track of because of the attention commanded by the more active issues.

As I'm trading these active issues, I can use iTradem to report my trades to the CBOE, calculate my hedging position, and execute a stock order on the New York Stock Exchange or the Nasdaq. Further, this device, which has been used on the CBOE since April 1999, also acts as my "eyes" in markets that I'm not actively monitoring.

Say, while I'm busy trading AOL or CMGI, unbeknownst to me Spyglass rises $3. Even though my attention is elsewhere, I don't have to miss out on that move. Rather, iTradem, acting as a robotic trading assistant, can be programmed to keep track of movements in a particular stock. So, for example, if Spyglass $60 calls move to a target of 3⅛, iTradem could generate a sell signal and in manual mode, send an alert to the screen to alert the trader, or in auto-hedge® generate a hedge in the underlying security.

The iTradem device allows you to preprogram your trading parameters to return to a market neutral position. Maybe you don't want to be long or short any more than 500 shares, or perhaps 1,000 shares. When you reach that limit, iTradem will generate a buy or sell order (depending if you're long or short) and transmit it to the New York Stock Exchange via the SuperDot system or to the Nasdaq through SelectNet or one of the ECNs that dominate trading on the Nasdaq.

We believe iTradem will not only find a place on the floor, but on the Web, with the Internet-version iTradempro.com, enabling us to offer this product to the professional off-the-floor audience and, in time, to the broader retail market. One of the CBOE traders who uses iTradem on the floor, would dial into the service via the internet from his vacation home in Michigan. With iTradem he could oversee every trade from his trading group, hedging their positions.

Moreover, I believe iTradem.com will assist active retail traders, speeding their options orders to a broker via the Internet or a stock order to any of the ECNs or the SuperDot system. In time, I believe iTradem, itself, will become an ECN, perhaps even the first options ECN, allowing orders to be viewed in a central marketplace where anyone with an iTradem screen—whether it's a trader on the floor or a retail investor in Dubuque, Iowa, or Naples, Florida—can see the bids or offers. We believe this product will significantly broaden the number of possible respondents to an order, instead of the limited number of market makers on the trading floor.

The electronic in-roads made by iTradem and competing products will speed a process that is bogged down in too many intermediaries. Today, a customer order goes to an upstairs broker who may or may not have direct access to the trading floor, who then routes it to a floor broker, who executes the trade, and then transmits the confirmation back up the food chain. Soon, the customer will be able to bypass the upstairs broker and direct his or her order through a brokerage site (which will make sure they have sufficient capital and paperwork on file), to an ECN like iTradem.com for execution.

I believe ECNs for options will succeed, just as they have in stocks, because of the narrowing of spreads that will likely occur as a result of the increased access to the marketplace. Stock ECNs helped bring about a more efficient market in Nasdaq, with narrower bid/ask spreads, which empowers the individual investor. A faster, more efficient market will lead to an explosion in options volume as well. Volume is already picking up. On April 18, 2000, daily options volume set a new record at the four U.S. exchanges, with 4,812,712 contracts traded. The previous record had been set on January 21, 2000, at 4,646,849 contracts.

There is both a need and demand for options among retail investors who, as we've seen, are invested in the market through retirement plans, mutual funds, and speculative investments. But options will lag the growth of stocks until the same online access enjoyed via Charles Schwab, E*TRADE, Ameritrade, Datek, and all the rest spreads to options.

The growth of the future is going to occur when the online investor can trade options using the Internet, to get their orders to the floor in a millisecond and back again in a millisecond. I believe this will lead to growth in options volume that will parallel what we've seen in equities, from 2.5 million options traded each day at the four U.S. exchanges to 10 million contracts per day. That will be accompanied by a growing realization among retail investors that, instead of just trading stocks, they can define their risk ahead of time using options. By coupling better risk parameters with a fast, accessible and responsive online marketplace, the options market is poised for growth unlike any we've experienced thus far.

The reason this is happening is, simply, the world is a faster place. And the marketplace is far more dynamic than it was 5 or

10 years ago. Retail participation, both as speculative money and 401(k) and other retirement investment, has burgeoned. When I began trading, the New York Stock Exchange did about 50 million shares a day; 55 million was a big day. Today, 50 million shares would signal a dull opening hour of trade. On a daily basis, 800 million to 1 billion shares trade on the New York Stock Exchange and, as of this writing, the Nasdaq has had some 2-billion-share days.

The growth experienced in those markets directly reflects the increased speed and the greater access. This is not just a professional arena any more. The world has come to the market, and the markets are opening up to the world.

Whether you're trading stocks through a full-service brokerage like, PTI Securities & Futures, or a discount cyber brokerage such as Datek, CyberTrade, Tradescape, or iTradem.com, customers—not just professional traders—can get to the New York Stock Exchange, Nasdaq, or ECNs via the Internet (albeit with a brokerage in between). All you need is an account. Once you execute your order online, a computer program at the brokerage firm confirms that you have enough money in your account to execute that trade. Then, any of the above named brokers will speed your order to the destination you thought provided the best price. They cost slightly more than the deep discount brokers that sell your order flow to firms like Knight Trimark (NITE) or Maddoff, but the savvy customers know the pennies saved can cost 10 to 20 times as much as routing your order to the best bid or offer yourself.

This is a far cry from the marketplace of the 1960s and 1970s, when customers called their brokers, who may have called back 10 minutes later with a trade. Now, transactions at discount brokers take 10 to 15 seconds without a live broker and half that time for the top cyber brokerages.

The derivatives markets and options haven't grown at the speed seen in stocks. Granted, overall option volume grew by nearly 60 percent last year. That looks great on the surface, but not when you realize it took us 20 years to get there! Just 10 years ago, we were doing 600,000 or 700,000 options a day at the CBOE. Now with three or four times the number of stocks, we do double the amount of volume. The reason is simple: The customer doesn't have the same fast access to the options market as they have in equities. For retail options trades, it's still much the 1970s model seen in equities.

Since options are a derivative of stocks, you might have expected that the growth in options trading would match, proportionally, the increase in stocks. So if the New York Stock Exchange went from 50 million shares a day to 1 billion a day, wouldn't you expect to see a 20-fold increase in options volume? The reason options have lagged stocks can be summed up with one phrase: electronic access.

The technology has been available for years, but the trading floors have not embraced it. That's not to say that every exchange member doesn't recognize that there's a value for the public to trade 10 times more often than they do, but the cost of new systems and turf battles have kept up barriers in hopes of preserving a time/place advantage of being a floor trader. That insular world of floor trading, however, is going to face some major competition. Enter the electronic options marketplace.

The International Securities Exchange (ISE) bills itself as the first entirely electronic options market in the United States. The ISE's application for registration as a national securities exchange was approved by the SEC in February 2000. Trading began in late June of 2000. The ISE eliminates the need for floor brokers since orders are inputted by broker/dealers directly into the electronic order book. I believe that the ISE will be able to move as rapidly as technology—and the SEC will let them, to establish and promote a fully electronic options exchange. Adding credibility to the ISE, several Wall Street giants—Goldman Sachs, Morgan Stanley Dean Witter, among others—have committed to be primary market makers. These firms and many other members of the ISE have made significant investments in ECNs to hedge their bets as to the future direction of Wall Street. (In fact, my partners and I have sold a majority of what is now known as the ECN Primex to Maddoff, Goldman Sachs, Merrill Lynch, Salomon Smith Barney, and JP Morgan.)

I contend that these name players are committing to the ISE to hedge their bets. If the ISE succeeds in attracting order flow away from traditional open outcry markets, the major participants can't be the last to the table. Even before the ISE and CBOE began to compete head-to-head, the traditional exchanges fired the first shot in the competitive battle by making significant reductions to the transaction costs they charge to nonmarket makers. In an interview with the Chicago Tribune, CBOE Chairman William Brodsky acknowledged that the ISE is a "serious competitor." But the CBOE is responding with increased trading capacity, as well as automatic execution for small trades and big block orders. Further, the CBOE has "reduced fees and we plan to keep them down," he added.

Eventually, firms executing orders for customers will be charged absolutely nothing. But traditional marketplaces like the CBOE have tremendous overhead to shoulder, and "zero" transaction costs will be a crushing burden. As of this writing, the market makers are bearing both sides, the fees formerly paid by the customer and the fees market makers have always paid. How much more can the open outcry markets pay and still have a worthwhile advantage? What's next? And even after the launch of the ISE, there still will be significant advantages to being market maker at the CBOE, including exemption from margin requirements on purchased or sold stock. There will be some time/place advantage of being at the CBOE. But we must remember that the options market, overall, is maintained to the benefit of the customer. That's why the impact of the ISE on the marketplace cannot be ignored. It is but one step that will lead to the continued evolution of this marketplace.

The launch of the ISE will presage a fundamental shift in the way the CBOE is run, eventually opening the door for the Exchange to act more as a broker. The brick-and-mortar exchanges and even the electronic ISE have a limited number of memberships. To be a truly open platform and an even playing field for professional and retail traders alike, there will have to be a marriage of a traditional trading floor—such as the CBOE—with an electronic screen-based system.

The option industry must embrace an Internet-based, electronic, and instant-access venue to welcome the new breed of on-line investor, who will add liquidity, capital, and depth to this marketplace. Then, as the marketplace becomes more liquid and more efficient, we'll see a narrowing of the spread between the bids and the offers and greater liquidity across the board. Retail customers will be able to trade with the market they can view on the screen as opposed to seeing where the market "was" on the screen. Too often, the prices at which retail trades are executed are different from the quote the customer saw on the screen. But with more liquidity and narrower bid/ask spread, there will be greater ease— or less "friction" as we say—to get into and out of the market. Instead of five market makers trading a particular issue, thanks to electronic access, some day there may be 500 or 5,000 traders who are interested in the orders.

My pro-customer perspective may set me apart from the traditional floor broker who wants to defend his or her turf. But, thanks to my involvement in our brokerage operations and the seminars that we participate in around the country, I'm on all three sides of the business. I manage a floor-trading/specialist operation on the floor of an exchange, so I know what works and what we need to be successful in the markets. It keeps me mindful of treating the customer right so they will want to return to our markets again. On the brokerage side, I know what the customers' complaints are and what their needs are. And I hear from the customers, themselves, not some hearsay or focus group telling the moderator what he wants to hear. When it comes to retail trading, customers are indeed concerned about commissions and they care about speed of execution. They know a lousy execution can cost them more than the next 10 commissions, so they want brokers who know the difference between a fast execution and a good one.

As an industry, we should care about open access to all participants. I'd rather see my traders making 10,000 trades a day for a one-sixteenth than 800 trades a day for half. I'd rather make a smaller increment on 10,000 trades than a bigger increment on 800. More liquidity will not increase my risk. Rather, it will give me a chance to spread my risk over more trades and the more volume, the more attractive it is for additional customers to enter the market.

Increased liquidity is the trader's friend since it increases the number of participants and the volume of trades being made. That's good protection against the dreaded "Roach Motel" position that you can check into but can't check out of (to paraphrase the insect-killer slogan).

But first, options must be demystified for people which was one purpose of writing this book. When I speak at seminars around the country, I invariably hear from the skeptics: "If options are so great, why doesn't everybody do this?" Maybe they've made their "millions" in real estate or some other field. They understand stocks, but with knowledge of options, could they do as well? The answer is yes, as long as the investors are committed to educating themselves. To understand options does take a little work. I remember well that during my first three months at the CBOE I was miserable because I couldn't fathom what was going on. It seemed to me to be a big secret because no one was teaching me.

Thankfully, that has changed. There are plenty of reputable places to learn about options. With more education, retail participation will increase. Then a natural market process will occur—the bid/ask spread will narrow, making a more competitive marketplace for all participants.

Those who take the time to educate themselves will find they have an important advantage in the marketplace. They're going to be miles ahead of those who just jump into buying and selling options without understanding time decay or knowing that volatility is the key component that moves the price of an option up or down. The educated investor/speculator will be attuned to when the market is nervous or overly confident. Those who take the time to study and prepare for this market will know that if you're buying options ahead of earnings, you're setting yourself up to lose, because that's the time that the premium—thanks to volatility—is as pumped up as it could be and if they really want to play directionally, they'd better be spreading.

Are options trading courses necessary? Not really. Do they accelerate the learning curve? Yes. You could read this book—or any other on options trading—and put yourself through the paces. But that would take you longer than if you sat through a two-day seminar. It also will depend on how active an investor you intend to be. For example, if you're driving to the grocery store, you don't need a Ferrari. A mini-van will do the job. But if you're going to the racetrack, you better have a racecar! By the same token, if you're going to buy a couple of options contracts a year, do you need to have the $3,000 software package? Probably not. But if you're going to trade actively or if you hope to support yourself by trading options or enhance your income substantially, then you better have all the tools at your disposal. You will need to understand far more than bull call spreads if you want to trade the market in all conditions. But if you're only going to trade in a bull market, you could rely on that one strategy.

There is no one strategy that is always going to work. Your trading arsenal needs to include the knowledge of bull call spreads, bear call spreads, iron butterflies, and so forth, because the market is constantly changing. What worked in the last six months won't work in the next six months. The market rotates in and out of sectors. It doesn't go straight up or straight down; there are always gyrations in between.

As retail investors continue on the options learning curve, this will create more and more demand for faster access to our market. Increasingly, the world is demanding instant gratification. You can buy everything from groceries to books to movie tickets online. As this retail audience becomes more acquainted with options, they are going to push for that kind of instant access.

Unfortunately, a retail options-trading is a much slower process. You have to go through a broker, who makes sure you're qualified to trade options. You have to have a margin account to trade options. You have to sign disclosure statements that you understand that options have a limited life. Admittedly, certain people shouldn't trade options, especially if the money they have to invest—if ever lost—would affect their livelihoods or their lifestyles.

As I've seen in the seminars I've given around the country, there are a growing number of retail investors who will readily come to the options marketplace, with an understanding that options allow you to define your risk when you enter your trade. Plus, the volatility of the overall equities market has also shown a clear case for options. Investors see hot stocks like eBay, Qualcom, and JDS Uniphase. They see Internet issues go from $40 to $300, and they want in on some of that action. But who can buy a $300 stock? Very few people. And the risk at lofty prices (as we've seen in the April 2000 "correction") is that the price could very well decline from $300 to $200 or $100 or even lower! With those prospects, most of us wouldn't want to buy 1,000 shares of a $100 stock to speculate.

With options, I could put on a trade and control 1,000 shares of a $100 stock for, $5,000, $10,000, or $20,000, depending on my timeframe. What does that mean? For one-tenth or one-twentieth of the money, you could put on a limited-risk trade and benefit in the same way as the risk-taker, who bought the stock at $300 a share and hoped it didn't tank.

Additionally, you can risk a lot less money and never have a margin call for buying and selling options. Once you've paid for the option, that's it. There is no margin call because of an adverse market move. That could be some very good news for Internet-stock investors who bought on margin and then faced some hefty margin calls in April 2000.

Options speculators are coming from the ranks of people who took a stab at day-trading stocks. They understand that, with options, they could still take advantage of the upside and downside potential of a stock—but with less risk and, thanks to leverage that's inherent in options, less capital requirements. This could be a part-time job or their next vocation. Or, perhaps they've been investors who held only mutual funds and now want to create a portfolio of their own using stocks. They realize, too, that options can be part of that strategy, hedging stock risk and participating in market moves with defined risk and less capital. That's the direction that options trading is taking, and the growth could be off the charts.

Several dynamic factors are coming together, from electronic exchanges to Internet access for speculators. Along the way, retail investors are becoming more comfortable with the idea of managing and trading their own money. Investors want to be empowered. They want to make their own investment picks and put their money on the line. But they don't—and can't—be exposed to unlimited risk. That's where options come in. With a little homework and dedication, investors can do this. The marketplace is changing, and the savvy ones among us will embrace the change, and welcome the new participants.

glossary

American style option: A call or put option contract that can be exercised at any time before the expiration of the contract. Most exchange listed options are American-style options.

assignment: When an option is exercised by the holder of that option, the option is assigned to the writer of that option. The writer of a call option is obligated to sell stock at the striking price of the call option; the writer of a put option is obligated to buy stock at the striking price of the put option.

at the money (ATM):   An option whose strike price is approximately the same as the current price of the underlying stock or future. For example, with IBM trading at $110, both the $110 call options and $110 put options are at the money.

bar chart: A bar chart is a price chart that depicts each trading period (month, week, day, hour, minute, etc.) as a vertical line (bar) ranging from the low price to the high price. Most bar charts also include two small hash marks on either side of the bar: one on the left that denotes the opening price and one on the right that denotes the closing price.

bear call spread: Net credit transaction. Maximum loss = Difference between the strike less the credit. Maximum profit = Credit. Requires margin.

bear put spread: Net debit transaction. Maximum loss = Debit. Maximum profit = Difference between the strikes less the debit. No margin required.

bear spread: A one-to-one spread established by selling a lower strike option series and buying a higher strike option series. Both option series are on the same underlying asset, are of the same type, and expire in the same month.

bearish: Expecting a decline in the market in general or a decline in the price of one particular asset.

bid: The highest price anyone is willing to pay for a security.

Black-Scholes: Fischer Black and Myron Scholes developed a formula to compute the values of European-style call and put options.

breakout: A breakout occurs when price bursts out of a congestion pattern like a trading range, flag, or pennant, or through some other support or resistance level. Sometimes breakout is used to describe upside moves only, while breakdown is used to describe downside moves.

bull call spread: Net debit transaction. Maximum loss = Debit. Maximum profit = Difference between strikes less the debit. No margin required.

bull put spread: Net credit transaction. Maximum profit = Credit. Maximum loss = Difference between the strikes less the credit. Required margin.

bull spread: A one-to-one spread established by buying a lower strike option series and selling a higher strike option series. Both options series are on the same underlying asset, are of the same type, and expire in the same month.

bullish: Expecting an increase in the market in general or an increase in the price of one particular asset.

butterfly spread: A long butterfly usually refers to the sale of two contracts on one option series and the purchase of one contract of a lower option series and one contract of a higher series. All contracts are on the same underlying asset, are of the same type, and expire in the same month. A long butterfly is also the result of combining a short straddle with a long strangle, or of combining a bull spread with a bear spread.

call: This option contract conveys the right to buy a standard quantity of a specified asset at a fixed price per unit (the striking price) for a limited length of time (until expiration).

candlestick chart: A price chart that uses rectangles that range from the opening price to the closing price of each trading session. The rectangle is dark (usually black) if the closing price is lower than the opening price (a down day), or light (usually white) if the close is higher than the open (an up day). Candlestick charts, which originated in Japan, are very similar to bar charts, although they predate them by a number of years. The high and low price extremes extend as vertical lines above or below these rectangles, forming "wicks" to the bodies of the "candles" represented by the rectangles. If the high and low of the day are identical to the open and close, no wicks will exist; conversely, if the open and close are the same price, no rectangle (body) will exist. Like bar charts, candlestick charts can be constructed on any timeframe.

close (or closing price):   The final trade price of the day (or other time period). In futures markets, the close is a representative price of the last minute of trading. In stocks, the close is the last recorded trade price.

closing transaction: Selling a previously purchased option or buying back a previously written option, effectively canceling out the position.

collateral: This is the legally required amount of cash of securities deposited with a brokerage to insure that an investor can meet all potential obligations. Collateral is required on investments with open-ended loss potential, such as writing naked calls or puts.

commission: This is the charge paid to a broker for transacting the purchase of the sale of stock, options, or any other security.

condor: A type of butterfly where instead of selling two options of the same series, two adjacent option series are sold. See **butterfly spread.**

congestion: A period of nontrending or sideways price movement, often in a narrow range (or an increasingly narrow range, as in the case of triangles and pennants). See **trading range.**

continuation pattern: Price action that interrupts a trend and implies a continuation of the trend (rather than a trend reversal) when the pattern is complete. Triangles, pennants, and flags are examples of continuation patterns.

contract size: The number of units of an underlying asset bought by exercising a call option or sold by exercising a put option. In the case of stock options the contract size is 100 shares of the underlying asset. In the case of options on futures contracts, the contract size is one underlying futures contract. In the case of index options, the contract size underlying asset is an amount of cash equal to parity times the multiplier. In the case of currency options, it varies.

correction: A shorter-term countertrend move. See also **pullback.**

cost of carry: The interest cost of holding an asset for a period of time. This is either the cost of borrowing funds to finance the purchase, in which case it is called the real cost, or it is the loss of income because funds are diverted from one investment to another, in which case it is called the opportunity cost.

covered: A short option is considered covered if there is a correspon-
ding offsetting position in the underlying security or another option
where no margin requirement results from the short option.

Cox-Ross-Rubenstein: John Cox, Stephen Ross, and Mark Rubenstein:
the inventors of the binomial option pricing model.

cup-and-handle pattern: A cup-and-handle is a reversal pattern formed
when a market makes a rounded bottom (the "cup"), begins to rally, pulls
back (the "handle"), and resumes the uptrend. See also **running cup-and-
handle.**

daily range: The difference between the high price of the day and the
low price of the day.

delta: The theoretical rate of change of an option's price relative to the
price of its underlying, times the contract multiplier. Delta is positive for
calls and negative for puts. An option with a delta of 25 will move 25 percent as much as the underlying asset. The delta of an option changes with
the distance of the strike from the underlying. Delta also measures the
equivalent unhedged position in the underlying asset.

divergence: Occurs when two markets, or a market and a benchmark
index, or a market and an indicator move in opposite directions. Common
examples include one stock index (e.g., the Dow Industrials) moving
higher while another stock index (e.g., the Dow Transports) moves lower,
or when price makes a new high and a momentum oscillator (like the RSI
or stochastics) makes a lower high. The implication is that by moving in
the opposite direction, the indicator (or secondary market or index) is not
confirming the price move in the market from which it is diverging. Corrections or reversals sometimes result in such circumstances.
    Note: Oscillators often produce multiple divergence signals in
strongly trending markets before the trend actually reverses; view such
signals conservatively. See **oscillator.**

double bottom: A reversal pattern consisting of two price troughs: The
market declines to a new low, retraces, then falls again to the approximate price level of the first trough and retraces again. The implication is
that by failing to break below the first price low, the market is hitting
support and the down trend (especially if it has been an extended one)
could reverse.

double top: A reversal pattern consisting of two price peaks: The market rallies to a new high, retraces, then rallies again to the approximate
price level of the first peak and retraces again. The implication is
that by failing to penetrate the first price peak, the market is hitting

resistance and the up trend (especially if it has been an extended one) could reverse.

earnings per share: After-tax profits divided by the number of outstanding shares. This is one of the most important fundamental measures of a stock's prospects for future price gains.

European-style option: A call or put option that can only be exercised at the expiration of the contract.

ex-dividend: Without dividends. Stocks purchased on the ex-dividend date are purchased without rights to the recent dividend. Owners of the stock are entitled to all future dividends.

exercise: The demand of the owner of a call option that the contract size number of units of an underlying asset be delivered at the exercise price. The demand by the owner of a put option contract that the contract size number of units of an underlying asset be bought from him or her at the exercise price.

exercise price: The price at which the owner of a call option contract can buy an underlying asset. The price at which the owner of a put option contract can sell an underlying asset.

expiration: The date the option contract becomes void unless previously exercised. All stock and index option contracts expire on the Saturday following the third Friday of the expiration month.

fair value: The mathematically calculated value of an option. It is determined by (1) the strike price of the option, (2) the current price of the underlying, (3) the amount of time left until expiration, (4) the volatility of the underlying, and (5) dividends.

far term: Expiration months further from expiration.

Fibonacci series: A mathematical series in which each consecutive number is the sum of the two preceding numbers: 1, 2, 3, 5, 8, 13, 21, 34, 55, 89, 144, and so on. As the series progresses, the ratio of a Fibonacci number divided by the immediately preceding number comes closer and closer to 1.618, the Golden Mean, a ratio found in many natural phenomena as well as manmade objects like the Parthenon and the Great Pyramid. (The inverse, 0.618, has a similar significance.) Traders use various permutations of Fibonacci numbers to project retracement levels, among other things.

fill or kill: Trade orders that are canceled if they are not filled almost immediately (typically after being bid or offered three times), that is, "If it doesn't get filled, it gets killed," also (FOK).

flag: A short-term congestion pattern (perhaps one to three weeks on a daily chart) that appears as a small consolidation within a trend. The upper and lower boundaries of the flag should be contained in horizontal trendlines; if the lines converge, forming a small triangle, the pattern is referred to as a **pennant.**

follow-up action: The term used to describe the trades an investor makes subsequent to implementing a strategy. Through these trades, the investor transforms one option strategy into a different one in response to price changes in the underlying asset.

gamma: Expresses how fast delta changes with a one point increase in the price of the underlying asset. Gamma is positive for all options. If an option has a delta of 45 and a gamma of 10, then the option's expected delta will be 55 if the underlying asset goes up one point. If delta is considered to be the velocity of an option, then gamma is the acceleration.

gap: When the low of the current price bar is higher than the high of the preceding price bar, or the high of the current price bar is lower than the low of the preceding price bar. Some traders also use gap to refer to an opening price that is higher than the high (or lower than the low) of the preceding price bar (an opening gap).

generals: Refers to the major buy side institutions such as Mutual Funds.

good-till-canceled (GTC) order: A trade order that remains open until you cancel it (in practice, for perhaps 60 days; check with your broker); there is no need to re-enter it day after day.

guts: A strangle made up of in-the-money options with the underlying asset centered between the strikes.

head-and-shoulders pattern: A reversal pattern consisting of three price peaks (in the case of a head-and-shoulders top) where the middle peak (the head) is higher than the peaks on either side of it (the shoulders). A head-and-shoulders bottom is simply the inverse of this pattern.

high-level pattern: A pattern that develops near the top of the recent trading range. For example, a consolidation that occurs at the top of an up trend could be called a high-level consolidation.

historical volatility: The degree of movement in a market over a past time period, typically 100 days. It is normally expressed as an annualized percentage. A 100-day historical volatility of 32 percent, for instance, means that over the last 100 days the market has fluctuated in such a way that it would be expected to fluctuate about 32 percent in a year's time.

If the market is currently priced at exactly 100, one would expect to see values between 68 (100 percent − 32 percent) and 132 (100 percent + 32 percent).

implied volatility: A calculated value of the options pricing model. To calculate the implied volatility, an investor would use the last sale (bid price or asked price) as the theoretical value of the option and solve the model to determine what volatility would have been required to calculate that value.

in-the-money (ITM): An option whose strike price is below the current price of the underlying stock or future (for call options) or above the current price of the underlying stock or future (for put options). With IBM trading at $110, both the $100 call options and $120 put options are in-the-money.

inside day: A day with a higher low and lower high than the preceding price bar.

intrinsic value: What an option's premium would be if the price of the underlying asset would remain at its current level until expiration. For an in-the-money option, it is the difference between its striking price and the price of the underlying asset. The intrinsic value of an at-the-money or out-of-the-money option is zero dollars.

key reversal: A one-day reversal pattern that occurs when a market makes a new high (or low), preferably a spike high (or low), and then reverses to close at or near the low (or high) of the price bar. The implication is that the market has experienced an extreme intraday sentiment change and a reversal is likely.

legging: The term used to describe a risky method of implementing or closing out a spread strategy one side (leg) at a time. Instead of utilizing a spread order to insure that both the written and the purchased options are filled simultaneously, the investor gambles that a slightly better deal can be obtained on the price of the spread by implementing it as two separate orders.

limit move: The largest one-day price move allowed in a future contract, up or down. During limit up and limit down days, it is impossible for traders to trade at a price above a limit up move or at a price below a limit down move.

limit order: A trade order with a specified execution price, for example, "Buy 100 shares of Microsoft at $147\frac{3}{4}$," or "Sell 10 June T-bonds at $118\frac{17}{32}$ *limit.*" Your broker cannot pay more than $147\frac{3}{4}$ for your shares or sell for less than $118\frac{17}{32}$ for your contracts. A standard limit order is good for the remainder of the day it is entered unless you give specific instructions to cancel the order. At the end of the day, your broker will cancel the order automatically, and you will have to place it again the next day if necessary.

liquidity: The amount of trading activity, and thereby the ease with which you can get in and out of a market. Measured by volume (and open interest in the case of futures markets).

long: Purchasing an asset with the intention of selling it at some time in the future. An asset is purchased long given the expectation of an increase in its price.

low-level pattern: A pattern that develops near the bottom of the recent trading range. For example, a consolidation that occurs at the bottom of a downtrend could be called a low-level consolidation.

margin: See **collateral.**

market order: A trade order executed immediately at the best possible price currently available, that is, at the market. If you wanted to buy Microsoft using a market order, you could tell your broker, "Buy 100 shares of Microsoft at the market."

market-on-close (MOC): Trade orders executed as market orders, but only during the closing of a particular market.

market-on-open (MOO): Trade orders executed as market orders, but only during the opening of a particular market.

marking a position to market: The act of comparing the historic cost of a position to its current market value.

McClellan oscillator: Measures the momentum of market breadth by calculating the difference between the 40- and 20-day exponential moving averages of daily advancing issues minus declining issues on the New York Stock Exchange. The idea behind the indicator is that more stocks will advance than decline in bull markets and vice-versa in bear markets. Generally, markets are considered oversold when the oscillator is below −100, and overbought when it is above +100.

The McClellan oscillator is not a stand-alone indicator. It measures the trend strength of advancing and declining issues, and not necessarily market turns. Leadership in a handful of stocks has characterized many bull markets, defying the premise that the broad market must advance for stock indexes to hit new highs.

measured move: A price projection based on previous price swings. The idea is that different legs of a price move will be roughly the same length. For example, if a stock trading at 100 rallies 20 points to 120, then pulls back 5 points to 115, a measured move projection would set a price objective of 135 if and when the rally resumes—another 20 point move from the low of the pullback.

momentum: Refers to the speed or strength of price movement. It also is the name of a specific technical study that measure the difference between today's closing price and the closing price N days ago. See also **rate of change.**

moving average: Calculations that smooth price action to reveal the underlying trend.

There are several types of moving averages. The most basic is the *simple moving average (SMA)*, which is the sum of closing prices over a particular period divided by the number of days in that period. For example, a 5-day simple moving average would be the sum of the closing prices of the 5 most recent trading days, divided by 5; a 20-day moving average would be the sum of the 20 most recent closing prices divided by 20, and so on. Each day the most recent closing price is added to the equation and the most distant day is dropped off.

A *weighted moving average (WMA)*, the most simple of which is referred to as a *linearly weighted moving average,* multiplies closing prices by a weighting factor that emphasizes recent price action. The oldest price in the calculation is multiplied by 1, the second oldest by 2, the third oldest by 3, and so on. For example, a standard 5-day weighted moving average would multiply the closing price of the fifth most recent trading day (5 trading days ago) by one, the fourth most recent trading day by 2, the third most recent trading day by 3, the second most recent trading day by 4, and the most recent trading day by 5: These products would be summed and *then* divided by the sum of the weighting factors (in this case, $1 + 2 + 3 + 4 + 5 = 15$) to derive the linearly weighted moving average value for the current day. Other weighting schemes can be used to increase or decrease the emphasis of more recent prices.

An *exponential moving average (EMA)* is actually a specific type of weighted moving average. It uses a constant (a smoothing factor) between 0 and 1 in the following manner: the current closing price (C) multiplied by the smoothing constant (S) added to the product of the previous day's exponential moving average value (PEMA) and 1 minus the smoothing factor, or:

Today's EMA = S*C + (1 − S)*PEMA

While the description and formula seem somewhat confusing, the approach is actually simpler to calculate than other moving averages because all you need is today's closing price and yesterday's EMA value.

The preceding descriptions use daily closing prices. Moving averages can be constructed on intra-day, weekly, or monthly timeframes, and substituting the open, low, high, or average price of a bar for the closing price.

One distinct type of moving average is the adaptive moving average (AMA), which dynamically adjusts the number of days in the moving average calculation to current market volatility: In high-volatility periods the number of days would increase (making the average less sensitive and less prone to whipsaws), and in low volatility periods the number of days would decrease (making the average more sensitive to smaller price swings).

naked: An uncovered option strategy. It is an investment in which options sold short are not matched with either a long position in the underlying or a long position in another option of the same type which expires at the same time or later than the options sold. The loss potential with naked writing is virtually unlimited.

near term: Expiration month closest to expiration.

offer (asked):   The lowest price at which anyone is willing to sell a security.

one-eighties (180s):   A two-day reversal pattern for strongly trending stocks described by Jeff Cooper in his book *Hit and Run Trading.* For buys, on day one, the stock must close in the bottom 25 percent of its daily range. On day two, the stock must close in the top 25 percent of its range. The pattern is reversed for sells.

open (or opening price):   The first trade price of the day (or other time period). In futures markets, the open is a representative price of the first minute of trading. In stocks, the open is the first recorded trade price.

opening transaction: The implementing of a new position.

open interest: The cumulative total of all option contracts of a particular series sold but not repurchased or exercised.

option premium: The price of an option.

oscillator: A technical indicator that measures (usually) the velocity of shorter term price action to determine whether a market is overbought or oversold. Well-known oscillators include the relative strength index (RSI) and stochastics. See also **momentum** and **rate of change.**

out-of-the-money (OTM):   An option whose strike price is above the current price of the underlying stock or future (for call options) or below the current price of the underlying stock or future (for put options). With

IBM trading at $110, both the $100 put options and $120 call options are out of the money. Out-of-the-money options have no intrinsic value.

outside day: A day with a high price higher than the previous day's high and a low price lower than the previous day's low.

overbought: When a market has presumably risen too far too fast and is due for at least a short-term correction. See **oscillator.**

oversold: When a market has presumably fallen too far too fast and is due for at least a short-term correction. See **oscillator.**

par: Refers to a price of 100, for example, "Stock XYZ rallied over par today, closing at $101\frac{5}{8}$."

pennant: A short-term congestion pattern (perhaps one to three weeks) that narrows into the form of a small triangle. (Pennants are essentially shorter duration triangle patterns.) See also **flag.**

pivot: When a market is rallying and today's low is lower than the low of the highest day in the rally, that high becomes a pivot, or swing high. When a market is declining and today's high is higher than the high of the lowest day, then that low becomes a pivot, or swing low.

point-and-figure chart: Differs from other price charts in that its time axis is not constant—prices are not plotted day by day or week by week. Instead, point-and-figure charts use columns of ascending Xs and descending Os to portray up moves and down moves (of a certain magnitude), respectively, in a market. For example, every X might represent a .5 point rise (referred to as the *box size*) in the stock's price. Price declines would only be denoted by a column of Os if price fell, say, 1.5 points (three boxes, referred to as the *reversal amount*). In this case, if the stock rose from 25 to 25.5 to 26 to 26.5, you would add three Xs to your column of Xs, one for each .5 point rise from 25 to 26.5. If it rose only a quarter point or a half-point, or declined only a point, you would do nothing. Only when price dropped by 1.5 points or more would you stop adding ascending Xs and start a column of descending Os immediately to the right.

   The larger the box size and reversal amount you use, the less sensitive your chart will be to smaller price fluctuations. Because a one-point move (or whatever increment you use for your box size) may occur in one hour or two days, the price action depicted in a point-and-figure chart is independent of time.

position: The specific instance of a chosen strategy. An option position is an investment comprised of one or more options.

premium: The price of an option contract.

pullback: A shorter-term countertrend move. Pullbacks offer opportunities to enter existing trends. See also **correction.**

put: This option contract conveys the right to sell a standard quantity of a specified asset at a fixed price per unit (the striking price) for a limited length of time (until expiration).

put/call ratio: Used by many as a leading indicator. Computed by dividing the four-day average of total put volume by the four-day average of total call volume.

rate of change: A momentum calculation that divides today's closing price by the closing price N days ago. Except for the scale, this study is virtually identical to the momentum technical study, which measures the *difference* between today's close and the close N days ago.

resistance: A price level that acts as an overhead barrier to further price gains. Prices will frequently rally to these levels and then retreat. Resistance (like support) is rarely a specific price; it is more often a relatively contained price range, frequently in the vicinity of past technical patterns. One of the basic precepts of support and resistance is that once a support level is violated it becomes a likely new resistance level and when a resistance level is penetrated, it becomes a new support level.

reversal: A short underlying asset position protected by a synthetic long underlying asset position. The synthetic long underlying asset position consists of the combination of a long call option and a short put option. Both options have the same strike price and expire the same month.

reversal patterns: Price patterns that suggest a trend reversal rather than a continuation of the current trend. Double and triple tops/bottoms, head-and-shoulders patterns, cup-and-handle patterns, and V tops and bottoms are some examples of reversal patterns.

rollover: When one futures contract expires and the next contract in the cycle becomes the new front month.

runaway: A strongly trending stock or future.

running cup-and-handle pattern: Occurs in an existing up trend. In this context, the pattern functions as a continuation pattern (a pause in the trend) rather than a reversal pattern. See **cup-and-handle pattern.**

short: An obligation to purchase an asset at some time in the future. An asset is sold short given the expectation of a decline in its price.

slim jim: A narrow-range, intraday consolidation pattern that forms at or near the high or low of the day. Generally, the longer and tighter the consolidation, the more explosive the eventual breakout.

spike: A price bar that extends much higher or lower than the surrounding price bars.

spread order: A type of order for the simultaneous purchase and sale of two options of the same type (calls or puts) on the same underlying asset. If placed with a limit, the two positions must be traded for a specific price difference or better.

stochastics: An oscillator based on the position of the current close relative to the absolute price range over the last N days. Consists of two lines: %K, which is the basic calculation, and %D, which is a moving average (typically three days) of the %K line. Usually, stochastics refers to an additionally smoothed version of the formula, whereby the original %D becomes the new %K line and a moving average of this line becomes the new %D line (this version is sometimes called "slow" stochastics, while the original calculation is called "fast" stochastics).

stop order: A trade order placed above or below the market's current price level that is intended either to liquidate a losing trade (a stop-loss order) or to establish a new market position.

Stop orders become market orders as soon as their prices are touched. A *stop-limit order* specifies the worst price at which a stop can be filled, for example, "sell 100 shares of DAL at 45 on a stop, 43 limit."

straddle: A long or short position in both call and put options. The options share the same exercise price, expiration month and the same underlying asset. A short straddle means that both call and put options are sold short. A long straddle means that both call and put options are bought long.

strategy: One of various kinds of option investments, (i.e., long call, covered write, bull spread).

strike price: The fixed price per unit, specified in the option contract.

support: A price level that acts as a floor to further price declines. When a market repeatedly declines to a particular level and then rallies, the market is said to be offering support at that level.

Support (like resistance) is rarely a precise price; it is more often a relatively contained price range, frequently in the vicinity of past technical patterns.

One of the basic precepts of support and resistance is that once a support level is violated it becomes a likely new resistance level and when a resistance level is penetrated it becomes a new support level.

tail: A new high bar that opens and closes near its low, or a new low bar that opens and closes near its high.

theta: The daily drop in dollar value of an option due to the effect of time alone. Theta is dollars lost per day per contract. Negative theta signifies long option positions or debit spreads; positive theta signifies short options or credit spreads.

the "Turk":   A reference to what appears to be a calculated market stabilizing action by the Federal Reserve or its appointed ally, such as large broker-dealers who do program trading and are active in the futures. The Turk has had a tendency to "save the day" during many potential crisis occasions, such as when it looks like the market is about to crash.

tick: The minimum price increment a stock, future, or option can trade in. For example, in a stock that trades in minimum increments of $\frac{1}{16}$th of a point, a move of $\frac{1}{16}$ up or down would be a one-tick move. In the S&P 500 futures, a tick is .10, in crude oil futures, a tick is .01, and so on.

tick indicator: Measures the difference between the number of up-ticking NYSE stocks vs. the number of down-ticking NYSE stocks throughout the day. (Do not confuse with the term **tick,** used to describe a minimum price fluctuation.)

time spreads: A long time spread is created by selling a near term option and by buying a longer term option. Both options are on the same underlying asset, are of the same type, and have the same exercise price.

time value: This is the amount that the premium of an option exceeds its intrinsic value. If an option is out-of-the-money then its entire premium consists of time value.

trading range: Nontrending, sideways price action with fairly defined upper and lower boundaries.

trailing stop: A stop order that is raised (in a rising market) or lowered (in a declining market) to follow an open position and lock in profits.

trendline: A straight line defining a price trend. Up trendlines connect the lows of several price bars while down trendlines connect the highs of price bars.

triangle: A longer term (approximately a month or more on a daily chart) consolidation/continuation pattern in which prices progressively converge in a series of lower highs and higher lows.

TRIN indicator: Compares advancing issues/declining issues to the up volume/down volume ratio.

triple bottom: A reversal pattern consisting of three price troughs at roughly the same price level. The implication is that by failing to move through such levels after three attempts, the market is meeting significant support and could reverse. See also **triple top, double bottom,** and **double top.**

triple top: A reversal pattern consisting of three price peaks at roughly the same price level. The implication is that by failing to move through such levels after three attempts, the market is meeting significant resistance and could reverse. See also **double top.**

true range: A volatility calculation developed by Welles Wilder that modifies the standard range calculation by accounting for gaps between price bars. True range is defined as the largest value (in absolute terms) of today's high and today's low (the standard daily range calculation); today's high and yesterday's close; and today's low and yesterday's close.

Average true range (ATR) is simply a moving average of true range calculated over N days. True range and average true range are common volatility measurements.

two-step pullback: A combination of two pullbacks, where the second pullback tests the level of the first pullback. See **pullback.**

uncovered: See **naked.**

underlying: This is the asset specified in an option contract, which, except in the case of cash-settled options, is transferred upon exercise of the option contract. With cash settled options, only cash changes hands, based on the current price of the underlying.

vega: The sensitivity of an option's theoretical price to changes in volatility. It is the dollar amount of gain or loss, per contract, you should theoretically experience if volatility goes up one percentage point.

volatility: A measure of the amount by which an asset has fluctuated, or is expected to fluctuate, in a given period of time. Assets with greater volatility exhibit wider price swings and their options are higher in price than less volatile assets.

volume: The number of shares or contracts traded in a particular market in a given time period (usually day). See also **liquidity** and **open interest.**

weighted moving average: See **moving average.**

whipsaw: When price repeatedly thrashes above and below a moving average (or support or resistance level) triggering multiple false trading signals. The same term applies to indicators that behave similarly (e.g., when an oscillator like the relative strength index (RSI) repeatedly moves above and below its overbought or oversold level).

wide-range day bar: A high-volatility price bar, that is, one whose range is much greater than the preceding price bars (or alternately, one with a range much greater than the average range over an N-day period).

write: An investor who sells an option contract not currently held (selling the option short) is said to have written the option.

index